Tudor Prelates and Politics

PRINCETON STUDIES IN HISTORY

Volume 8

Tudor Prelates and Politics

1536-1558

BY LACEY BALDWIN SMITH

PRINCETON, NEW JERSEY
PRINCETON UNIVERSITY PRESS
1953

TO
N. H. S.

PREFACE

*I*T is almost impossible to approach the period of the English Reformation with a complete sense of objectivity. It was an age of hyperbole and contradiction, of fervent idealism and blatant self-interest, of servile compliance and heroic martyrdom. Whether the historian is dealing with the clash of religious ideologies or the personal rivalries of such vivid personalities as Anne Boleyn and Catherine of Aragon, the nature of the conflict inevitably produces bias. The fascination of this militant age has varied from generation to generation but has never slackened, and though the books on the Reformation are to be numbered in the thousands, none has achieved complete neutrality; nor does the author claim to be an exception. If the reader detects a certain penchant for Stephen Gardiner and his conservative followers, it is because the author sees mirrored in the history of Tudor England some of the tensions which plague our modern world. The ideological conflict between the Catholics and Protestants, the endless, futile series of conferences to secure peace between two passionately held positions, the fears, the uncertainties and confusions, and above all the slow polarization of society into two militant groups are suggestive of our own age. During these violent years it was the mild, middle-of-the-road conservatives who were driven by the course of events to renounce their moderate and liberal humanism, and the insecurity and uncertainty of their position is reminiscent of many middle-of-the-road groups today. This tendency to see reflected in the past the problems of the present is avowedly a perilous concept for anyone endeavoring to understand the past in terms of its own standards, but it must be admitted that much of the attraction of the Reformation and many of the author's sympathies and antipathies are in fact a reflection of his twentieth century environment.

In a very real sense the research on which the following pages are based was made possible through the sacrifices of the last war, and when the debit and credit sheet for those years is tabulated the Fulbright Act and the scholarships which have been given to American students for study abroad must be listed in evidence that good does on occasion stem from evil. I wish to express my thanks to the officials of the Fulbright office in London for their kindness and cooperation during my stay in England, and I am also grateful to the officials of the British Museum and the Public Record Office for permission to consult books and manuscripts and for their constant help in locating essential material.

Of the many people who have contributed their time and advice, I am particularly indebted to Professor E. Harris Harbison of Princeton University and Professor J. E. Neale of University College, London; the former for his constant encouragement when the going became painful, and the latter for his kindness to a novice in Tudor history and his efforts to transform what was originally a vague theory into a manageable and worthwhile historical study. I also owe a great deal to the members of my family who have accepted without complaint the toil of correcting and proofreading the manuscript, and have suffered in silence the tedium of a surfeit of Tudorism in their lives.

L.B.S.

CONTENTS

Tudor Prelates and Politics

INTRODUCTION

ON SUNDAY, the first of June, 1533, in the twenty-fourth year of the reign of Henry VIII, the townsmen of the city of London commenced preparation for the coronation of Mistress Anne Boleyn, the climax of days of celebration and ceremony. The streets were hung with scarlet and crimson, and wine was free to those loyal subjects of the King whose duty it was to make the streets ring with enthusiastic cheering. Burgher and commoner were attired in all their finery and the lords temporal had donned their parliamentary robes. As the coronation procession began to move slowly from the Tower of London towards Westminster Abbey, abbots in their "robes of black cloth lined with satin and sarcenet" and bishops in cloaks of "scarlet furred with white lettice" and "hoods of the same" took their place, lending divine recognition and sanction to a travesty which had begun many years before as a passionate and lively love affair. In the Abbey Thomas Cranmer, the new Archbishop of Canterbury, stood before the altar waiting to bestow the coveted crown which had kept the diplomatic couriers of Europe moving restlessly back and forth between Rome and London, Paris and Madrid, for the past six years. Finally, down the aisle of Westminster walked the aspiring Queen herself "in a surcoat and robe of purple velvet furred with ermine, in her hair coif and circlet" and "over her was borne the canopy by . . . porters all crimson with points of blue and red hanging on their sleeves, and the bishops of London and Winchester [to] bear up the laps of the Queen's robe." These episcopal pages were John Stokesley, Bishop of London, and Stephen Gardiner, Bishop of Winchester, two men who were to regret bitterly their participation in the events of this day.

The story of the first of June, 1533, is more than a mere

pageant, for the crowning of Henry's second wife was both the culmination of the first stage of the English Reformation and the commencement of that last act which was to end in the coronation of Protestantism as the state religion of England in the person of Queen Elizabeth, Anne Boleyn's as yet unborn daughter. For those present at this memorable occasion, the sight of these two newly consecrated bishops must have symbolized both the support that youth, energy, and ability had given to Anne's ambition to be Queen of England, and the desire of that "most serene and invincible Prince" for a young and attractive wife who could secure the succession through a male heir. But if we bring to this picture the clarity of historical perspective, the symbolism is subtly modified. Gardiner and Stokesley are no longer men who have attained rank and promotion in the wake of royal marriage, but are the outstanding opponents of the coming religious changes embodied in this Lutheran Queen. Instead of being porters aiding and abetting Mistress Boleyn at her coronation, they become men who are clinging to her robes in a desperate attempt to prevent not only her own coronation, but more important, the crowning of her Protestant beliefs by the waiting hands of Thomas Cranmer. Both mental images are correct, for it was Catholic humanism, Catholic learning, and Catholic legal training which had made the divorce and the breach with Rome possible, and it was to be, to a great extent, these same men who stubbornly opposed the Reformation forces which were set free when Henry's conscience "crept too near another lady" of the court.

Embodied in this picture as painted by the chronicler, Edward Hall, is the symbol of the coming conflict between conservatism and reform, or, in terms of personalities, between Stephen Gardiner and Thomas Cranmer, the two outstanding leaders of the opposing parties. The history of this duel is the story of intrigue and personal malice, of religious passion and human prudence, of ideals dissipated by human corruption, and of men who faced martyrdom for the sake of conscience. The levels on which the battle was fought were many and complex, for the fanaticism of faith was to enter the political panorama of Europe, upset the dynastic designs of kings, embitter national politics, and finally, was to force each protagonist to wage his own battle—to resolve the universal dilemma between certainty of mind and security of body.

The solution to the ubiquitous problems of their age reached by Stephen Gardiner and his episcopal colleagues, the attitude of mind which they brought to bear upon the religious-political issues of the century, are closely and intimately related to their past experiences and environmental training. This work, then, is a study in conservatism, in the relationship between ideas and the biographical and social matrix from which they evolve.

The conservative members of the Episcopal Bench during the first years of the English Reformation were by preference and training administrators and statesmen, and only by chance and patronage were they ecclesiastical figures. They were essentially bureaucrats and humanists, forced by the demands and exigencies of their position to lay down and administer religious policy, and the criticisms and prejudices which they held towards the violent religious upheavals of their day were basically those of the secular, politically-minded administrator who judges truth in terms of human prudence, theory in terms of expediency. It is this worldly and secular spirit which they brought to the religious problems of Henry's reign that differentiates them from their idealistic and reforming colleagues on the Episcopal Bench; it both exaggerated the growing bitterness between them and confronted such men as Gardiner, Stokesley, Heath, and Bonner with a hopeless personal dilemma. Being bureaucrats, owing their careers to the patronage of the crown, and being responsible for the security and efficiency of the Tudor governmental machine, they naturally opposed any religious change which might upset that

[5]

fixity of belief, that discipline of religious thought which was the basis of mental and, in Tudor times, of national security. At the same time, however, this point of view led them to place national and outward unity of religion above their own personal inclinations. They were men trained in diplomacy, and thus in compromise, masters of verbal interpretations which veil a multitude of meanings and mental reservations. Thus, while opposing religious change for both personal and political reasons, they were willing and ready to accept compromise for the sake of general conformity and national security.

I do not pretend or aspire to offer a complete explanation for conservative thought among these men, for to do so would mean describing the entire matrix of bewildering elements that went to make up England of the Renaissance. However, if these bishops are to be understood, their problems appreciated, they must be judged by the standards of their age. In part the failure to do justice to these conservatives has been because historians have judged them in the light of what did happen and not in the darkness of what might have happened. They have been attacked for being reactionaries and sycophants; the first because they made the unpardonable historical error of failing to predict the future, the second, because they escaped with their lives, despite the passion and recrimination of religious conflict. The historian too often forgets that human action cannot be judged solely by what did occur, but is also explained by the fear of what might have occurred. Moreover, ideas unrelated to action are spirits without bodies, as elusive and unprofitable as a poltergeist, for not only do ideas motivate action, but physical events, by stimulating fear and confusion, can determine an infinite series of further actions which are quite unrelated to formal ideas and opinions.

All this is by way of an apology for what may appear to be an unnecessary emphasis on political and social history in a study which is presumably an intellectual analysis. However, if the living age is to recreate the mind of a dead generation, the conflicting passions and loyalties of the era must be conjured up as the backdrop necessary to give the protagonists the warmth and color which is their right. To claim that administrative and diplomatic training was the sole determining element in the composition of conservative thought is not only historically incorrect, but also makes of these men deities insulated from the fears and intellectual confusion which beset all men. Ideas are too volatile and actions too mercurial to be stereotyped; only through the careful reconstruction of the foundation and pattern from which sixteenth century conservative thought evolved can we hope to relate specific ideas to broad intellectual programs and individuals to clear party affiliations—an attempt which will not be essayed until Chapter v of this work. Then, and only then, can we follow the recipe laid down by the Colonel of Dragoons when he said: "Take of these elements all that is fusible, melt them all down in a pipkin or crucible, set them to simmer and take off the scum, and a Heavy Dragoon is the residuum!" In this case, the residuum will be an analysis of conservative religious thought from 1536 to 1558.

CHAPTER I

THE FRATERNITY OF SCHOLARS

ISTORY has rarely seen fit to mark the young men on whom she will later bestow her munificent gifts, and, in the eyes of a contemporary at least, there was little to differentiate the group of aspiring youths who attended Oxford and Cambridge during the second decade of the sixteenth century. That Stephen Gardiner would become Bishop of Winchester and Lord Chancellor under Queen Mary, or that Thomas Cranmer would rise to be Primate of all England, was unguessed and unknown. Had, however, a prophetic classmate been able to foresee their respective careers, it would hardly have warranted more than passing notice, for the annals of both Oxford and Cambridge are crowded with the deeds of distinguished statesmen and divines. The fading medieval society must have thrown up to its surface many a "Little Bilney," young sensitive misfits, obsessed with the sense of their own sin, who a hundred years before would have found solace and relief in some secluded Franciscan order. Few would have prophesied that Thomas Bilney's modest mysticism or Hugh Latimer's fiery indiscretions would have led to imprisonment and eventually to the stake. No one yet realized that the time had passed when their respective virtues and vices could have found their place in the healthy stream of contemporary life, the one as a recluse, the other as an itinerant friar. As yet the legions of martyred disciples had not been sacrificed to a "living God," and at Cambridge, where tradition and institution alike reflected the past and not the future, the bishops of a later Episcopal Bench were still schoolboys, still untainted by a history of their own creation. Only the prelude of the Protestant Reformation had begun, and as yet the warm breath of humanistic spring had not been succeeded by the scorched heat of religious controversy.

To the eyes of the youthful master, who at the beginning of the fall term traveled about the country picking up boys from parents who were reluctant to see their sons travel alone to Cambridge,[1] there must have been little to differentiate his unruly protégés. Nor has the passage of four hundred years clarified the picture. Incipient reformer and conservative alike were cast in the same mold, products of that almost unique English institution referred to as the "second son." Neither they nor their fathers were inheritors of great wealth, but usually there was a rich uncle or cousin on whom they could call for financial help and the exercise of influence in obtaining a government position or church benefice. Thus, for instance, Nicholas Ridley was put through Cambridge by his uncle, a distinguished scholar and divine,[2] and Arthur Bulkeley, later Bishop of Bangor, was brought to the attention of Thomas Cromwell through the influence of his "cousin," Richard Bulkeley, the Vice-Chamberlain of Wales.[3]

It was understood that the eldest son would inherit the bulk of his father's estates, and there was usually little left for the younger members of a large household. If he was lucky, the younger brother would marry an heiress or be set up in business by his father, but more often it was towards the church that a careful parent directed the interests of his younger sons. William Barlow, for example, was the youngest of four sons in an old landed family made suddenly destitute through their association with the Perkin Warbeck plot of the previous century. Three of the four sons were thus forced to make

[1] Mullinger, *University of Cambridge,* I, pp. 345-346. Cambridge is emphasized at the expense of Oxford in the course of this chapter because Cambridge, not Oxford, was the center of the "New Learning" during the period 1510 to 1530, and either by accident or design the great majority of the future bishops went there.

[2] Ridley, *Works,* p. ii and App. III, p. 492.

[3] *L.P.,* XII, pt. ii [1537], No. 998. See also App. II *infra.*

careers for themselves in the church.[4] The will of William Goodrich, father of Thomas, Bishop of Ely, affords another instance of what must have been common practice among the more well-to-do of the country gentry. Thomas was to be "found at school till he be 30 years old, so that he will be priest by that time, and to have such necessary charge as [he] shall need at any degrees taking. And if he be a priest by that time or afore, he [is] to have 10 pounds a year till he be beneficed to the value of xvi pounds a year clear." Thus young Thomas was to be maintained by his family until he could obtain a church benefice of sufficient income to support him. In the meantime, of course, the bulk of his father's estate was entailed to his elder brother.[5] This was on the whole a very typical and eminently satisfactory arrangement, and is exceptional only in that Master Thomas seems to have been slightly better off than some of his university colleagues. A similar arrangement was devised in the case of Thomas Cranmer. Again, he was the second son of an ancient Nottinghamshire family whose estates were insufficient to endow two young sons. His brother John stayed with the land, neither aspiring to a university education nor to a chance to make his fortune in London. He remained a lusty squire whose family duty was to oversee his farms and to propagate the name of Cranmer.[6] That Thomas was also to sire a family was, at least during the early years of the century, decidedly unexpected and on

[4] The most available and recent account of the Barlow family may be found in Rupp, *English Protestant Tradition*, ch. IV, "The Early Career of Bishop Barlow," p. 63 *passim*. The Barlow pedigrees are given in *N. and Q*, vol. 183 (Nov., 1942), p. 327, and Meyrick, *Visitations of Wales*, I, pp. 117-118.

[5] His will, registered at Somerset House (Ayloffe—7) and dated 1517, refers to him merely as William Goodrich, but in the family pedigree he appears as "Edward or William" (*Lincolnshire Pedigrees*, H.S., LI, pp. 415-417). For abbreviations used in footnotes see Table of Abbreviations, p. 297.

[6] See his pedigree in *The Visitation of the County of Nottingham*, H.S., IV, pp. 70-71; cf. Pollard, *Thomas Cranmer*, ch. I, "Parentage, Birth and Early Years."

the whole undesired. In fact, it is surprising how many of the later bishops had their start in the landed tradition of the country squirearchy. Nicholas Ridley's father, Christopher, was the younger son of an old and somewhat turbulent York-shire family;[7] Edward Lee's grandfather had been twice Mayor of London, and in 1470 was sheriff of Kent, while his father, Richard Lee, was a country gentleman of Delee Magna, Kent.[8] The future conservatives, Richard Sampson, Cuthbert Tunstal, Edward Fox, John Voysey, William Rugge, Roland Lee, John Skip, and George Day, and the later Protestants, John Wakeman, Henry Holbeach, Robert King, and Robert Holgate all came from country families whose propensity for numerous offspring forced them to send their sons into the church.[9]

The Reformation was to show little respect for economic or social groupings and it is not difficult to find families which were divided against themselves. George Day, the future Bishop of Chichester, refused his brother William, later the Elizabethan Bishop of Winchester, money to buy books, and if we can believe Fuller, is said to have remarked on this occasion that "he thought it not fit to spend the goods of the

---

[7] Foster, *Pedigrees Recorded at Heralds' Visitations of Northumberland*, p. 102; *Visitation of Yorkshire*, H.S., XVI, p. 263. William Turner wrote John Foxe that Ridley "was born in my own county of Northumberland, and descended from the noble stock of Ridleys. One of his uncles was a knight; the other, Robert Ridley by name, a doctor in divinity, not only of Cambridge but also of Paris. . . ." Ridley, *Works*, p. 492.

[8] For his pedigree, see *Gentleman's Magazine*, New Ser. xv (1863), pt. ii, p. 337.

[9] The pedigree of Edward Fox may be found in the *Visitation of Shropshire*, H.S., XXVIII, pp. 191-194. This pedigree makes Bishop Fox the brother of Charles Fox of Bromfield who was still living in 1583. Inasmuch as Edward died in 1538 this seems unlikely, and he was probably an uncle to Charles. However, the Bishop did have, as the pedigree claims, a brother named Edmund (*L.P.*, IV, pt. ii [1528], No. 4479) and was certainly a member of the Fox family of Shropshire (cf. the Bishop's arms recorded in Bedford, *The Blazon of Episcopacy*, p. 61, and the family coat of arms in their pedigree). For Roland Lee's pedigree, see *The Visitation of Shropshire*, H.S., XXVIII, pp. 189-190. The pedigrees of the other bishops are given in App. III *infra*.

church on him who was an enemy of the church."[10] Again, Nicholas Ridley and Cuthbert Tunstal were relatives, but Nicholas died at the stake under Mary while Tunstal was deprived of his see by Elizabeth.[11]

But in 1515 the prejudices of religion had not yet confronted brother against brother, uncle against nephew, friend against friend. The young men enrolled at Oxford and Cambridge still retained a community of interests and experiences. If great riches and family fame were denied them, they were at least the inheritors of that substantial county life which for those who entered the rough and ready governmental service was of unique value. Many were the official reports written by young bureaucrats, clerks of the Cardinal's household, or even royal secretaries who were forced to labor late into the night after a long day in the field in attendance on their sport-excelling sovereign.[12] Not only did physical prowess and endurance affect their future careers by bringing them to the attention of their royal master, but it was an indispensable attribute in the long peregrinations which ecclesiastical administrators had to endure. Often the pomp of an episcopal train and the more doubtful comforts of an ecclesiastical mule had to be discarded for the speed and urgency of the post, when the exigencies of international diplomacy so demanded.[13]

Not all the future bishops, of course, stemmed from the countryside. Stephen Gardiner was the son of a successful clothmaker in Bury Saint Edmunds in Norfolk,[14] while Nicholas Heath was reared and educated in London. His father, William Heath, was a "citizen and cutler of London" who bequeathed in 1535 what must have constituted a sizeable

---

[10] Fuller, *Worthies*, pp. 588-589.

[11] Sturge, *Cuthbert Tunstal*, p. 296; *DNB*, Art. "Nicholas Ridley."

[12] Stephen Gardiner, the King's Principal Secretary, wrote his patron, Cardinal Wolsey, that he had "been forth from morn to night a-hunting by the King's Highness' commandment." *L.P.*, IV, pt. iii [1529], No. 5831.

[13] *L.P.*, IV, pt. i [1525], No. 1803; XIII, pt. ii [1538], No. 59.

[14] Muller, *Stephen Gardiner*, p. 1.

fortune to his wife Agnes and her two sons, Nicholas, "Clerk and Master of Arts," and William, a "mercer."[15] Thomas Thirlby's father is said to have been the town clerk of Cambridge, a position which is difficult to assess, but his grandfather was a Campion and "a gentleman of London."[16] It would be incorrect to assume that the division of town and country created a barrier between these families, for almost all of the landed gentry had relatives who had turned to the city to make or recoup their fortunes. William Heath was undoubtedly related to the Heaths of Twickenham in Middlesex and was probably a second son either of that family or a cadet line.[17] Edward Lee's grandfather was twice Mayor of London,[18] while William Rugge's brother, Robert, became mayor of Norwich.[19]

As far as the records show, none of the future episcopal figures seem to have come from the lower classes, but some whose families have been obscured by passing generations may have indeed been of humble origin. The closest approach to such a status was Hugh Latimer, whose father was a yeoman, but it is almost impossible to distinguish between the lesser gentry and the upper yeomanry. Certainly his father was a man of some substance who delighted in his reputation for hospitality, and had the means to send young Master Hugh to Cambridge.[20] Generally speaking, it is indicative of the

[15] His will is recorded at Somerset House (Dyngeley—3). He was educated at St. Anthony's School, London, where Sir Thomas More was also a student. Stowe, *Survey of London*, p. 69.

[16] Cooper, *Athenae Cantabrigienses*, I, p. 287; *Visitations of Essex*, H.S., XIV, p. 556.

[17] See the pedigree of John Heath of Twickenham in Middlesex (*Visitation of London*, H.S., I, p. 37) and compare his arms with those of Bishop Heath (Bedford, *Blazon of Episcopacy*, p. 138). Nicholas also had an uncle living in Norwich (see his father's will, Somerset House, Dyngeley—3), and the *DNB* says that the Heath family was descended from the Heaths of Apsley, Tamworth.

[18] See his pedigree recorded in *Gentleman's Magazine*, New Ser. XV (1863), pt. ii, p. 337.

[19] See his pedigree in the *Visitations of Norfolk*, H.S., XXXII, p. 229.

[20] *DNB*, Art. "Hugh Latimer."

overall status of the Episcopal Bench during the latter years
of Henry's reign that seventeen of the bishops living in 1549
are mentioned in family pedigrees, while the origins of three
more of the total 27 are perfectly clear, either through the
wills of their fathers or the similarity of their coats of arms to
other landed families.[21]

On the other hand, few of the boys matriculating at the
two universities could prove relationship to noble houses.
When they could claim the blue blood of England's aristocracy
in their veins, it was usually tainted by the bar sinister. Edmund Bonner was distantly connected with the Earls of Derby
through his blood relationship with George Savage of the
Savages of Cheshire (see Appendix 1), and Cuthbert Tunstal
could claim a family link with Richard Neville, Earl of Warwick, but here again the relationship was marred by illegitimacy.[22] Only Thomas Stanley, Bishop of Sodor and Man,
was of direct noble descent,[23] but he and the successors to his
see are not legitimately part of this history, for his diocese did
not give him the right to vote in Parliament as a spiritual
lord.[24] The only other bishop of the final years of Henry's

---

[21] See App. III *infra.*

[22] Sturge, *Cuthbert Tunstal,* ch. II, "Family and Early Life," and App.
I. Bishop Tunstal himself was not a blood relation of the Neville family,
but his brothers were. Their mother was Alice, dr. of George Neville, Bishop
of Exeter and Archbishop of York, brother of Richard Warwick, the King-
maker. Cuthbert Tunstal, however, was the son of Thomas Tunstal's second wife, dr. of Sir John Conyers, who married his father some years
after Cuthbert's birth.

[23] Thomas Stanley was the second son of the first Lord Monteagle who
was the fifth son of Thomas Stanley, first Earl of Derby, by his first wife,
Eleanor, dr. of Richard Neville, Earl of Salisbury and sister of the King-
maker. *DNB,* Art. "Thomas Stanley."

[24] The Bishopric of Sodor and Man is technically independent of the
English ecclesiastical organization. The bishop, though he has a seat in
the House of Lords, exercises no vote, and although the see belongs to the
Archdiocese of York, it has its own Convocation. During the Reformation
the Bishopric was not directly affected by the Reformation Acts of Parliament, and the dissolution of the monasteries on the Isle of Man did not depend upon an act of Parliament but instead upon the personal actions of
Henry VIII. See the *Encyclopaedia Britannica,* XVII, Art. "Isle of Man,"
pp. 536-537; XXV, Art. "Sodor and Man," p. 343.

life who was in any way affiliated with a baronial family was Roland Lee, who is referred to as a "cousin" of the Earl of Rutland.[25] However, the term "cousin" in Tudor times might mean almost anything, and his connection is too far distant to appear on any of the pedigrees.

Socially and economically the future bishops had much in common, and it is not surprising to discover that many of these episcopal families had fortified their community of interests by family marriages. Edmund Bonner and Arthur Bulkeley were distantly related through the marriage of Margarette Savage and Sir Richard Bulkeley.[26] George Day and Roland Lee lived to see a nephew and niece joined in matrimony,[27] while as we have already noted, Cuthbert Tunstal and Nicholas Ridley were distant cousins.[28] If such fami-

---

[25] *L.P.*, vi [1533], No. 546. Some of the bishops were related to families which later attained noble rank. Arthur Bulkeley was connected to the Bulkeleys of Beaumaris and Thomas Bulkeley was eventually made Viscount Bulkeley of Cashel by Charles I in 1643 (Earwaker, *East Cheshire*, I, pp. 181-183). Robert King was related by marriage to Thomas Cromwell, who was elevated to the title of Earl of Essex by Henry VIII, and to John Williams who was knighted in 1537 and elevated to the peerage in 1554. Bishop King's brother, William of Devonshire, married Anne, dr. of Sir John Williams of Burfield, Bucks., who was a nephew of Thomas Cromwell (see B.M., Add. 24488, f. 1, and *DNB*, Arts. "Robert King" and "Thomas Cromwell"). William Barlow's sister, Elizabeth, was lady-in-waiting to Queen Margaret of Scotland and eventually became Lady Elphinstone, while his first cousin, Anne Barlow, married Lord Gray (Rupp, *English Protestant Tradition*, pp. 63, 65). Cuthbert Tunstal, besides being indirectly related to the Neville family, was directly connected with the Parr family through his father, Thomas Tunstal, whose aunt, Alice Tunstal, married Sir Thomas Parr, the great-grandfather of the Marquis of Northampton (1513-1571) and Catherine Parr, last wife of Henry VIII. Thus the Queen was third cousin to the Bishop (see Sturge, *Cuthbert Tunstal*, App. 1).

[26] See the Bulkeley pedigree in Earwaker, *East Cheshire*, I, pp. 181-183, and the Savage pedigree in the *Visitation of Cheshire*, H.S., XVIII, pp. 203-204. More important than the marriage itself is the fact that the two families were old acquaintances and the Bulkeleys undoubtedly knew Edmund Bonner before he became a bishop, P.R.O., S.P.1, vol. 74, f. 200 (*L.P.*, vi [1533], No. 179).

[27] *Visitation of Shropshire*, H.S., XXVIII, p. 162. For the Fowler-Lee pedigree see *Visitation of Staffordshire*, Staffordshire Historical Collections, v, pt. ii, p. 135.

[28] Sturge, *Cuthbert Tunstal*, p. 296.

lies must be placed within the deterministic theory of class divisions, it would not be far wrong to say that they were members of that vast and undefined section of society commonly known as the middle class, which supplied the ability and loyalty on which the Tudor administrative machine relied. Robert King, Bishop of Oxford, was related by marriage to Thomas Cromwell,[29] a connection which proved profitable for himself and his brother. Arthur Bulkeley was a cousin of Richard Bulkeley, one of Cromwell's factotums and Vice-Chamberlain of Wales.[30] John Taylor was probably the nephew or cousin of John Taylor, lawyer and councillor under Henry VIII,[31] while William Barlow's brother, after trying his hand as a merchant in Spain and associating with Sebastian Cabot, returned to England to share in the spoliation of the church land, and died Vice-Admiral of the Pembroke coast.[32]

Under normal circumstances such boys could have expected little in regard to their future careers, and had they entered Oxford or Cambridge only a generation earlier, their lives would have been very different. Cranmer would have been destined to obscure security as a professor of sacred theology, while Edmund Bonner might have settled for the same life as his natural father, George Savage, parson of Daneham.[33] Stephen Gardiner might have remained at Cambridge as professor of civil and canon law, and even when he entered Wolsey's service he could hardly have expected the success which he later achieved. The position of a bishop was a coveted reward predicated on long and arduous years of government service and loyalty, and that Gardiner became bishop of the wealthiest see in England[34] at the age of thirty-

---

[29] *DNB*, Art. "Robert King."
[30] *L.P.*, XII, pt. ii [1537], No. 998.
[31] *DNB*, Art. "John Taylor."
[32] Rupp, *English Protestant Tradition*, pp. 63, 65.
[33] *Visitation of Cheshire*, H.S., XVIII, p. 205; see also App. I *infra*.
[34] Muller, *Stephen Gardiner*, p. 42.

four[35] was a precocious advancement which in a previous age had been limited to those of royal blood. Richard Sampson could have expected some help from his elder brother, a clerk of the Council, but except for chance he might have remained an unknown minion.[36] John Skip, John Taylor, and Nicholas Ridley would have continued as professors of divinity, known only in the annals of their university as masters of their colleges,[37] not a bad life, not an insignificant career, but certainly not one which leads to the Episcopal Bench, and in one case at least to the stake.

What these men had in common was ability and wit and the rare historical fortune to have lived in a moment of rapid if sometimes alarming change. Above all else, it was the Reformation with all its theological, administrative, and diplomatic ramifications which swept them into prominence. Stephen Gardiner, Edward Lee, and John Stokesley owed their promotion to the King's "Great Matter,"[38] while the story of Cranmer's chance meeting with Gardiner and Edward Fox, and his subsequent suggestion of sounding the opinion of the universities of Europe concerning the issue of the King's divorce, is too well known to warrant detailed discussion here.[39] However, the decision to gather the opinions of the learned divines of England and Europe was to have a far-reaching effect on the lives of otherwise ordinary professors, for it brought them to the attention of the court and

---

[35] *Ibid.*, p. 3. According to Muller, Gardiner was probably born in 1497. He was elected to the See of Winchester in September of 1531 and was installed on December 27.

[36] *Visitations of Berkshire*, H.S., LVII, p. 207; B.M., Add. 5524, f. 157 (163). His brother seems to have been Robert Sampson of Bynfeld, Berks., "Clerk of the Council to Henry VII and Henry VIII." See App. III for further details.

[37] They were masters respectively of Gonville Hall (1536-1540), St. John's (1538-1546), and Pembroke Hall (1540-1553).

[38] *L.P.*, V [1531], No. 432. Chapuys wrote on 26 September, 1531, saying he suspected that both Lee and Gardiner had been promoted in order to gain two more votes in the House of Lords in favor of the divorce.

[39] Pollard, *Thomas Cranmer*, pp. 38-39.

focused on them the uncertain light of royal approval. When Fox and Gardiner arrived at Cambridge in February of 1530 to solicit the opinion of the university, they met with considerable opposition. That the motion in favor of the King's divorce would eventually be sanctioned was, of course, merely a matter of time, but in the process of the debate the extent of the opposition became quite clear, and Gardiner was careful to report to Henry the names of those who favored and those who opposed "the King's question." Needless to say, none of the men who eventually attained episcopal rank were listed in the opposition, while the names of five future bishops appear among those who favored the divorce.[40] For the theologian and lawyer alike, it was the divorce which brought them fame and advancement by placing a new and often dangerous premium on the "right" knowledge of divinity and canon law. But in 1515 England was still Catholic in faith, Henry still seemingly devoted to Catherine, his first wife. The waves of a future religious storm were only ripples on the calm waters of English life, and both master and undergraduate had more immediate concerns than to worry about an as yet unrevealed future. For the moment, at least, it was education and university life which occupied them.

The number of Reformation figures who received their degrees from Cambridge during the first decades of the century is outstanding; of the forty-six bishops holding office between 1536 and 1551, thirty-three are registered at her colleges, and during the years 1510-1520 no less than twenty-two were in residence.[41] For a brief moment their lives were brought into conjunction, and it was cruelly ironic that persecutor and persecuted, incipient reformer and conservative should have

[40] *L.P.*, IV, pt. iii [1530], No. 6247, sec. ii. They were John Salcot, Nicholas Shaxton, Hugh Latimer, John Skip, and Nicholas Heath.

[41] Of this number six are claimed by both Oxford and Cambridge, thus leaving 27 for Cambridge and 13 for Oxford. These figures are based on Foster, *Alumni Oxonienses*; Venn, *Alumni Cantabrigienses*, pt. i, I-IV; and the Cambridge *Grace Book B*. pts. i and ii, vols. II and III.

lived in equality and even friendship during these few years at college. The bitter antagonism that was to brand their later careers was still non-existent, while the warm breath of Christian humanism augured reform not revolution, peace not war. It would be impossible to attempt to narrate the undergraduate lives of each of these young Cantabs, and it must suffice to take one of their number as the thread of Ariadne to guide us through this labyrinth of personalities. Possibly the most gregarious and by far the most popular of these future bishops was Thomas Thirlby, later to be Bishop of Westminster.

Master Thomas's lineage is not altogether clear, and for lack of better evidence we must accept the word of Cooper who says he was born in the parish of St. Mary the Great, Cambridge, and that his father, John, was "scrivener and town clerk" of the university town.[42] What is better substantiated is that his mother, Joan, was the daughter of William Campion, "a gentleman of London,"[43] and that he was a cousin by marriage of William Blackwell, one of the wealthiest citizens of London. It is highly probable that the Thirlbys had relatives living in Norfolk, which, if true, would help to explain Thomas's later friendship with the Walpoles of that county.[44] Moreover, the exact date of his entrance into Cambridge is uncertain, but it was certainly not later than 1518.[45]

[42] Cooper, *Athenae Cantabrigienses*, I, p. 287.

[43] *Visitations of Essex*, H.S., XIV, p. 556.

[44] Thomas Thirlby's first cousin, Margaret Campion, married William Blackwell of London whose daughter, Mary Blackwell, married William Walpole. See *Visitations of Essex*, H.S., XIV, p. 556; and Jessopp, *One Generation of a Norfolk House*, p. 125, n. 10. For the Thirlbys of Norfolk, see Carthew, *History of the Hundred of Launditch, Norfolk*, pt. ii, p. 677.

[45] Cooper, *Athenae Cantabrigienses*, I, p. 287, claims that Thomas Thirlby was born "about 1506." Assuming that he was 14 or 15 when he entered Trinity Hall, it is difficult to fit the date of his birth with the fact that he received his bachelor's degree in Civil Law in 1520-1521, only a year after arriving at Cambridge, and graduated Doctor of Civil Law in 1527-1528 and Doctor of Canon Law in 1529-1530 (Venn, *Alumni Cantabrigienses*, pt. i, vol. IV, p. 220). On the basis of the dates of his degrees, it seems far more likely that the Bishop was born about 1500. If Cooper, on

The Cambridge of that year when Thomas Thirlby may be presumed to have matriculated, was in many ways not a pleasant prospect for a normal boy. The average age of admittance was fourteen or fifteen,[46] and the university officials treated their young first-year men accordingly. The "boys" were rarely allowed beyond the confines of their college gates except when accompanied by a Master of Arts, who evidently combined the duties of advanced scholarship and juvenile disciplinary drudgery. Master Thomas was probably housed with three or four other boys of the same age in a single room which supplied the needs of study and dormitory alike. Should high spirits or flagging intellectual ambitions lead them into trouble, the birch cane was always handy and generally administered by a practiced and expert hand.[47] Nor was university food particularly appetizing, and then as now was the butt of constant ridicule. "A penny piece of beef among four," and a "little porridge made of the broth of the same beef, with salt and oatmeal" may have been an exaggerated description of university fare.[48] However, Sir Thomas More probably expressed the general regard for collegiate well-being when just before his execution and when his own fortunes were at their lowest ebb, he commented to his family that there was no need as yet to "descend to Oxford fare" and for the time being they could manage on "Lincoln's Inn diet."[49] University life was markedly severe even in an age accustomed to daily discomforts, and it is not difficult to imagine the truth of one college master's description of learned dons and young

---

the other hand, is correct, then Thirlby was a Bachelor of Law at 14, a Doctor of Civil Law at 21, a Doctor of Canon Law at 23, and a bishop at 34. It is difficult to believe that even Thomas Thirlby was quite so precocious.

[46] Mullinger, *University of Cambridge*, I, p. 346.
[47] *Ibid.*, p. 369.
[48] Lever, *Sermon Preached at Pauls Cross* (1550), p. 122.
[49] Chambers, *Thomas More*, p. 67.

bachelors running or walking up or down for "half an hour to get a heat in their feet when they go to bed."[50]

But there was the lighter side of undergraduate life apart from the discomforts of medieval standards and the sixteenth-century rigorous academic schedule. The river Cam always afforded food and sport while the perennial dispute between town and gown concerning fishing rights supplied a constant topic of speculation. The blatant disregard on the part of the university for the claims of the municipality to the sole monopoly of fishing on the Cam led to the amusing picture of the Mayor and the Prior of Barnwell laying "violent hands on each other," and when the town officials farmed out their rights to "poor men" whose poverty, it was hoped, would make them more solicitous of protecting their property, the only result seems to have been to give the university students the amusement of driving them off by showering them with stones and cutting their nets. In such diversion we can well imagine that Master Thomas Thirlby with his intimate knowledge of the bickering of town and college was a leading figure. Besides fishing, there was cockfighting, the cross bow, and long walks in the country, which by university statute had to be taken in pairs.[51]

But the young man coming to Cambridge was not expected to be beguiled by such recreation or his ambitions dulled by such Spartan democracy. For lack of conflicting evidence, we must take the description of the Master of St. John's as the norm, when he wrote in 1550 that industrious scholars rose at five, heard chapel for an hour, studied from six till ten, dined on a meagre repast, and returned to their studies until ten in the evening, with time out only for a sparse supper "not much better than their dinner."[52] Young Thomas was registered at Trinity Hall where he was studying for a

---

[50] Lever, *Sermon Preached at Pauls Cross* (1550), p. 122.
[51] Mullinger, *University of Cambridge*, I, pp. 373-374.
[52] Lever, *Sermon Preached at Pauls Cross* (1550), p. 122.

law degree, and the student of civil law was expected to spend ten years, if he were not already a Master of Arts, for a doctorate. He had to read the *Digestum Vetus* twice and to have lectured himself on the *Institutes*, and be able to show that he owned or had borrowed and presumably read all the books required in his course of studies. Long hours, under the worst possible conditions in badly lit rooms, were needed to meet the prescribed standards. Nor was it possible to indulge in the modern technique of cramming, for books were still scarce and those in most constant use were generally chained to tables in the library. In an age when books were still treasured, the lecture assumed important proportions, for often the spoken word had to substitute for the printed page. Should the student go on to a degree in canon law, as most of them did, he had to attend lectures on the Bible for at least two years and to have himself lectured on one of the books of the *Decretals*.[53] As for Thomas Thirlby, he seems to have completed his studies in the shortest possible time, having received his bachelor's degree in 1521, his doctorate in civil law in 1528, and two years later the equivalent degree in canon law.[54]

Were this a complete description of university life during the sixteenth century, it would vary little from that of a hundred years before. The physical structure of academic life was, in fact, relatively unchanged throughout the course of years, but a new spirit, a new criticism, had entered both Oxford and Cambridge as the fifteenth gave way to the sixteenth century. Old bottles were being dusted off and the heady wine of the "New Learning" was replacing the medieval vintages.

The Catholic Church of the Middle Ages had been a vast edifice of faith and ceremony each complementing the other, and the two welded into an institutional structure by the

[53] Mullinger, *University of Cambridge*, I, p. 364.
[54] Venn, *Alumni Cantabrigienses*, pt. i, vol. IV, p. 220.

crystallizing nature of vested interests and tradition. Safe in its Catholicism, the church could afford to countenance within its fold the divergent ideas and destructive nature of intellectual curiosity as long as dangerous intellectualism remained quarantined in the monastic cloister or the college hall. But as soon as inquiry and inquisitiveness acquired political and social implications, when ideas and innovations first born in the sanctuary and seclusion of the scholar's ivory tower, were translated into popular action, both the state and church alike were forced to take immediate and drastic counter measures. It was assumed that heresy and sedition went hand in hand, and that a threat to the church was equally a threat to the state. However, the church of the fifteenth and early sixteenth centuries was relatively secure, but security and universality breed tolerance and negligence, and, for the most part, the church, even if it did not altogether approve, at least allowed the spread of this new intellectual quickening known as the "New Learning." It was only when words were no longer savored and appreciated like fine wines by a handful of intellectuals, and when the intoxicating spirit of innovation was tasted by the masses, that the generous policy of tolerance was replaced with persecution.

It is not part of this thesis to inquire into the details of the new critical atmosphere which was stimulating the thought and curiosity of scholars during the early decades of the century. It moved up from Italy and slowly rolled across Western Europe and into England. Generically it is described as the "New Learning," but its species and variations were multitudinous. It fostered a vast and slavish respect for pagan literature and art, and indulged in ridicule and laughter at the expense of older scholars who, in the words of one humanist, had made the universities "nests of gloomy ignorance."[55] It attacked the prevalent ignorance of pure Latin and even the simplest Greek; it scoffed at the determined

[55] Petrarch, quoted in Mullinger, *University of Cambridge*, I, p. 382.

and uncritical respect for Aristotle and the later medieval commentators; it scorned the mercenary if not illogical attitude of the canonists and civilians who studied law not for the sake of Ciceronian orations and classical style, but as a preparation for the future and a financially profitable life. Rhetoric replaced logic as the staple of education, while scholastics were condemned for groveling "in the grossest kind of sophistry." As the clear and somewhat precious air of skepticism, cynicism, and revolt moved northwards across Germany, the Lowlands and the Ile de France, it was transformed into the clouds of the Christian humanistic spirit, acquiring moisture from the stream of northern religious fervor and mysticism which was shortly to fall again as rain to nourish both the weeds and flowers of the Protestant Reformation.

In England the "New Learning" found a close and friendly ally in the growing discontent over the religious forms and rituals then in common practice. Catholicism had lost some of its spiritual strength during the course of centuries, and ceremonies and religious observances had become stereotyped and meaningless. Superstition had crept into the church transforming pilgrimages, images, and the worship of saints into mechanistic means of salvation in themselves. Many churchmen and laymen alike looked with disgust upon bishops who in their worldly preoccupations had little knowledge of, and less interest in, the "innumerable souls" of their dioceses. Preachers and ministers were obsessed with the uncertain and transcendental nature of life. The plague, the sweating sickness, and the severity of daily existence brought death close upon the world, and at any moment the wrath of an omnipotent God might descend to take "away thy wife, thy husband, thy child, thine heir, thy goods, thy worldly comforts that thou haddest so much pleasure in." In an age when social barriers were being disregarded and when the "common sort" were dressing like gentlemen, and a blacksmith's son could become a minister of state, the words of the evangelical preachers had real and personal meaning. Men felt insecure and the fear of divine retribution fell heavily upon their hearts. "I was born and came into this world bare and naked, and bare and naked I shall go from it. . . . Yea, both Emperors and Kings, Queens and ladies, lords and gentlemen, rich and poor, All, All, All are born naked and bare, and as barely shall they again depart this world. . . . This fair body of thine which you make so much of, which you deck so preciously, which you set so much by, it shall away. . . . It is but earth, ashes, dust and worm's meat. . . . Serpents shall inherit thy body as thou do naturally inherit thy father's lands. Even so serpents, worms and toads shall inherit thy body . . . shall gnaw, eat and devour thy beautiful face, thy fair nose, thy clear eyes, thy white hands, thy goodly body. Remember this thou lord and lady. Remember this thou Christian man and woman."[56] The men of Tudor England, even in the midst of their wealth and worldly interest, were too close to death to forget such words, and they demanded more from death than to be forgotten and devoured by serpents, toads, and worms. The church, however, no longer seemed to afford the certainty of salvation which such a life made necessary, and men turned from the still well-marked road held out to them and plunged into the byways of individual interpretation and into the uncertainty of personal inquiry.

This then was the new wine which was filling the old bottles at Cambridge, a new approach to scholarship with its criticism of past standards, and a growing desire for an evangelistic broom within the church itself. But a changed atmosphere, a new spirit, has no existence unless translated into the lives of men, and it is here that we must return to the story of Thomas Thirlby in order to relate this new mood to personalities and social contacts.

Exactly whom young Master Thomas knew at Cambridge is

[56] Longland, *A Sermon spoken before the Kinge his Maiestie at Grenwiche* (1536), sig. E II - E III.

not recorded, but the assumption is that such a gregarious individual must have been acquainted with most of his future colleagues on the Episcopal Bench. Both he and the diminutive Thomas Bilney were Trinity Hall men and received their bachelor degrees the same year, and Thirlby roomed just beneath "Little Bilney," at least until that introspective and conscience-stricken young man gave up law for the evangelical study of the Gospel. John Foxe, the Martyrologist, has preserved the story of Thirlby, an accomplished musician, entertaining his friends on the recorder and consequently reducing Bilney, who detested music, to a flood of prayers. Whether such an effect could always be counted on and whether Master Thomas and his friends maliciously planned to plague the long-suffering and charitable Bilney is not disclosed, but the future bishop and diplomat must have had little sympathy for the intense and esoteric experience of a would-be mystic.[57]

The list of distinguished Norfolk men at Cambridge is unique. In 1518 Stephen Gardiner was a new Bachelor of Civil Law, John Skip had just received his Master of Arts and was going on to study divinity at Gonville College, while Nicholas Shaxton was working for his degree of Doctor of Divinity. There also were Robert Barnes, John Lambert, and "Little Bilney" himself, three men who were to swell the list of future martyrs. County associations tended to transcend collegiate particularism, and Norfolk men were notorious for their cliquishness.[58] With his probable Norfolk connections, Thirlby must have been intimately acquainted with most of these men. Gardiner was a Trinity Hall student himself and is said to have instructed Master Thomas in the mysteries of the law,[59] and Bilney, as we have already noted, was his close neighbor. Whom else he knew is difficult to say. He eventually became the close friend of Thomas Cranmer, then a Fel-

[57] Foxe, IV, p. 621.
[58] Mullinger, *University of Cambridge*, I, pp. 239, 563.
[59] Muller, *Stephen Gardiner*, p. 11.

low of Jesus College but not yet a Bachelor of Divinity, and it was through Cranmer's influence that the young law graduate was later brought to the attention of the King and Cromwell.[60] Nicholas Heath, Robert Holgate, and Nicholas Ridley were students like himself, while Thomas Goodrich had already become a Doctor of Divinity at Corpus Christi College. Roland Lee was just finishing his studies for a doctorate in canon law, and Hugh Latimer was still a conservative and orthodox Fellow of Clare College and until 1524 neither a reformer nor a Bachelor of Divinity. Robert Warton, George Day, and John Taylor were, like Thirlby, young men just starting their university studies in 1518, while Henry Holbeach was not to enter Cambridge for several years. Some of the older men whom Thomas Thirlby was to know in later life had already left college. Edward Lee by 1518 was a chaplain of Henry VIII and already being groomed by Cardinal Wolsey for the diplomatic service; John Capon had just the previous year left Cambridge to become Abbot of St. Benet's in Norfolk, while Richard Sampson, Gardiner's old teacher in the law, was already in the Lowlands working for his patron, Thomas Wolsey. Cuthbert Tunstal had left years before to study for his doctor of law degree in Italy, and William Rugge had returned to the monastic life. But the span of years separating these men is slight. Lee, Sampson, and Capon had only just left Cambridge when Thirlby arrived, and only Tunstal, Clerk, John Bell, and John Kite can be said to have belonged to an older generation, a generation which preceded the arrival of Erasmus at Cambridge. As for John Scory and John Poynet, they were in 1518 still children under ten.

For years the "dry and biting sublety" of scholasticism had been the dominant motif of medieval education. What had commenced as a magnificent attempt to unite God and man within a rational religion, built soundly upon the dual rock of

---

[60] Foxe, VIII, pp. 71-72; *L.P.*, VII [1534], Nos. 257, 703.

divine revelation and human reason, had become by the sixteenth century a self-perpetuating study for specialists who
blindly accepted the premises of the great schoolmen and indulged in pedantic haggling over details. Thirteenth-century
knowledge had become antiquated, its logic stereotyped, and
its faith dulled and forgotten in a forest of academic arguments. Endless speculation revolved around such points as
"whether God could have taken upon Himself the likeness
of a woman? Or of a devil? Or of an ass? Of a gourd? Of a
piece of flint? Then how would that gourd have preached,
performed miracles, or been crucified?"[61] No doubt this is a
highly prejudiced quotation made by a very partial observer,
but although such "finespun triffles" may indeed have been
a fascinating pastime for those versed in the intricacies of
medieval logic, for many men it was inconsequential and
demoralizing. To Erasmus, More, and John Colet it was the
grossest kind of mortal presumption to pollute "the majesty
of sacred theology by silly, sordid terms and sentiments."[62]
God was to be loved, not analyzed; religion was to be founded
upon the sure rock of faith, not upon the uncertain sand of
human reason and speculation.

In England the man who did most to free religion from
the suffocating hold of academic specialists, to strip the Scriptures of the multitude of allegories which had concealed its
more obvious lessons, was Desiderius Erasmus. Erasmus was
invited to Cambridge in 1511 at the instigation of John Fisher,
Bishop of Rochester. He stayed only two years, being driven
away by the cold, the plague, and the vile beer, but during
these few months he prepared his *New Testament* which was
published at Basle in 1516. For the first time the principles
of the "New Learning" were being applied to the sacred
sphere of divine revelation. What Valla had done for the
Donation of Constantine and Grocyn for Dionysius' *Celestrial*

[61] Erasmus, *Praise of Folly*, pp. 78-79.
[62] *Ibid.*, p. 83.

Hierarchy, Erasmus was doing for the Bible. All were being held up to the light of new scrutiny, based on a sounder knowledge of Greek and the early Latin authors. Much that for centuries had been taken as authoritative, even perfect, was now exposed to the scrutiny of human criticism, and centuries of tradition were set aside for the judgment of presumptuous contemporaries. Stripped of allegories sanctified by years of acceptance, the Scriptures became the source from which the individual drew his personal religion. Neither Catholic nor Protestant, Lutheran nor Anabaptist, doubted the ultimate nature of that source, but the conflict over the authoritative interpretation had commenced, and was to continue for four hundred years until a modern and more skeptical age grew weary of the quest for ultimate truth.

Youthful lawyers and humanists read the new work for its Latin, while the young critics of contemporary society bought it, as they had bought the *Praise of Folly* and later the *Colloquies*, for the implied attack which it made on the secularized and superstitious elements which were degrading the divinity and ritual of the church. The *New Testament* was a startling innovation but in 1516 it was eminently orthodox, having received the enthusiastic approval of Fisher, Tunstal, Archbishop Warham and even the Supreme Pontiff. It was no exaggeration when Erasmus wrote that he had the support, not only of bishops and archbishops, but of "the Pope himself."[63]

The spell of Christian humanism affected these Cambridge scholars in various ways: some directly as a consequence of the *New Testament*, some by the presence of Erasmus at Cambridge, and some merely by the intoxicating effect of the "New Learning." It was not mere coincidence that Cranmer turned to humane letters the year Erasmus arrived at Cambridge and five years later, in 1516, began his ponderous but fruitful study of the Scriptures. Robert Aldridge, the future

---

[63] Erasmus, *Epistles*, II, p. 331.

Bishop of Carlisle and sincere opponent of the Reformation, escorted Erasmus on his scoffing pilgrimage to Our Lady of Walsingham, acting as guide and interpreter, and joined the Dutchman and his company in their scornful ridicule of the credulous who traveled to venerate "a stinking bundle of old bones."[64] Stephen Gardiner, drawing from his knowledge of Greek and the general atmosphere of reform, transformed the study of the *Institutes of Justinian* into something new and stimulating, winning from the antiquarian, John Leland, the praise that he was "the seat of fluent eloquence and of the Pierian chorus."[65] While Aldridge learned to scoff and laugh, while Gardiner lent grace to the drudgery of the law, and Cranmer moved cautiously through the Scriptures, it was "Little Bilney" who caught and savored a mystical experience from reading the *New Testament*. He began, like any other young humanistic lawyer to read it for its Latin, and ended by finding Christ. His own words are majestic testimony of that vast source of inspiration and comfort which lies hidden within the Gospel. "But at last I heard speak of Jesus," he wrote, "even then when the *New Testament* was first set forth by Erasmus; which when I understood to be eloquently done by him, being allured rather by the Latin than by the word of God (for at that time I knew not what it meant), I bought it even by the providence of God, as I do now well understand and perceive: and at the first reading . . . I chanced upon this sentence of St. Paul . . . 'It is a true saying, and worthy of all men to be embraced, that Christ Jesus came into the world to save sinners; of whom I am the chief and principal.' This one sentence, through God's instruction and inward working, which I did not then perceive, did so exhilarate my heart, being before wounded with the guilt of my sin, and being almost in despair, that immediately I felt a marvelous comfort and quietness, insomuch 'that my bruised bones leaped

[64] Erasmus, *Colloquies*, p. 245.
[65] Leland, *Collectanea*, V, p. 157.

for joy.' "[66] Many other men were to find solace and support in these words and to feel themselves sustained and protected by their personal knowledge of the Scriptures.

This atmosphere of criticism and revolt was not confined to the study of the Bible but occasionally took on physical aspects, and Bass Mullinger in his history of Cambridge has preserved one such incident which led to a serious university scandal. In 1517 or thereabouts, the Papacy distributed for local publication a series of indulgences, carefully noting the various species of crimes and the charges necessary for expiation. The notice was duly posted on the "gate of the common school" and during the night a youthful Norman student named Peter de Valence proceeded to scribble across the notice the words: "*Beatus vir cujus est nomen Domini ejus spes, et non respexit in vanitates et insanias falsas (istas).*" Next morning Bishop Fisher "summoned an assembly" and after trying to explain the reason for indulgences, called upon the undergraduate vandal to confess. Peter de Valence, however, preferred to enjoy his defiance in secret, and the affair was eventually forgotten.[67] There are several versions of this story and only Bass Mullinger has connected it directly with the fatal declaration of indulgences of 1517 which drove the young monk of Wittenberg to post his ninety-five Theses.[68] Whether the two events are related makes but small difference, for what in Germany had such far-reaching results, in England was regarded as an undergraduate prank. Cambridge students may have been radical and defiant, but as yet they were not heretical.

In the year that Thirlby entered Cambridge, however, a much more significant event took place, for in 1518 or possibly the preceding year, a group of young apostles of reform began to meet at the White Horse Tavern. Many historians

---

[66] Foxe, IV, p. 635.

[67] Mullinger, *University of Cambridge*, I, pp. 556-557.

[68] Smith, *Henry VIII and the Reformation*, p. 252; Fuller, *History of Cambridge*, p. 99.

would have us believe that the first meetings were the result of the edict of 1520 banning all Lutheran books in England.[69] Canon Smith, however, has pointed out that these informal gatherings commenced several years earlier, and were decidedly not the work of venerable and religiously inspired Protestants who crept together to avoid the bigoted arm of a persecuting church.[70] Until the end of 1520 Lutheran books were quite legal, while Erasmus' *New Testament* was being freely circulated. Moreover, we must accept with caution Bass Mullinger's statement that for "the first time, the noble thoughts of Luther sank deeply into many a heart," and that Lutheran "doctrines, if not invariably accepted, were tested by honest and devout enquiry and by the sole standard of Scriptural truth."[71] It is much more probable that enquiry was far from being devout, and that the standards were not always those of "Scriptural truth." Many of the young men who gathered at "little Germany," as the Tavern was scornfully dubbed, were merely youthful critics and scoffers, and there is no evidence at all that Thomas Cranmer, who was indeed interested in "honest inquiry" and "Scriptural truth," ever attended the sessions. The members were, on the whole, young and gregarious, and attendance, if not completely respectable, was certainly open and aboveboard.[72] At worst, the White Horse Tavern can be called a "fellow travellers' society," and in fact was probably much closer to a coffee house in the reign of Queen Anne, as Canon Smith has described it.[73]

The meetings afforded a chance to discuss and criticize current ideas, and it is probably not far from the truth to say that the personal idiosyncrasies of college dons came up for undergraduate scrutiny far more often than Martin Luther's newest book. That Lutheran ideas and unorthodox opinions were

---

[69] Mullinger, *University of Cambridge*, I, pp. 571-572.
[70] Smith, *Henry VIII and the Reformation*, p. 252.
[71] Mullinger, *University of Cambridge*, I, p. 574.
[72] Smith, *Henry VIII and the Reformation*, p. 253.
[73] *Ibid.*, p. 252.

voiced cannot be doubted, but what is important to this narrative is that the gatherings at the White Horse Tavern epitomize the equality which existed between later reformers and conservatives during their Cambridge days, for both groups met and savored of this embryonic heresy. Whether Thomas Thirlby himself was ever a regular disciple is doubtful but that he went on occasion is highly probable, considering his friendship for those who attended more regularly. If we keep in mind the history of their future careers, the names of those who gathered at "little Germany" are indeed remarkable. There were the three incipient conservatives, Stephen Gardiner, Nicholas Heath, and John Skip, the two Protestant martyrs, Thomas Bilney and Nicholas Ridley, the Protestant author Coverdale, the future diplomat Edward Fox, and the uncertain reformer Nicholas Shaxton.[74] How many of the later bishops attended is impossible to say, especially since the meetings extended over a number of years, but probably most of them at one time or another attended or accompanied friends, drawn by idle curiosity and a glass of beer. The coterie of the White Horse Tavern consisted mostly of young men, their average age being well under thirty. Among their group were enthusiastic critics of church, state, and university alike, youthful humanists, and indiscreet students who enjoyed the chance to express personal opinions without regard to authority. If most came out of curiosity or for the sake of conversation, a few attended for "honest and devout inquiry." Only the year before the first recorded meeting, Bilney had been converted to a pseudo-Protestantism and was fervent in his efforts to reconcile both friend and foe to his beliefs, and Robert Barnes, "a merry scoffing friar," found a sympathetic audience for his indignation against the injustices and inanities of governmental and university bureaucracy and red tape.

What must be impressed upon the reader is that this was

[74] *Ibid.*, p. 253.

not heresy. It may have "savoured of the frying pan," but as yet the church had not defined its dogma in preparation for the coming conflict, and indiscriminate criticism was still safe. Future Protestants had not yet learned the power of the "Gospel" and future Catholics its dangers. It was not heresy to scoff at pilgrimages, to criticize the superstitious worship of images and saints, or to read Lutheran tracts. Stephen Gardiner, who was a conscientious defender of Barnes in his early lapses into heresy, wrote of these men that "there was not then in them malice, and they maintained communication having some savour of learning; I was familiar with such sort of men. . . ."[75] Nor was Gardiner alone among the later conservatives who were familiar "with such sort" and who "loved them for their learning." John Skip, Roland Lee, Thomas Thirlby, and Nicholas Heath were friends of such men as Bilney, Shaxton, Latimer, Lambert, and Joye, and, as we shall see in a later chapter, they retained their desire for reform even after they had left Cambridge.

When then did malice creep into the new doctrines? When did church and state feel that youthful innovators had gone too far? The case of Robert Barnes shows how easy it was for the respectable reformer to slip into heresy. In reminiscing about Barnes, Gardiner wrote in 1546: "A doctor of Divinity he was, but never like to have proved to be either martyr or confessor in Christ's religion; and yet he began there to exercise railing (which, among such as newly profess Christ, is a great piece of cunning, and a great forwardness to reputation, especially if he rail of bishops, as Barnes began, and to please such of the lower sort as envieth ever authority) chiefly against my Lord Cardinal, then . . . having the high administration of the realm."[76] But Gardiner was careful to point out that insubordination, and such "railing of bishops" as referring to the Cardinal as "Carnal Wolsey" were not Barnes' real crimes.

[75] Gardiner, *Letters*, No. 81, "Gardiner to George Joye," (1546) p. 166.
[76] *Ibid.*, pp. 165-166.

Such epithets were commonplace witticisms at Cambridge, and Gardiner himself must have joined in undergraduate criticism of reactionary dons who disapproved of the teaching of Greek or the publication of Erasmus' *New Testament*. But the authorities were beginning to take alarm when men began to preach to "please such of the lower sort," and when Barnes was brought before Cardinal Wolsey and Bishop Fisher, the Bishop could find little wrong with his sermons but strongly reprimanded him for preaching "this before the butchers of Cambridge."[77] What made the case against Friar Barnes serious was not his remarks about pardons being sold "as openly as a cow and an ox" or even his refusal to pray for souls in purgatory, but his statement that no Christian could sue a fellow Christian.[78] What had moved his crusading spirit was the pitiable plight of a friend who had been thrown into debtor's prison, and Barnes had made the mistake of giving vent to his feelings in a public address. When the Friar was brought before the majesty of the law in the person of Thomas Wolsey, he proved himself a brash and impudent man, but as Gardiner confessed: "And yet that railing, in a friar, had been easily pardoned, if Barnes had not fondly persisted in the Anabaptist's opinion, denying suits to be lawful among Christian men."[79] Fortunately for Barnes, he was induced to recant and to do penance, and he eventually left for Europe where, no doubt, he found a more sympathetic audience.

What is significant about this story is that Barnes was not merely condemned for heresy and collegiate defiance, but was ordered before the Lord Chancellor for preaching in a public pulpit, before butchers and apprentices, ideas which were dangerous to the whole social structure of the nation. He probably did not realize at the time the full implication of what he was preaching and was only attacking the injustices of a specific case in general terms, but to his audience, and certainly to the

[77] Barnes, *Supplication*, p. 206. [78] *Ibid.*, pp. 205-217.
[79] Gardiner, *Letters*, No. 81, "Gardiner to George Joye," (1546) p. 166.

Cardinal, his words were pregnant with social disorder. To deny the right of lawsuits was equivalent to denying the entire doctrine of the law itself. It was at this point that church and state decided that collegiate enthusiasm preached before the "common sort" might lead to sedition, and accordingly it was dubbed Anabaptist and heretical. Malice had indeed crept into Cambridge, and astute churchmen and government officials were quick to perceive the danger of ideas and theories which could lead to the destruction of all organized institutions and endanger all authority and "good order." Ideas suddenly joined to the catalyst of social distress could be transformed from the plaything of intellectuals into the weapons of revolutionaries, and the spectre of social revolution was constantly before the eyes of every Tudor administrator.

By 1530 the graduates of both Oxford and Cambridge had attained manhood, and had been taught all that the sixteenth-century academic life could offer them. Then and only then did these future bishops begin to part both mentally and physically. The doctors of the two laws went forth into the violent duplicity and ceaseless intrigue of court life, while those in divinity remained behind in the isolated atmosphere of the academic world or were recalled to their monastic institutions. Cranmer, Shaxton, Latimer, and Ridley continued as professors of theology, while Holgate, Salcot, Hilsey, Hooper, and Holbeach retired to their monasteries. For both these groups, it was the Reformation which destroyed the obscurity surrounding their lives and plunged them into the world of events and sordid realities. On the other hand, Sampson, Gardiner, Bonner, and Roland Lee left their universities, proudly to lay their new degrees in civil and canon law at the feet of Cardinal Wolsey; there these future conservatives remained, to be fostered and reared under the crimson velvet of the Cardinal's patronage.[80] Nor could they have selected a

---

[80] Edward Fox and Edward Lee were Doctors of Divinity, but unlike Cranmer and Shaxton they did not remain in the academic environment.

better path to fame and worldly success than through the household of this Chancellor, who was only secondarily a cardinal of the church. The collegiate association of Doctor of Divinity and Doctor of Law was over, and while the Cranmers and Ridleys stayed behind in the already heretical air of Cambridge, the new ecclesiastical lawyers began their training under Wolsey as diplomats and administrators. They were still humanists, they were still humane, but they had little time for scholarship for its own sake, for they were too busy learning that government is the result, not of ideas but of expediency, not of policy but of inertia, not of God but of man. From a common starting-point their paths began to diverge until they met again in the House of Lords as bishops and councillors of the Privy Council. By that time these Cambridge graduates were poles apart in temperament, experience, and wisdom, and the passions of religious controversy were to place them in opposite parties.

Instead they were quickly drawn into the Cardinal's household and a worldly career. Tunstal, John Bell, and William Knight were like Gardiner, Doctors of Law, but their names are not included here because they had joined Wolsey's entourage long before 1530.

CHAPTER II

LAW AND HUMANISM

*T*HE study of law in any age is exacting and tedious work, but in the sixteenth century the reward for long hours poring over the decrees of the *Corpus Juris Canonici* and the *Institutes of Justinian* was a substantial one. The knowledge of canon law had become the criterion for clerical promotion. Bishop's chancellors, diocesan vicars-general, and archdeacons were all trained in the intricacies of church law. The probate of wills, civil and criminal cases involving the clergy, trials of heresy, and disputed contracts and marriages were decided in clerical courts.[1] Bishops had little time for their episcopal responsibilities and their administrative burdens were delegated to their vicars-general and archdeacons while their spiritual duties were passed on to Irish and suffragan bishops who did the work of consecration, baptism, and the overseeing of the "innumerable souls" of a diocese.[2] This mountain of judicial and administrative business on which the machinery of the church relied assured immediate advancement for the youthful university jurist who had spent years preparing for the day when he would step into the office of an ecclesiastical advocate or vicar-general. Roland Lee became Chancellor to Bishop Blythe;[3] John Voysey began as Vicar-general and Chancellor to Arundel, Bishop of Coventry and Lichfield;[4] Richard

---

[1] Maitland, *English Law and the Renaissance*, p. 48, n. 18; p. 62, n. 33; *ibid.*, *Roman Canon Law in the Church of England*, ch. II, "Church, State, and Decretals."

[2] Smith, *Pre-Reformation England*, p. 28. John Stokesley, Bishop of London, for instance, was described by the Spanish ambassador as a man who, until July 1535, had "never preached in his life on account of his stammering and bad speaking." *L.P.*, VIII [1535], No. 1019.

[3] *DNB*, Art. "Roland Lee."

[4] *DNB*, Art. "John Voysey." See also Oliver, *Lives of the Bishops of Exeter*, pp. 120-132, 294. Voysey was placed in the household of Elizabeth

Sampson filled the post of Cardinal Wolsey's Chancellor in his troublesome See of Tournay;[5] and Cuthbert Tunstal in 1509 commenced his career as Chancellor to Archbishop Warham.[6] Voysey, Tunstal, and Sampson were valued administrators long before the issue of Henry's divorce with Catherine placed the trained canonist at a premium, but for many of the younger and more obscure lawyers, it was the King's "great matter" which pushed them into prominence. From being minor legal advisers to the Cardinal or lesser ecclesiastical advocates, they were suddenly called upon to prepare the royal lawsuit when it was presented before the Legate's court at Blackfriars in 1529, or to draw up the endless stream of legal documents which were dispatched to Rome. Thus John Bell rose from being Vicar-general of the See of Worcester and one of the commissioners of the Court of Audience to become one of the legal advisers of the King,[7] and Edmund Bonner, who up to the time of the Cardinal's fall in 1529 had been "master of my lord's faculties and spiritual jurisdictions" became by 1532 one of the ambassadorial advocates of the royal divorce.[8]

But the young law graduate of Oxford and Cambridge had yet another string to his bow, for he was usually doctor of both laws, canon and civil, and while the former assured him

---

of York in 1498, made Vicar-general and Chancellor to Bishop Arundel in 1502, was registrar of the Order of the Garter in 1515, and was consecrated Bishop of Exeter in November of 1519 at the age of 50.

[5] *DNB*, Art. "Richard Sampson." He was chaplain and Chancellor to Wolsey at Tournay as early as April 1514. See *L.P.*, 1 [1514], No. 4982.

[6] Sturge, *Cuthbert Tunstal*, p. 18. He entered Warham's service probably in 1508.

[7] *DNB*, Art. "John Bell." He was Vicar-general of the See of Worcester in 1518. See *L.P.*, III, pt. ii [1522], No. 2178, and *L.P.*, Add. [1527], No. 528. For his position as a Canon Law adviser to Henry VIII, see B.M., Royal 11 B. XI; *L.P.*, IV, pt. iii [1529], No. 5518.

[8] Cavendish, *Wolsey*, p. 212. The description "Master of my Lord's faculties" actually means very little. Bonner was probably one of the Cardinal's many legal advisers. See P.R.O., S.P.1, vol. 53, ff. 286-287 (*L.P.*, IV, pt. iii [1529], No. 5533). His first mission to Europe and Rome was in January 1532.

rapid promotion within the legal hierarchy of the church, the latter was his preparation for government service. Sir Thomas More, statesman, diplomat, and Lord Chancellor of England, was quick to realize the value of legal training, and in writing to his own university of Oxford he took pains to remind the academic officials "that not all who come to you, come for the study of theology. The State needs men learned in the law."[9] Both international diplomacy and the principles of equity as practiced in the Court of Chancery were based on the civil law, and diplomat and lord chancellor alike were expected to be skilled civilians.[10] It was not mere bravado that Trinity Hall, Cambridge, the college of jurists, had for its motto: learning "for the advantage, rule, and direction of the commonwealth"; it was not mere coincidence that three of her graduates, Richard Sampson, Stephen Gardiner, and Thomas Thirlby, each in turn the pupil of his predecessor,[11] should have become statesmen, ambassadors, and members of the King's Privy Council. The story of their administrative careers must await a later chapter, but here we must note that it was the knowledge of the civil and canon law which made their future success possible, for the astute Thomas Wolsey was not slow to appreciate the ability and value of such men and to utilize their talents. Gardiner became his private secretary; Tunstal left the Archbishop's service to become a young negotiator for the Cardinal in the Lowlands; Sampson reluctantly took over the management of the Lord Chancellor's household, a veritable court of 500 persons.[12] Roland Lee along with Stephen Gardiner and Thomas Cromwell proved themselves competent administrators in dissolving and administering the monastic houses which were taken over in order to support and endow their patron's new college at

[9] Quoted in Stapleton, *Life of More*, p. 41.

[10] Nicholas Heath is an important exception to this generalization. As Lord Chancellor to Queen Mary, he was not trained in law but in divinity.

[11] Muller, *Stephen Gardiner*, p. 11.

[12] Cavendish, *Wolsey*, p. 36.

Oxford. In all these posts the knowledge of the law was an essential ingredient.

Erudition in the law was a common bond between these men, for it not only gave them a similar educational background, but it led them into related careers where their lives were bound to cross, and it is not too great a generalization to say that every one of these lawyer-bishops was intimately acquainted with the other. Gardiner, Sampson, Bonner, and Roland Lee were all members of Wolsey's vast entourage in 1528; Tunstal, Sampson, and Sir Thomas More were old associates who had worked together on the diplomatic and mercantile commission sent to the Lowlands in 1515; John Clerk and John Bell were colleagues in their duties as legal advisers in the King's divorce; Thomas Thirlby was briefly associated with Tunstal on the Council of the North, the former as a young clerk, the latter as President of the Council; and John Voysey was for years Lord President of the Council of Wales and an intimate friend of Sir Thomas More.[13] Moreover, their legal training and judicial interests brought them together in the same clubs, for many were members of Doctors' Commons, either as practicing advocates of the Court of the Arches or as individuals who found common bonds of interest with such a company. Doctors' Commons was an association of canonists and civilians most of whom were affiliated with the Court of the Arches. They lived together and dined at a common table in a small house on Pater Noster Row. The Commons at its inception in 1509 was not restricted to advocates and rapidly became a meeting place of distinguished men, many of whom were secular lawyers or divines. There was John Voysey, Cuthbert Tunstal, John Clerk, Richard Sampson, Roland Lee, Arthur Bulkeley, Edmund Bonner, John Bell, and Thomas Thirlby, all men with law degrees. Among those who did not qualify as legitimate members

[13] For the details of their administrative and diplomatic careers see ch. III, *passim*.

but were enrolled in an honorary status were Sir Thomas More; John Stokesley, later Bishop of London; John Colet, the Dean of St. Paul's; Thomas Winter, Wolsey's natural son; Polydore Vergil, the historian; and William Grocyn, the eminent scholar and humanist. Such men must have joined Doctors' Commons for its agreeable and sympathetic company and the desire to have temporary lodgings in London when they arrived for short visits.[14]

Statistics are often misleading but they cannot be dismissed as inconsequential. Of the eleven bishops who graduated from Oxford or Cambridge in law or acquired their degrees in Europe, not one can be called a reformer.[15] Gardiner, Tunstal, and Bonner were the outstanding leaders of the conservative party, and each in turn lost his bishopric when the Protestant elements took control of the government.[16] Richard Sampson avowedly admitted his distaste for religious innovation and came perilously close to losing his head for being too closely associated with the Gardiner-Tunstal clique.[17] John

[14] A. C. Ducarel, *A Summary Account of the Society of Doctors' Commons*, Lambeth Palace Lib., Ms. 958, has the most complete list of members. C. Coote, *Sketches of the Lives and Characters of Eminent English Civilians*, has the most accessible description of the organization and its members. See also E. J. Davis, "Doctors' Commons, its Title and Topography," *London Topographical Record*, xv (1931), pp. 36-50. John Voysey, Cuthbert Tunstal, John Clerk, Polydore Vergil, William Grocyn, and John Colet were probably original members, joining before 28 May, 1511, when the first date of admission occurs. Richard Sampson was enrolled on 20 March, 1514; Sir Thomas More on 3 December, 1514; John Bell on 21 November, 1516; Roland Lee on 8 October, 1520; John Stokesley on 22 October, 1525; Arthur Bulkeley on 16 April, 1526; Edmund Bonner on 15 April, 1526; Thomas Winter on 29 October, 1530; Thomas Thirlby on 7 February, 1535. There also were Henry Morgan and David Pole, the Marian bishops of St. David's and Peterborough; Nicholas Wotton, diplomat under four reigns; and Richard Laiton, Dean of York and Thomas Cromwell's handy factotum.

[15] See App. IV for a list of reformers and conservatives.

[16] Gardiner was deprived on 14 February, 1551; Bonner lost his see on 1 October, 1549 under Edward VI and again under Elizabeth on 30 May, 1559; Tunstal was deprived on 14 October, 1552 and for a second time under Elizabeth on 28 September, 1559.

[17] *L.P.*, xv [1540], No. 737.

Clerk was one of the few men with the courage openly to oppose the Submission of the Clergy in 1532,[18] while Roland Lee was dubbed by his contemporary, Stephen Vaughan, "a papist, an idolater, and a fleshly priest."[19] Arthur Bulkeley for all his compliance was imprisoned and attainted for treason and papal affection,[20] while John Bell, William Knight, and John Voysey were open adversaries of the Reformation.[21] Even Thomas Thirlby, despite his friendship for Thomas Cranmer and his acute sense of loyalty to the crown and government, finally refused to comply with the wishes of Elizabeth and consequently lost his see.[22] This, of course, does not mean that all the conservatives were civilians and canonists, but of the leaders of the conservative group, only Nicholas Heath was a Doctor of Divinity.[23]

Professor Muller in his life of Stephen Gardiner makes a statement which we might well apply to all these lawyer-bishops. "His studies," he wrote referring to Gardiner's training in the law, "foreshadowed his career. They did more; they determined the fashion of his thinking. They gave him, or at least strengthened in him, that legal temper of conservatism which even his enthusiasm for humanistic studies

---

[18] Atterbury, *Rights, Powers, and Privileges of an English Convocation*, p. 94. John Clerk also obstructed and opposed the course of the King's divorce (Burnet, I, p. 211) and it was rumored in 1530 that he, Fisher and Bishop West of Ely had all been arrested (*Cal. St. P. Ven.*, III, Nos. 629, 634, 664).

[19] P.R.O., S.P.1, vol. 80, f. 80 (*L.P.*, VI [1533], No. 1385).

[20] *L.P.*, XIX, pt. i [1544], No. 1035, grant 140.

[21] *L.P.*, VIII [1535], No. 859; P.R.O., S.P.1, vol. 115, pp. 166-167, (*L.P.*, XII, pt. i [1537], No. 308); *Archaeologia*, XXIII (1831), p. 59. The position of William Knight is difficult to assess. He rarely expressed an opinion except on diplomatic or administrative affairs, and he died (29 September, 1547) before a final decision on religion was necessary. However, he was a business acquaintance and personal friend of Sir Thomas More (*L.P.*, IV, pt. ii [1526], Nos. 2536, 2541).

[22] Thirlby was transferred from Westminster to Norwich under Edward VI and from Norwich to Ely by Queen Mary. He was deprived by Elizabeth in April of 1559 and died 26 August, 1570.

[23] Stephen Gardiner, Cuthbert Tunstal, Edmund Bonner and Thomas Thirlby were all canonists or civilians. See App. IV. *infra*.

did not destroy. While the revival of learning made skeptics or reformers of the theologians, the study of things classical caused the ecclesiastical lawyers merely to transfer allegiance from Pope to king, to clothe the king in the garments of the Roman emperor, and thus to magnify the Civil at the expense of the Canon Law; but the legal habit of thought was unchanged—the shrinking from innovation, the demand for order and for submission to existing conditions, the spirit which asks what is, rather than what ought to be."[24] It is in this last sentence that Professor Muller has placed his finger on the attitude of the conservatives. The study of law more than any other of the professions is the study of the relationship between fact and theory. The law may exist by itself as a Platonic idea or an emanation of divinity, but it acquires meaning only when related to physical events. It fosters a clear and logical method of thinking, and cultivates a mode of thought which tends to translate ideals into the mundane facts of daily existence. Stephen Gardiner expressed just such an attitude of mind when he wrote in *De vera obedientia* "What folly it is then, that one man, whom we may call John, living in England, should admit allegiance to the Prince as head of the state, but when called a Christian, to deny that he is subject to the King in the same way. Indeed, since he lives in England he is of the realm; and in truth, as a Christian living also in England he must be regarded as being of the church of England. The King, they say, is head of the state but not of the church, and yet the English church is nothing more than the congregation of men and women, clergy and laity, living in England and united in Christ's profession. It [the Church of England] is rightly to be called a church, since it is a communion of Christian people; and rightly to be called Anglican because of the place in which it is located, as also is the case of the French church, the Spanish

[24] Muller, *Stephen Gardiner*, pp. 8-9.

church, and even the Roman church."[25] Here is a theory of the English church in terms of living people, of flesh and blood; to men like Gardiner "Christ's profession," or any other social institution, had little meaning unless solidly planted upon the foundations of human actions. It was a close approximation of the truth when one foreign observer remarked that Bishop Gardiner argues more like a lawyer than a theologian.[26]

The reformers were thoroughly cognizant of the dangerous opposition to be expected from men who placed legality above salvation, and their scorn for these clerical procurators was based upon both the deep religious conviction that such men were the devil's advocates and the astute political realization that the ecclesiastical lawyer was their most pernicious rival. The disdain of John Poynet was boundless when he wrote to Bishop Bonner saying "thou . . . allowest nothing to be well done (by whatsoever authority it be done) except it be lawful, nor nothing to be lawful that is not agreeing to thy canon law."[27] Bonner was to live up to this characterization when, during the discussion of the Book of Common Prayer of 1549, he expressed his complete disapproval of the Protestant principles on which the new book rested by informing his spiritual colleagues that "When anything is called into question, if ye dispute it, ye must see whether it be *decent, lawful* and *expedient*."[28] To Bonner and his kind the new theology of Cranmer and Ridley was none of these.

The relationship between religious conservativism and a legal education may have been exaggerated by the loquacious martyr, Hugh Latimer, but there remains an element of truth

[25] Janelle, *Obedience in Church and State*; Gardiner, *The Oration of True Obedience*, p. 95.

[26] *L.P.*, XVI [1541], No. 667; Muller, *Stephen Gardiner*, p. 95; Smith, *Henry VIII and the Reformation*, p. 184.

[27] Quoted in Maitland, *Essays on the Reformation*, p. 73.

[28] B.M., Royal 17 B. XXXIX, "Certain notes touching the disputation of the Bishops in this last Parliament assembled of the Lord's Supper"; printed in Gasquet and Bishop, App. V, p. 406. The italics are my own.

in his statement that a canonist is "one that is brought up in
the study of the Pope's laws and decrees; one that will set
forth papistry . . . and one that will maintain all superstition
and idolatry. . . ."[29] What these canonists believed was certainly neither superstitious nor idolatrous; it was not always
even Catholic. But Latimer was quite right in assuming that
a man trained in the canon law would regard the legal aspects
of the Reformation as equal to the spiritual. The passionate
martyr had good cause to view such men with a jaundiced eye,
for when the storm of the Reformation swept England it
found these lawyer-bishops solidly opposed to indiscriminate
religious innovation; they could never escape the discipline
of years spent laboriously absorbing the principles of Roman
law and the details of a multitude of papal decrees. The reformer George Joye showed remarkable insight into the
minds of many of the conservatives when he wrote of Stephen
Gardiner that "Winchester now teacheth and writeth mixing
the observance of the law with the grace of the gospel. . . ."[30]

It is here that the first breach between the common background of the reformers and conservatives appears. While
Cranmer, Latimer, Ridley, and the other Protestants remained
within their colleges "singing pleasantly" to themselves, while
such theologians were poring "over chestfuls of the great
corpus of divinity," and were "manfully waging war against
lice and fleas," the lawyers were out gathering "goodly free-
holds with broad acres." They may have been "asses" as
Erasmus disdainfully named them, but even Erasmus had to
admit that "great matters and little matters alike are settled
by the arbitrament of these asses."[31] These ecclesiastical "asses"
were for the most part hard-bitten business men who were
quick to use the law to their own advantage. Young Thomas

[29] Latimer, *Sermons*, "Sermon of the Plough" (1548), p. 70.
[30] Gardiner, *A Declaration of true Articles* (1546), f. xxiiii. All that
remains of Joye's original attack on Gardiner is what the bishop cared to
preserve in his own book.
[31] Erasmus, *Praise of Folly*, p. 45.

Winter had a deep respect for Edmund Bonner's legal abilities and in 1528 he hastened to warn a friend of the dangers of going to law against such a man. Master Winter had himself been a victim of Bonner's legal machinations when the young archdeacon threatened to deprive him of all his preferments "by the canon law." Chastened by this experience, Winter wrote to a friend in England saying he could not "sufficiently wonder at the rashness of my Father Hampton. I hear he has taken the law against Bonner, who will certainly be more than a match for him."[32] Whether the warning was heeded or whether Archdeacon Bonner was more than a match for the innocent Father Hampton is unknown, but neither the future bishop nor the other ecclesiastical lawyers were men easily outwitted in their own metier. Knowledge of the law and the intrigues of courtroom maneuvering were important elements of their careers, and when the vicissitudes of history thrust them into the heated religious controversies of their age, they tended to treat questions of doctrine and faith with the same strict legality. In fact, there was considerable truth in the assertion of the bellicose reformer Robert Barnes when he said that ". . . these lawyers, these justiciares, that say that a man may lawfully ask his own good afore a judge and contend in judgment, have destroyed all patience, devotion, and faith in Christian people."[33] To Friar Barnes there was little of the milk of Christian kindness in men who were so coldly skeptical of the innate goodness of their fellow men, and who preferred their social obligations to be solidly grounded upon legal contract and enforced by the machinery of the law. It must constantly be borne in mind when later we analyze the conservative attitude towards religion, that many of the leading figures within the conservative party were lawyers, but, in the meantime, we must turn to another ele-

[32] P.R.O., S.P.1, vol. 71, ff. 142-145 (*L.P.*, V [1532], Nos. 1452-3).
[33] Barnes, *Supplication*, p. 207.

ment which many of the future conservative bishops had in common.

The dinner conversation which went on around the common table at Doctors' Commons was not restricted to the vagaries of the law, but must have run the gamut of human knowledge. Sir Thomas More was trained in the common law and was ignorant of the ecclesiastical code; John Stokesley, though a member of the King's Council and constantly burdened with the business of the Star Chamber, was educated in divinity and physics; John Colet was happily unaware of the solemnity of court protocol or the niceties of a lawyer's brief. But even had these distinguished laymen and divines been absent from the company, the presence of John Voysey, Bishop of Exeter, with his extravagant tastes and courtly manners, of Edmund Bonner and Cuthbert Tunstal with their vast fund of merry tales of diplomatic and foreign intrigue, must have lent an ecumenical flavor to the conversation. These men were all votaries of the "New Learning," had eaten of the apple of the tree of knowledge, and their interests were humanistic in the widest sense of the word. From Oxford and Cambridge, where they had studied Greek and dabbled in embryonic heresy at the White Horse Tavern, from the universities of Padua and Bologna where many had gone to study law and imbibe the secular atmosphere of Italian culture, they had returned to London to reestablish old associations and friendships. John Clerk and the musician and humanist, Richard Pace, had been scholars together at Bologna, had commenced their careers in the entourage of Cardinal Bainbridge, and after his death had returned to England to accept the patronage of Thomas Wolsey.[34] Tunstal was one of Sir Thomas More's closest friends and an old diplomatic colleague of Richard Sampson, while all three were intimates and admirers of Erasmus.[35] Whether it was around the communal

---

[34] See ch. III, pp. 72-73.
[35] Sturge, *Cuthbert Tunstal*, ch. v, "Tunstal and the English Humanists,"

table at Doctors' Commons, or as young members of Cardinal Wolsey's household, or as diplomats on common mission, or just as constant visitors to each other's homes, their interests and daily lives were intricately related.

The "New Learning" had not yet come to mean the heretical study of Protestant doctrines, and scholars could still inspect the classics and the language of the ancient Greeks with impunity. A few reactionaries, it is true, condemned the entire revival of learning as heretical and dangerous, but to men like More and Gardiner, the advocates of the "New Learning" had "not then in them malice." When Tyndale accused More of hypocrisy for countenancing the translation of "ecclesia" as "congregation" and "presbyter" as "elder" by Erasmus but condemning it in his (Tyndale's) translation of the Bible, More could write with open conscience that he had not found in "Erasmus, my darling, the cunning intent and purpose that I found with Tyndale. . . ."[36] The study of the classics had not yet sunk into the pedantic stupor which was already paralyzing the humanism of Italy, and for these worldly and scholarly bishops it was still in essence "the study of human affairs." In upholding the knowledge of Greek and Latin against the reactionary "trogans" of Oxford, Sir Thomas More wrote of the duties and aim of a university education that "A knowledge of human affairs, too, must be acquired, which is so useful even to a theologian, that without it he may perhaps sing pleasantly to himself, but will certainly not sing agreeably to the people. And this knowledge can nowhere be drawn so abundantly as from the poets, orators and historians."[37]

The growing chasm between the reformers and conservatives was nowhere more marked than in their respective attitudes toward secular preoccupations. The men who remained

---

and esp. p. 23; Erasmus, *Epistles*, III, No. 744, pp. 275-276; No. 780, pp. 347-348; *L.P.*, III, pt. i [1520], No. 968; *L.P.*, II, pt. ii [1517], No. 3850.

[36] Quoted in Stapleton, *Life of More*, pp. 39-40.

[37] *Ibid.*, p. 41.

behind at Oxford and Cambridge as professors of divinity had little experience and even less interest in "human affairs."[38] Ridley, Hooper, Ferrar, and Cranmer were absorbed with salvation, not law, with God, not man. They studied the "New Learning," its Greek and Latin, with vigor, but not for the sake of the classical poets and historians. They were progressive in the sense that they broke with the past, with the authority of the medieval scholastic scholars, but they were never humanists. They contemplated divinity, not humanity. "Little Bilney" read Erasmus' *New Testament*, as most of the humanists did, for its Latin, but he ended by finding a new god, a god who would not countenance the divided allegiance of human interests. Bilney found "marvelous comfort and quietness" and his "bruised bones leaped with joy," but he never again studied law. These learned dons struggled with classical Latin in order to meditate upon Saint Ambrose, not to savor a Ciceronian oration; they practiced Greek in order to learn the customs of the primitive church, not to read of the heroes of Homer. They learned that the words image and idol might mean the same thing, and that the word *episcopus* or bishop might be translated merely as superintendent.[39]

The reformers had little knowledge of the workings of the law. They spent their time comparing God's law to that of man and found it piteously lacking and corrupt.[40] They tended to take literally the words of Matthew that "Men worship him [God] in vain with the precepts of men."[41] Above all, they lacked the humanity, the association and experience, to appreciate the words of Roland Lee, Lord Presi-

---

[38] Only one of the reformers can be described as a humanist. Paul Bush, Bishop of Bristol, is said to have been a celebrated poet, a master of Greek, Latin, Hebrew, an architect, a chemist, and a botanist. *DNB*, Art. "Paul Bush."

[39] Strype, *Ecc. Mem.*, II, pt. ii, "Ponet to Dr. Martin" (1553), pp. 141-142.

[40] For example, see Hooper, *Early Writings*, pp. 273-274.

[41] *Ibid.*, "An Oversight and Deliberation upon the Holy Prophete Jonas" (1550), p. 441.

dent of the Council of Wales and Bishop of Coventry and Lichfield, in defending young Doctor Ellis before Cromwell when he said, Ellis "is young and must have a time, for the tree groweth not to be an oak at the first day."[42] Instead, Bishop Hooper warned against such leniency. "Beware," he once wrote, "of this ungodly pity, wherewith all men for the most part be very much now-a-days cumbered withal, which will for pity rather let a fool or an evil man to enjoy his benefice, than a thousand souls to be brought to knowledge: this is no pity, but rather a cruelty and killing of the soul."[43] Well might Tunstal, Gardiner, Sampson, and Voysey and the other clergy who in the eyes of Hooper were "dumb bishops, unpreaching prelates," say, as the man said of his surly mistress: "She hath too much Divinity for me. Oh! that she had some more Humanity."[44]

The young humanistic lawyers and ministers of state had little time in the midst of their legal and government duties to indulge their literary tastes, and few of them have left evidence of their abilities. As the flood of the Reformation and the divorce poured over them, they were forced into the religious polemics of the period. Cuthbert Tunstal began by writing a textbook on arithmetic and ended by defending the Catholic concept of the mass.[45] Stephen Gardiner, though never trained in theology, is now remembered for his defense of the old religion, but he did find time when imprisoned in the Fleet under Edward VI to copy out from memory a series of Latin and Greek proverbs and verses.[46] Richard Sampson had composed motets in his younger days in honor of Henry VIII,

[42] P.R.O., S.P.1, vol. 87, f. 42 (*L.P.*, VII [1535], No. 1443).

[43] Hooper, *Early Writings*, "The third sermon upon Jonas" (1550), p. 481.

[44] Fuller, *Worthies*, p. 809.

[45] They were *De Arte Supputandi* (1522) and *De Veritate Corporis et Sanguinis Domini nostri Jesu Christi in Eucharistia* (1554). See Sturge, *Cuthbert Tunstal*, ch. IX "The 'De Arte Supputandi' " and ch. XXVII "Tunstal's Theology and Faith."

[46] Muller, *Stephen Gardiner*, p. 204.

but he finished by writing a monograph in defense of the Royal Supremacy and the breach with Rome.[47] If the record of their humanistic works is small, the testimony of humanists like Erasmus, More, and Richard Pace is eloquent evidence of their many talents, while their friendship with such men is added proof of their wide cultural associations. "Such men as More, Mountjoy, Linacre, Pace, Colet, Stokesley, Latimer, Tunstal, and Clerk," Erasmus wrote in 1519, "are a credit to the court of Henry VIII."[48]

To add to the testimony of Erasmus, we have the words of Richard Pace who considered Stokesley, Bishop of London, as "his best friend on earth; a man of the keenest judgment, excellent, and indeed marvelous, in theology and philosophy, and not only skilled in Greek and Latin, but possessed of some knowledge of Hebrew."[49] Richard Sampson, the young chaplain to Wolsey and future bishop of Chichester, was the admired friend of Erasmus, while Thomas Aldridge had not only been his "imprudent and flippant guide" on the Dutchman's pilgrimage to Walsingham, but in 1525 again won the scholar's praise and gratitude through his help in collecting and translating old manuscripts.[50] Tunstal, Thomas More, and John Stokesley were the executors of the will of their friend, Thomas Linacre, the King's distinguished physician.[51] John Longland, Bishop of Lincoln, was the personal confidant of Thomas Wolsey and patron to Erasmus to the extent of "ten angels" a year,[52] while his nephew, Richard Pate, was a classmate of the Cardinal's baseborn son, Thomas Winter.[53]

---

[47] He was author of *Oratio quae docet hortatur admonet omnes potissimum Anglos regiae dignitati cum primis ut obediant* (1533), B.M., Royal 11 E. XI (*L.P.*, VIII [1535], No. 1602, sec. 1).

[48] *L.P.*, III, pt. i [1519], No. 394.

[49] Quoted in Gasquet, *The Eve of the Reformation*, pp. 31-32 from Richard Pace, *De Fructu*, p. 99.

[50] *L.P.*, IV, pt. i [1525], No. 1840.

[51] Johnson, *Linacre*, pp. 272-277, 330-333; Sturge, *Cuthbert Tunstal*, pp. 25-26.

[52] *L.P.*, IV, pt. i [1526], No. 2128.

[53] *Ibid.*, pt. ii [1528], No. 4514.

Edward Fox, later to be Bishop of Hereford, a "habile gallant" as the Spanish ambassador described him,[54] was highly praised by Reginald Pole, the future Cardinal and Legate for England under Mary, for his "prudence, diligence and learning,"[55] while both Fox and his close colleague, Stephen Gardiner, were constant visitors to the abode of Thomas Lupset at Paris where Master Winter was receiving his education during the final years of his father's life.[56]

To this celebrated group we must add the name of Edward Lee, chaplain to the King, ambassador to the court of the Emperor, translator of a "Collection of the Lives of Saints and other Narratives,"[57] and shortly to become Archbishop of York. Lee was a boyhood friend of More, a friendship which withstood the strain of Lee's quarrel with Erasmus. In every dispute there are two sides to the story, but unfortunately for the young man's later reputation, the word of Erasmus has carried the greater weight, and consequently Edward Lee has been labeled a reactionary and an opponent to the study of humane letters. The controversy began in 1519 when Erasmus asked him to help in the correction of a revised edition of the *New Testament*.[58] A scholar's squabble ensued and Lee accused Erasmus of using many of his suggestions without giving him sufficient credit, and of ignoring what Lee considered to be useful suggestions. Erasmus, on the other hand, discarded Lee's aid as unsolicited, and referred to the younger man's notes as the "miscellaneous jottings of a beginner in Greek." During the course of the quarrel, More wrote his friend saying: "You ask me, my dear Lee, not to lessen my affection for you in any way. Trust me, good Lee,

[54] *L.P.*, v [1531], No. 238.

[55] P.R.O., S.P.1, vol. 57, pp. 248-249 (*L.P.*, IV, pt. iii [1530], No. 6505).

[56] *L.P.*, IV, pt. ii [1528], No. 3955.

[57] B.M., Harl. 423, ff. 148-200.

[58] The most complete description of both sides of this quarrel is in Gasquet, *The Eve of the Reformation*, pp. 154-155. See also *L.P.*, III, pt. i [1519-1521], Nos., 242, 262, 382, 408, 471, 554, 929, 930; More, *Correspondence*, pp. 137-138.

I shall not. Although in this case my sympathies are with the party which you are attacking, yet I trust that you will withdraw your troops from the siege with perfect safety."[59] While More was trying to smooth ruffled academic tempers, Fisher, Colet, and Pace all wrote Master Lee begging him to keep his peace. Unfortunately, however, Erasmus was not so easily silenced and he added fuel to the dying embers of the dispute by writing Lee sarcastically that "possibly the Pope, out of admiration for such a fine genius, will resign the sceptre to you, and make you censor of all the world, that nothing shall come abroad without Lee's *imprimatur*."[60] This was hardly conducive to the soothing of injured and youthful pride, and a bitter literary fight ensued. Lee accused Erasmus of "adulation" and said that, for himself, he had "no belief in any one who, having made a mistake, is not willing to acknowledge it."[61] Erasmus, in turn, scornfully dubbed the younger man a notoriety hunter and "would-be saint." The older scholar was correct in saying that the quarrel would hurt Lee's reputation more than himself, and though the young Archdeacon strenuously denied that he was either hostile to the study of "letters" or to Erasmus' *New Testament* as a whole, later generations have usually classified him as a pig-headed opponent of the humanists and the Reformation alike. He eventually became a staunch conservative, but he was certainly never an obscurantist.

Finally, to this list of scholars and men of "letters," we must add two more men: the dilettante and courtly John Voysey, already Bishop of Exeter, and the popular and ubiquitous Thomas Thirlby, "one of the most accomplished and graceful scholars of his age,"[62] and the close friend of Stephen Gardi-

---

[59] More, *Correspondence*, No. 85, pp. 211-212, translated in Stapleton, *Life of More*, p. 47.

[60] Erasmus, *Epistolae*, IV, No. 998, p. 11 (*L.P.*, III, pt. i [1519], No. 382).

[61] Quoted in Gasquet, *The Eve of the Reformation*, pp. 154-155, note 1 from Edward Lee, *Apologia* (no reference given).

[62] Jessopp, *One Generation of a Norfolk House*, p. 116.

ner. Sir Thomas More knew John Voysey well, and in a letter to his daughter Margaret relates an episode which helps
to explain the Bishop's popularity. "I happened this evening,"
he wrote, "to be in the company of his Lordship, John, Bishop
of Exeter, a man of deep learning and of a wide reputation
for holiness. Whilst we were talking I took out from my desk
a paper that bore on our business and by accident your letter
appeared. He took it into his hand with pleasure and examined
it," and "began to praise it in the highest terms . . . for its
pure latinity. . . ." Then much to the secret pleasure of the
proud father, the Bishop "took out at once from his pocket a
portaque which you will find enclosed in this letter. I . . . was
unable to refuse to take it to send to you as a pledge and token
of his good-will toward you," but "it annoyed me to have to
accept for you. But, as I have said, he is so good that it is a
happiness to be able to please him." Then More ends his
letter with the time-worn advice to a child: "Write to thank
him with the greatest care and delicacy. You will one day be
glad to have given pleasure to such a man."[63]

It would be straining the limits of the meaning of humanism to include all the conservative bishops as humanists, but
only one, William Rugge, Abbot of St. Benet's and later
Bishop of Norwich, is a clear exception, and even he is referred to by the poet Leland as "theologus ad unguem doc-
tus."[64] As for John Skip, Nicholas Heath, George Day, William Knight, John Bell, and Arthur Bulkeley, they were all
men who associated with learned and cultured disciples of the
"New Learning," and were constant visitors at the royal court
during these early years of the sixteenth century when, in
the words of Erasmus, Henry's court seemed "not a Court,
but a temple of the Muses."[65] The evidence is not clear, but

[63] More, *Correspondence*, No. 108, pp. 257-258, translated in Stapleton,
Life of More, p. 116.

[64] Quoted in Venn, *Biographical History of Gonville and Caius College*,
I, p. 18.

[65] Erasmus, *Epistles*, III, p. 361.

what little there is points to the fact that they had far more in common with the worldly ecclesiastics and laymen than with the Protestant divines. George Day was chaplain to Bishop Fisher and probably was acquainted with Erasmus through his master, and when he became Master of St. John's College, his academic colleague, Richard Brandesby, mournfully remarked that "he tarries altogether in the Court now."[66] Nicholas Heath for all his training in divinity was a traveled and accomplished diplomat; he became Lord Chancellor of England under Mary on the death of Stephen Gardiner, and under Elizabeth was one of the few Marian bishops who was able to command the respect and friendship of the new Queen. There is no evidence, however, that either William Knight or John Bell were intellectually inclined; they were loyal and able Tudor workhorses, and it is significant that both men waited for promotion many years after the "bright young men" of Henry's reign had received their bishoprics.

There is, of course, a considerable difference between the ages of these men. Before the Cardinal's fall in 1529, Tunstal and Voysey, Bishop Kite of Carlisle, John Longland of Lincoln, and John Clerk were already bishops and distinguished men of affairs. Stephen Gardiner, Richard Sampson, Edward Fox, and the two Lees, Edward and Roland, were experienced officials of the Lord Chancellor and Cardinal Legate. Edmund Bonner, Nicholas Heath, Thomas Thirlby, and Arthur Bulkeley were just commencing their careers, while William Knight dated back to the days of Ferdinand of Aragon. Thirlby, of course, knew Gardiner at Cambridge; Bonner was a messenger boy for the Cardinal, carrying reports between his master and secretary Gardiner; and Arthur Bulkeley was chaplain to the Duke of Suffolk. These younger men were not to become the equals of their elders for some years, but they were all members of a similar section of society, and though age and personal idiosyncrasies divided them, they are

[66] P.R.O., S.P.1, vol. 133, ff. 19-20 (*L.P.*, XIII, pt. i [1538], No. 1169).

sufficiently alike to be treated as a class. With the exception of Tunstal and his friend Sir Thomas More, none were great scholars or outstanding humanists, but Erasmus could hardly say of them as he remarked of the wise man that "he can be of little use to himself, his country, or his family, and all because he is inexpert in everyday matters, and far out of step with general ways of thinking and modes of life among the folk."[67] The description fits far better the lives of the learned dons of Oxford and Cambridge.

The associations of these conservative bishops were broad and their interests secular, and in some cases, their tastes were extravagant and sensuous. John Voysey liked nothing better than to travel with an expensive livery of "four-score horse" and was known on occasion to have given "20 nobles in reward to the officers of the house" when he paid an official visit to the residence of Thomas Cromwell.[68] Stephen Gardiner was constantly criticized by puritanical reformers for his princely behavior and sumptuous household, and the scornful George Joye took pains to picture the Bishop as clad "in his velvets and satin aloft upon his mule trapped with velvet with gilden stirrups and bridle, and with his gentlemen bare headed chained with gold, before and after him." "Who will not say," he ridiculed, "but there rideth a princely prelate, a glorious Bishop to orne and honor a whole realm? See what a cleanly sort of tall men he hath about him, what costly liveries giveth he, what a many of idle bellies daily feedeth he."[69] Wily Winchester undoubtedly opened himself to the contempt of those who thought a bishop should be solely an "elder" and a guardian of souls, but to the "common sort" he was indeed a lordly prelate of the church to whom they humbly doffed their caps. Nor is Joye's description merely the bigoted exaggeration of a prejudiced observer, for Thomas Wriothesley, who was Gardiner's friend and pupil, remarked

---

[67] Erasmus, *Praise of Folly*, p. 33.   [68] *L.P.*, XIV, pt. i [1539], No. 967.
[69] Quoted in Gardiner, *A Declaration of true Articles* (1546), f. xcvii.

in writing to Cromwell in 1538 that "This Friday before noon, I met with my Lord of Winchester between Sitingburn and Rochester. His train is very galant; he hath 5 mulettes and 2 cartes . . . all covered with clothes of his colours, with his arms in garters embrowdered upon the same. . . ."[70]

Their interest and tastes were on the whole strikingly un-ecclesiastical. They enjoyed good food, good wine, good art, and, we may presume, not so good women. There are only two extant records written by John Skip, one, a sermon, the other, a recipe for apple tarts, and though it would be an injustice to judge from this that he was known equally for his culinary abilities as for his divinity, he certainly was not a man whose sole interest was dedicated to the problems of religious life.[71] Moreover, we may guess that Thomas Thirlby's table conversation was not entirely taken up with spiritual topics, for after that accomplished musician and scholar had visited Calais while en route to England, Lady Lisle, the wife of the Deputy Governor, wrote him to ask how "many pounds of sugar must go to how many pounds of quinces" for the good lady had "clean forgotten," and now that "the time of quinces is come . . . she would fain be doing."[72] Edmund Bonner had a deep appreciation for the arts and an astute eye for human anatomy. Though he protested his ignorance of the female form, a more skeptical generation may suspect his sincerity when he sent a print from Paris to Lord Lisle as a token of his esteem, and wrote that "This present, which of late was here imprinted" is said to be a very fine example of French Art. "The anatomy of the man is judged here to be done exquisitely. The anatomy of the woman pleaseth me not so much; howbeit Mr. Bekinsall that is married and hath had but one child, telleth me that that is the figure of women in their travail; to whose judgment, because I am ignorant, I leave the matter, thinking that he took consultation with some

---

[70] *St. P.*, VIII, No. DII, p. 51. [71] *L.P., Add.* [1536], No. 1057.
[72] *L.P.*, XIII, pt. ii [1538], No. 505.

midwife touching his sentence."[73] The Bishop's interests, however, did not stop with the fine arts; he was a determined gardener, an avocation which he enjoyed in common with his patron Thomas Cromwell, to whom he often sent seeds from "Rome, Bononye, and parts of Lombardy."[74]

John Voysey, as Sir Thomas More said, may have been esteemed for his "wide reputation for holiness," but neither he nor his colleagues can be characterized as saints. Fortunately, however, these lawyers and state officials made no pretense of a particularly godly life, and both Stephen Gardiner and Edmund Bonner were the first to admit their many human failings.[75] As humanists and disciples of a secular life, they must have been thoroughly versed in Erasmus' penetrating satire, *The Praise of Folly*, and must have savored its amusing anecdotes with deep appreciation. But it is difficult to imagine either Hugh Latimer or John Hooper ever smiling over the story of the man who presented his wife with a set of imitation jewels and then told her they were of infinite value. "Pray tell me," Erasmus wrote, "what difference did it make to the girl, so long as she joyously delighted her eyes and heart with glass, and carefully kept these trinkets in a safe place never far from her person? In the meantime, her husband had avoided expense, he had enjoyed his wife's delusion, and he had bound her to himself no less than as if he had given greater purchases."[76] The Thirlbys, Gardiners, Heaths, and Bonners of Tudor society could read such a tale and laughingly say that at worst it made but small difference, and at best it was a merry story of what undoubtedly happened in daily life. But the innocent wife of Erasmus' story was still the victim of a deception which could hardly have amused men who judged human action by the standards of heaven.

[73] P.R.O., S.P. 3, vol. 2, f. 39 (*L.P.*, XIV, pt. i [1539], No. 1307).
[74] *P.L.*, VI [1533], No. 158.
[75] Muller, *Stephen Gardiner*, p. 303; Foxe, VII, p. 355.
[76] Erasmus, *Praise of Folly*, p. 64.

It would be an injustice both to these "princely prelates" and the church in which they held office, to say that they were impious skeptics and secular agnostics. Tudor England was still an age when society expressed both individually and collectively the will of God, when man, even the most humble wage earner, was regarded as an unique organism imbued with a spark of divinity, a soul which was still worth saving. The twilight of the medieval world had not yet vanished before the artificial illumination of a brilliant but man-made civilization, and even among the apostles of avarice and egotism there were men who still held religion as more than a social obligation. For Catholic and Protestant alike religion was a living faith which had not yet been relegated to the afterworld. The conservatives may not have been pious, but they were still sincere Catholics; they may have had little time for their religious duties, but they were no supporters of the superstition which was creeping into the spiritual life of the nation. As products of a sophisticated environment, they tended to laugh at the man who spent his days "measuring out time to be spent in purgatory as if with an hour-glass," or he who fancied that the "laying down one small coin from his extensive booty" would purify "the whole cesspool of his life."[77] They had little sympathy for the man who burned a candle to a saint in order to ease the pain of a toothache or assist in a financial adventure.[78] Their humanistic training led them to seek for truth, and even after Luther raised the standard of revolt, they were unwilling to regard all that was Protestant as pernicious. Reginald Pole, the future Catholic cardinal, wrote early in his career that "heretics be not in all things heretics. Wherefor I will not so abhor their heresy that for the hate thereof I will fly from truth."[79] Sir Thomas

---

[77] *Ibid.*, pp. 56-57.

[78] H. M. Smith has a brief but admirable account of the religious situation during the early Tudor period in his *Pre-Reformation England*, pt. i, ch. IV, "Superstitions and Abuses."

[79] Starkey, *England*, p. 135.

[61]

More, who was later to die for his faith in an united Christendom, expressed almost the same feeling when he praised the English translation of the Bible as a worthy endeavor and said that "a commodity ought not to be kept back for the harm that may come of it."[80] As long as the reformers lived up to the limits of their name and maintained reform, not revolution, most of these early conservatives were willing to give their full cooperation.

The church was in need of a thorough housecleaning. Apathy, superstition, old wives' tales, perversion, and exaggeration had all crept into the ritual of the church, clouding and obscuring the essentials of Christianity. Both pious Protestants and sincere Catholics could join company in denouncing the folly of those "who think that they have done a lasting service to Christ, when they have invented a fable about some Saint, or a tragic description of Hell, which either melts an old woman to tears, or makes her blood run cold."[81] Such religious extremism was viewed by the conservatives with cold disgust whether they found it in their own church or in the actions of the Protestants. Moreover, the cult of the Virgin had entered into the church, and Europe had fallen captive to the charms of the Madonna whose power was regarded as equal to her Son's and whose depth of forgiveness exceeded that of Christ himself.[82] The Catholic church was tending more and more to become like its architecture, pure form and no soul. Like some gossamer ribbed and vaulted roof of the late Gothic style which by the very intricacy of its form conceals and destroys the nature of the stone itself, so the church's ceremonies and rituals were beginning to destroy the thing worshipped—God himself. Pilgrimages to the shrine of Saint Thomas à Becket were as prevalent as ever, but one wonders how many came to view for themselves its fabulous riches and

---

[80] More, *Works*, p. 244.

[81] This is More speaking. Quoted in Smith, *Pre-Reformation England*, p. 157.

[82] Erasmus, *Praise of Folly*, p. 57.

how many to worship at the sanctuary of his martyrdom. When the time came for the destruction of the shrine and the looting of its treasures, Stephen Gardiner was unable to defend the motives of those who made pilgrimages to Canterbury, and gave his open approval to the act of destruction.[83] In fact, there was a great deal of reform which the conservatives welcomed, and John Clerk when presenting Henry's book against Luther to the Pope dared even in the presence of His Holiness himself to suggest that a reformation was already long overdue. The Bishop was clear in his denunciation of the "prodigious poison" and "deadly bane" of Luther's *Babylonian Captivity* but he was not willing to dismiss Luther entirely as a "poisonous serpent" and admitted that the German's attack "against the wicked manners of our age . . . in some manner might have been borne with."[84] Thomas Aldridge, as we have already seen, joined Erasmus in his ribald criticism of the naive pilgrims to Walsingham; Richard Sampson, when he became Bishop of Chichester, tried to stop the superstition so prevalent in his diocese, and rudely condemned the Vicar of Tysherst as "a very fool" for preaching that the people should once again "offer up a candle to St. Lowye for their horses, and to St. Anthony for their cattle."[85]

On the whole, the conservatives approved of the work of John Colet and Erasmus; and John Longland, then Dean of Salisbury, in 1519 is said by Sir Thomas More to have admitted that more knowledge was to be found in Erasmus' *New Testament* than in all the other religious commentaries.[86] More himself went even further and in writing to Edward Lee in the same year, said that should the Pope rescind his approval of the *New Testament*, Luther's attack upon the

[83] *St. P.*, VIII, No. DII, p. 51.

[84] Clerk, "oration," printed as a preface to Henry VIII, *Assertio Septem Sacramentorum*, third page.

[85] P.R.O., S.P.1, vol. 133, ff. 51-53 (*L.P.*, XIII, pt. i [1538], No. 1199, sec. I and III).

[86] More, *Correspondence*, No. 83, p. 192 (*L.P.*, III, pt. i [1519], No. 567).

Papacy would appear to the civilized world as an act of piety in comparison.[87] The humanists were no more favorable to the scholastics than were the Protestants, and referred to the ancient schoolmen as a "marvelously supercilious and irascible race." They disliked the dogmatism of both the scholastics and the Protestants, and while Erasmus wrote of the reactionary Catholic theologians of his own day that they attempt to dispute "with unclean lips about holy things, which are rather to be worshiped than expounded,"[88] Nicholas Heath, while attempting to prevent Queen Elizabeth from reestablishing the Protestant faith, argued that "the highest mysteries of the faith . . . should be reverenced in silence, rather than be made the subject of popular debate."[89]

Possibly the greatest weakness of these conservative bishops was that their humanism was too aristocratic, and their belief in reform, though sincere and practical, lacked passionate conviction.[90] George Day and Nicholas Heath could work with Cranmer in abolishing the custom of crawling to the cross, of ringing bells on All Hallows Day, and of covering images during Lent;[91] Tunstal while Bishop of London could approve and foster such practical reforms as ordering that the feasts of dedication of churches in the city of London should be held on the same day,[92] but all these changes were essentially matters of church discipline and organization. The conservatives

[87] *Ibid.*, No. 85, p. 210 (*L.P.*, III, pt. i [1520], No. 640).

[88] Erasmus, *Praise of Folly*, p. 83.

[89] Sanders, "Report to Cardinal Moroni on the change of religion in 1558-59," *Catholic Record Society*, I (1904-1905), p. 26.

[90] Janelle in his *L'Angleterre Catholique à la Veille du Schisme*, p. 322, is probably correct in saying that the aristocratic nature of sixteenth-century humanism prevented such men as Stephen Gardiner from placing themselves "at the head of a popular movement" in defense of Catholicism. However, his conclusion that the vast and humanistic learning of the conservative bishops was hopelessly impracticable and divorced from reality completely ignores the very practical legal, administrative, and diplomatic aspects of their lives. Cf. Janelle with Bush, *The Renaissance and English Humanism*, pp. 78-79.

[91] *L.P.*, XXI, pt. i [1546], Nos. 109-110.

[92] Sturge, *Cuthbert Tunstal*, p. 130.

might approve of the abolition of such ceremonies as crawling to the cross because of its abuse, but they could never seriously consider that either its retention or abolition had any ultimate effect upon man's chances of salvation. They considered superstition to be ridiculous and Erasmus could expect the full support of the Bishop of Lincoln, John Longland, when he wrote him that there were many of his friends in England who thought highly of his *Colloquies*, but unfortunately there were others of "so vinegar a disposition" that they abhorred "everything playful."[93] What they could never appreciate, however, were the words of Hugh Latimer when in 1538 he suggested to Cromwell that the image of Our Lady of Worcester be destroyed because "she hath been the devil's instrument to bring many (I fear) to eternal fire. . . ."[94] Superstition, the abuse of images, the idle worship of saints, were all the result of stupidity and ignorance, and the conservatives could never conceive of a God who would condemn a man to eternal damnation because he was ignorant and knew no better. After a busy day in attendance on the King, writing official letters, or working in the law courts, they had little time or desire to wonder about the mystery of divinity or to question the nature of their Creator.

Their faith in humanism led them to believe that learning could extinguish both superstition and heresy, and Wolsey's new college at Oxford was dedicated to the extermination of "the many heresies and schisms, which had spread themselves over the Christian world."[95] It was hoped that "good learning" within the church itself would cure the institution of "Christ's profession" and then slowly seep down into the structure of society. The conservatives lacked any great faith in a popular religious revival and their long years in government merely confirmed in them their inbred suspicion of un-

---

[93] *L.P.*, IV, pt. i [1526], No. 2128.
[94] Latimer, *Sermons and Remains*, p. 395 (*L.P.*, XIII, pt. i [1538], No. 1177).
[95] Fiddes, *Life of Cardinal Wolsey*, p. 374.

controlled reform; the responsibility of reform came from above, not from below. Sir Thomas More greeted the translation of the Bible with approval, but, he warned, it should be an authorized version made by competent scholars, nor was it to be discussed by "every lewd lad . . . to keep . . . a pot-parliament upon."[96] Such men admitted that the Scripture was "the foundation and ground of all truth," but Stephen Gardiner was careful to point out that "it is dark and obscure to senses unexercised, and God giveth not to all the spirit of prophecy."[97] As for superstition, the Bishop of Winchester dismissed it as being primarily a characteristic of "the rude people," "a fault," he added, which is "annexed to the multitude, to do either too much or too little."[98] Upon this sound administrative maxim, he drops the matter.

Though their humanism was aristocratic and closely akin to intellectual snobbery, it was still a vast cloak of liberalism. Like Reginald Pole they were unwilling to abjure truth because of their hatred of heresy. They had attained that degree of broadmindedness which is able to see good even in one's opponents. This may be true Christianity, but it is certainly not the stuff of which martyrs are made, and once the Reformation commenced, they discovered that it was impossible to reform abuses without endangering the thing abused. Once the illusion of reform was destroyed and the passionate fanaticism of revolution replaced the tolerance of a more placid age, the liberal and middle-of-the-road spirit of compromise vanished. "I was a young man," the aged Bishop Day sadly confessed to Master Bradford at the young heretic's trial in 1555, "and then coming from the university, I went with the world."[99] This world of the 1520's of which George Day speaks was both liberal and enthusiastic, tolerant and complacent, but unfortunately it was not to last. The con-

[96] More, *Works*, pp. 245-246.
[97] Gardiner, *A Declaration of true Articles* (1546), f. lxxxiiii.
[98] *Ibid.*, ff. cviii-cix.   [99] Foxe, VII, p. 176.

servatives could hardly pretend tolerance when their religious rivals began calling Edmund Bonner a "brockish boar of Babylon, a swill-ball, a blockhead, a belly-god," and Richard Sampson "the double faced, epicureous, bite sheep of Coventry and Lichfield."[100] The bearers of such titles were confronted with the problem of maintaining their liberal, humane and tolerant spirit at the risk of sacrificing the main tenets of their religious and social beliefs. Like so many before and after them, they lived to see the middle ground of compromise cut from under them, and they were forced either to advance with the Protestant revolution or to retreat into the fastness of the Catholic reaction—almost to a man they chose the latter. Unfortunately much that was good was lost in the process of reaction for it was soon apparent to many conservatives that after all "a commodity" ought to be held back for "the harm that may come of it."

The withdrawal from the middle ground of liberal reform to the bitter hatred of religious strife varied with individuals. The prophetic More saw early where reform was leading, and Erasmus, slow himself to take sides in the spreading conflict, said of More in one of his letters, "He hates the criminal doctrines by which the world is now miserably troubled. So attached is he to piety that he does not hesitate to say that if he had to move in one direction or another, it would be towards superstition rather than toward impiety."[101] Sir Thomas More never moved toward superstition, but he took his stand long before his friends on the issue of Christian unity and faith. It was not, however, until the mediating hand of Henry VIII was removed that men like Gardiner, Bonner, Heath, and Day made their final decision and faced imprisonment rather than comply with the dictates of a Protestant government. Gardiner's decision came as something of a shock to his erstwhile

---

[100] Gardiner, *De Vera Obedientia*, "Roane" edition (26 October, 1553), "Preface" probably by John Bale (no pagination).
[101] Quoted in Stapleton, *Life of More*, p. 69.

friend, William Paget, who was reported to have said in connection with the Bishop's imprisonment in 1549 that Gardiner
"is quite intractable, and entirely different from what he used
to be: indeed I cannot get over my wonder at the change that
has taken place in him."[102] All these men changed, but it was
Nicholas Heath who expressed to Queen Elizabeth the bitter
disillusion of a lifetime of experience. "He had learned," he
said, "by experience in the course of a long life, to say nothing
of what he knew from study, that great mischief accrues to the
state from frequent changes, even in the laws relating to the
administration of justice. How much less then ought alterations to be attempted in religion, where evidence of antiquity
was accounted so great a commendation?"[103] But this is anticipation of events, for the history of the slow retreat of the conservatives from their liberal beginning is, in fact, the basis
of a large part of this study. We must again turn to the decades
of the 1520's and 30's to pick up the thread of their lives—this
time as diplomats and administrators.

[102] *Cal. of St. P. Span.*, IX, p. 187.
[103] Sanders, "Report to Cardinal Moroni on the change of religion in
1558-59," *Catholic Record Society*, I (1904-1905), pp. 25-26.

CHAPTER III

TRAINING FOR AUTHORITY

*T*HE humanism of the sixteenth century was undoubtedly both genteel and aristocratic, but it was rarely divorced from reality. The flippant scorn of Erasmus was directed against the frailties of man, not the fundamentals of religion. The reforms advocated by Tunstal, More, Heath, and Gardiner were leveled toward the corruption which had penetrated the physical observance of religion, against misuse, abuse, misrepresentation and deceit, but these liberal conservatives never doubted the ultimate truth and necessity of Catholicism. They may have needed the patrons of art and the benefices of the church to indulge their virtuosity, as Pierre Janelle claims,[1] but they never became intellectual parasites living off the bounty of a humanistic sovereign. The knowledge of "the poets, orators and historians" of ancient Greece and Rome was, as Sir Thomas More said, the source from which "a knowledge of human affairs" was derived, and these humanists were always willing to dedicate their time and talents to the burdens of state. As one author has said, "Since the middle of the fifteenth century, humanistic training had opened the way to political and eventually to ecclesiastical preferment."[2] But it must be remembered that the wealth of the church was open to them only as a reward for faithful and loyal service to the crown. They were statesmen and administrators by preference, and clerics and bishops only as an accident of patronage. Men trained in the law, fluent in French and conversant with Italian and German, were too valuable to the King and Wolsey to be allowed the dubious privilege of an intellectual's ivory tower.

[1] Janelle, *L'Angleterre Catholique à la Veille du Schisme*, p. 322.
[2] Zeeveld, *Foundations of Tudor Policy*, p. 19.

[69]

They were drawn into this world because of their learning, and from the time they entered Wolsey's service their interests and experiences were firmly based on political reality. Their milieu was no longer the White Horse Tavern, the aimless pouring forth of ideas and conjectures, but was now the world of diplomatic intrigue, of worried councillors meeting in secret conclave, of dynastic policy and court flattery.

Some of the humanistic statesmen, it is true, rebelled against such a secularity and longed to return again to the quiet of a scholar's life. Sir Thomas More begged Wolsey to allow him to escape the bickering of diplomats and the hardships of foreign travel so he might be "set afloat again" on the humanistic world he knew and loved.[3] Stephen Gardiner found time in the midst of his secretarial duties in 1527 to write nostalgically to Erasmus, reminiscing of their acquaintance sixteen years before and regretting his refusal of the scholar's offer to join his household. Gardiner was not the man to suffer long over what was past, and philosophically concluded his letter with the remark that he was "a fool to complain of what cannot be altered . . . ," but the future Bishop did regret that he no longer had time to gratify his love of learning or even keep abreast of Erasmus' publications.[4] The reactions of Richard Sampson, however, were not so stoical, and he made a strenuous effort to break away from the slavery of political success. He wrote in 1519 imploring Wolsey not to burden him with the management of the household, a task of which he was ignorant and which he considered "incompatible with his studies," for, he said, he had always wanted to "devote himself to letters" and wished "no such exaltation as all others would covet." "A court life," he added with youthful determination was "disagreeable to him."[5] More was probably honest in his

---

[3] B.M., Galba B. III, f. 260 (294) (*L.P.*, II, pt. i [1515], No. 679).

[4] Printed in Muller, *Stephen Gardiner*, pp. 4-5, and dated by him as being 28 February, 1527.

[5] P.R.O., S.P. 1, vol. 19, ff. 105-106 (*L.P.*, III, pt. i [1519], No. 515); *Ibid.*, ff. 77-78 (*L.P.*, III, pt. i [1519], No. 486).

complete indifference to worldly fame, but we may doubt the sincerity of the other two. Sampson's complaints had been chronic for several years and probably were related to the unpleasant task assigned him as Wolsey's chancellor and the King's proctor at the Flemish See of Tournay. He may have broken with his patron in 1519, but he was certainly back among the court personages by 1522 and was shortly cajoled into diplomatic service in Spain. As for Stephen Gardiner, he was soon off to Italy on behalf of the "King's Great Matter" and within three years was Bishop of Winchester. Once caught within the strands of the Cardinal's far-reaching web, it was difficult to escape the responsibilities of authority, and when Robert Aldridge dallied too long at Eton in his capacity of Provost, an irate Government peremptorily ordered him back to his duties as Bishop of Carlisle and commissioner of the border defenses.[6]

Duty to the state and loyalty to the crown were paramount principles of daily life in Tudor England, while resignation was tantamount to dismissal. Once the reflected light of royal patronage and favor had been lost, the dismissed servant retired into the darkness of friendless obscurity, for no one cared to know a man who had incurred the royal displeasure. An individual might still be loyal, as Sir Thomas Wyatt pointed out at his trial in 1541 and still "misliketh or repugneth his prince's proceeding," but, he added, "if misliking includes disobeying, I think him no good subject. . . ."[7] Even such an eminent statesman as Sir Thomas More was careful to make it quite clear that when he resigned the chancellorship in 1531, he did so because of ill health and not because he had fallen from royal grace.[8] The old proverb that "the king's wrath is death" was deeply etched on the minds of these civil servants, and they had cause to remember it both as ecclesiastics and statesmen.

[6] *L.P.*, xvi [1540], No. 286.   [7] *Ibid.* [1541], No. 641, p. 309.
[8] Chambers, *Thomas More*, p. 283.

But for the time being, at least, there was no question of resignation. Few of the future bishops had reached episcopal status before 1530 and most of them were still working for their patron, the Lord Cardinal. It was Wolsey, not the King, who induced these college graduates and traveled humanists into the royal service, and it was here, as members of the Legate's household or as his representatives at court, that there evolved a veritable community of bureaucrats, a society of men who were in constant contact with one another. At the zenith of the Cardinal's power in 1527, the two Cambridge class-mates, Stephen Gardiner and Roland Lee, had been in service for almost three years and both were, in the following year, associated with Thomas Cromwell in the dissolution of the smaller monastic houses whose revenues were absorbed by Wolsey's new seat of learning at Oxford.[9] Edward Fox in 1527 was still working for his degree of Doctor of Divinity and had not yet entered the Lord Chancellor's entourage.[10] Tunstal, Sampson, Knight, Clerk, Bell, and John Kite, Bishop of Carlisle, were of a still older vintage. John Clerk had been the friend and classmate of Richard Pace and together they had entered Cardinal Bainbridge's service. When that worldly prelate was murdered at Rome in 1514, they both had been loud denouncers of the Bishop of Worcester as the most likely assassin of their late patron. When the Bishop complained to Wolsey, that astute cleric replied that Worcester was at perfect liberty to send a citation into England against Mr. Clerk, at that moment en route home from Rome, and agreed with the

[9] B.M., Titus B. I, ff. 275-276 (281-282) (*L.P.*, IV, pt. ii [1528], No. 4755).

[10] The exact date of Edward Fox's degree of Doctor of Divinity is not known. He was a D.D. by 22 September, 1528, when he was elected Provost of King's College, Cambridge, and he received his M.A. in 1519-1520. Allowing eight years for a Doctorate, he probably graduated D.D., in 1527-1528. His name does not appear in the *Letters and Papers of Henry VIII* until 1528, though it is possible that he joined Wolsey's household late in the year 1527. See Venn, *Alumni Cantabrigienses*, pt. i, vol. II, p. 169; *DNB*, Art. "Edward Fox."

slandered Italian that Clerk was "one of the most malicious conspirators" against him. Curiously enough, within two years the same Master Clerk was a trusted and loyal tool of the Cardinal and was shortly to become the government's Italian expert. A man so intimately acquainted with the kitchen diplomacy of the Papal court was too valuable to lose despite the feeling of the Bishop of Worcester.[11] John Stokesley and Edward Lee, likewise, got their start under the Cardinal-legate, the former as Lord High Almoner to the King and member of the royal council, the latter as resident ambassador to Spain in 1526.[12]

Examples of this kind of early association are almost unlimited. More, Tunstal, Knight, and Richard Sampson were on a joint mission together to Flanders in 1515 attempting to smooth the snarled and acrimonious trade relations between the two countries.[13] Edmund Bonner was too young before the Legate's fall in 1529 to do more than run errands between the court and Wolsey's residence, but he certainly knew the old triumvirate, Roland Lee, Stephen Gardiner, and Thomas

---

[11] Wegg, *Richard Pace*, pp. 9-10, does not believe that the John Clerk who was with Pace in the Cardinal's entourage at Rome was the same John Clerk who eventually became Bishop of Bath and Wells. However, Pollard, *Wolsey*, p. 24, n. 3, assumes he was. Certainly Richard Pace states that his great friend, John Clerk, was with him studying in Italy (Wegg, p. 9), and the Bishop, John Clerk, received his degree of Doctor of Law at Bologna (Venn, *Alumni Cantabrigienses*, pt. i, vol. I, p. 342). Moreover, the ages of Pace and the Bishop would indicate that they had been associated in Italy as students, for the former was born in 1482 while the latter received his B.A. at Cambridge in 1499 and his M.A. in 1502, thus making the probable date of his birth about 1480. It is altogether too great a coincidence to suppose that John Clerk, later Bishop of Bath and Wells, should suddenly appear in 1516 as Dean of the Chapel Royal (*L.P.*, II, pt. i [1516], No. 2735, p. 875) and shortly thereafter be sent to Rome with Richard Pace as an expert in Italian affairs, if he were not the same John Clerk who returned from Rome in the fall of 1514. See *L.P.*, I [1514], Nos. 5365, 5465.

[12] *L.P.*, III, pt. ii [1523], No. 2954. Edward Lee had been Archdeacon of Colchester, chaplain and Almoner to the King, and had been sent briefly to Nuremberg in 1523 to present the Emperor with the Order of the Garter. *L.P.*, III, pt. ii [1523], No. 3275.

[13] *L.P.*, II, pt. i [1515], Nos. 520, 977.

Cromwell, and unlike these three remained with his patron after his fall from power during the concluding months of 1529.[14] It is one of the most ironic touches of this most mordacious age that "Bloody Bonner" should have been rescued the following year from obscurity and the consequences of his loyalty to his dying master by the friendship of that Protestant darling, Thomas Cromwell. Thirlby, Heath, and Arthur Bulkeley do not appear at court until after the issue of the divorce had absorbed the interests and vitality of the government and the Cardinal's name had become a distant memory. The future Bishop of Bangor, Arthur Bulkeley did not leave Oxford till around 1526-27 when he joined the Court of the Arches as a practicing advocate. Still as an expert in legal affairs, he entered the service of the Duke of Suffolk in 1530 with the deceptive title of "chaplain," a term which, in Tudor days, was almost synonymous with that of "clerk."[15] The young chaplain later had the misfortune to earn Cromwell's displeasure over a contested benefice which the Vicar-general desired for his nephew, the eight-year-old Gregory Williamson. Bulkeley refused to give it up even at Cromwell's request and tenaciously held to his position until family pressure finally induced him to give way to the wishes of Master Williamson's omnipotent uncle.[16] The year following this episode, however, in 1537, he succeeded in persuading his cousin, the Vice-Chamberlain of Wales to write to Cromwell on his behalf.[17] Whether or not he entered the Vicar-general's household is unrecorded, but within six years he became a sufficiently valued state official to warrant a bishopric. Bulkeley's career is unusual in that his success seems to have been predicated solely on his legal abilities and not on his experience as a diplomat and statesman. The case of John Bell, however, followed the

---

[14] *L.P.*, IV, pt. iii [1529-1530], Nos. 5881, sec. ii, 5964, 6411; Cavendish, *Wolsey*, p. 212.

[15] P.R.O., S.P. 1, vol. 126, f. 35 (*L.P.*, XII, pt. ii [1537], No. 998).

[16] *L.P.*, XI [1536], Nos. 1055, 1329.

[17] P.R.O., S.P. 1, vol. 126, f. 35 (*L.P.*, XII, pt. ii [1537], No. 998).

same pattern, and although Anthony Wood states that he was an experienced diplomat, there is little evidence to suppose so.[18] He studied law at Oxford and Bologna, became one of Wolsey's factotums and eventually a member of the royal council. He may have been Dean of the Arches, and in his early days was probably at Rome as Vicar-general to his non-resident Italian patron, Silvester, Bishop of Worcester. Less is known of Bell than of the other bishops of Henry's reign, and though he is rated by his Protestant contemporaries as a papist and a non-preaching prelate, there is little information concerning his willingness to conform to the Reformation policies of his sovereign.[19] Moreover, to add to the mystery, he resigned his bishopric of Worcester in 1543 for no accountable reason, after having held his see for only four years.

The majority of the conservative bishops, however, had grown old in the service of the state as itinerant ambassadors to the court of the Emperor, to the papal palace at the Vatican, and to the princely households in Germany. These future diplomats and administrators had been selected from among their university colleagues not only for their training in law but also for their social ease and polish, attributes absolutely necessary for a successful diplomatic career. It was here, in the role of ambassadors to foreign lands and as government administrators, that these incipient conservatives learned to regard the progress of the German Reformation with alarm and to view idealism with scorn. Their futures lay in the world of actuality inhabited by shrewd realists, an environment in marked contrast to that of the academic life of Cranmer and Ridley, Hooper and Latimer. Stephen Gardiner, for example, spent almost six years of his life carrying out the King's policy in foreign lands,[20] while Thomas Thirlby, his

---

[18] Wood, *Athenae Oxonienses*, II, p. 771.

[19] *L.P.*, IV, pt. ii [1528], No. 4488; VIII [1535], No. 962, sec. 24; II, pt. ii [1517], No. 2895; III, pt. ii [1522], No. 2178; *Archaeologia*, XXIII (1831), p. 59.

[20] Gardiner was with Wolsey in France from July to September 1527;

friend and pupil, passed a lifetime in attendance on the migrant court of Charles V. Edmund Bonner saw service in Rome, Paris, Spain, and the Lowlands, while John Clerk, after his early position as the English observer at the papal court, was given the delicate and embarrassing task of placating the Duke of Cleves, brother of the divorced Anne, Henry's fourth wife, and it was on this last mission in 1540-41 that he died old and exhausted from a long life in the service of the crown.[21] Such men had to be both cunning and gregarious, constantly skeptical of all they heard but able themselves to conceal their own intent. Deceit and subtlety were their constant implements; chicanery and prevarication were the fundamental principles of their profession.

One of their primary duties as high church officials was to entertain visiting dignitaries at their episcopal palaces, a task which Richard Sampson, for one, found exacting and annoying. In 1538 Sampson was instructed by Cromwell to receive the German ambassadors traveling to London for the forthcoming conferences on a religious union between England and the Protestant German princes. The Vicar-general had given the Bishop only a day's notice and Sampson complained bitterly that he had neither ale nor beer nor wine on hand, and, in an effort to avoid an unpleasant assignment, suggested that John Stokesley, Bishop of London, was better equipped to receive the honored guests than he.[22] Evidently Sampson's proposal went unheeded, for Stokesley was an open opponent of Crom-

---

on mission to Rome, February through September 1528; on assignment again to France, December 1531 to March 1532; with Henry VIII on the occasion of his meeting with Francis I, October to November 1532; on mission to Marseilles, September to December 1533; ambassador to France, October 1535 to July 1538; on mission to the Emperor, November 1540 to August 1541; and finally was sent as special ambassador to Charles V from October to November 1544, and again from October 1545 to March 1546.

[21] *L.P.*, xv [1540], No. 943. He died 3 January, 1541, and it was rumored that he had been poisoned. See *DNB*, Art. "John Clerk."

[22] P.R.O., S.P. 1, vol. 133, f. 250 (*L.P.*, XIII, pt. i [1538], No. 1295).

well's German policy and the government presumably felt it inexpedient to house the foreign Protestants at his London residence. But the See of London at other times came in for its share of government entertainment, and one of the reasons why Cuthbert Tunstal was promoted to the dignity of Bishop of London in 1522 was, as Archbishop Warham wrote Wolsey, because the new bishop was "a man of so good learning, virtue, and sadness, which shall be right meet and convenient to entertain ambassadors and other noble strangers at that notable and honorable city in the absence of the King's most noble grace, if it shall then fortune your good grace to be also absent."[23]

When not entertaining "noble strangers" in London, these ecclesiastical statesmen were often sent to Europe on missions which required both polished deceit and detailed knowledge. William Knight in 1532 was required to negotiate with the Emperor's delegates in Flanders, men, who in the opinion of Stephen Vaughan, were the "polytikist fellows in all this land."[24] The dispute had a more than modern atmosphere about it, and Knight must have been an expert in financial and mercantile relations, for his mission was designed to placate the Flemish merchants' complaint that bills and obligations made in foreign currencies were not payable in England and that the English wool-growers had been practicing dishonest methods by false packing and weighing of wool.[25]

Likewise, the youthful Nicholas Heath, on his first trip to Germany in 1534, was made responsible for what must have been a highly delicate diplomatic mission. The English government expected him not only to place Henry's divorce in the best possible light, but he was also instructed to paint for the German divines an ingenious if questionable picture of Anne Boleyn's many talents and virtues which were, in the words of

[23] P.R.O., S.P. 1, vol. 23, f. 271 (*L.P.*, III, ii [1522], No. 1972).
[24] B.M., Galba B. x, f. 3 (*L.P.*, v [1532], No. 804).
[25] *L.P.*, v [1532], No. 843.

[77]

his instructions, "the purity of her life, her constant virginity, her maidenly and womanly pudicity, her soberness, her chasteness, her meekness, her wisdom, her descent of right noble and high parentage, her education in all good and laudable thewes and manners, her aptness to procreation of children, with other infinite good qualities, more to be regarded and esteemed than the only progeny, [all of which] be of such approved excellency as cannot be but most acceptable unto Almighty God, and deserve His high grace and favor, to the singular weal and benefit of the King's realm and subjects."[26] Unfortunately, there is no record of how successful the young ambassador was in persuading the Germans of the truth of this eulogy, but when two years later he and Edward Fox, Bishop-elect of Hereford, returned to Germany to discuss the possibilities of a political and religious alliance with the Lutheran princes, Heath proved himself a far more popular man than his superior. The young archdeacon won from Melanchthon the praise that he excelled all the others of his party in "courtesy and learning" and that he was "fit for purer doctrines,"[27] while Edward Fox was considered a pompous and worldly opponent of the Lutheran faith. The evidence of the German doctors probably does an injustice to the Bishop of Hereford, who was regarded by the English Protestants as an extremely liberal man, but Fox was an imperialist and probably disapproved of any political union between England and the German princes.[28] Moreover, Henry had no intention of reforming the English church to fit the Lutheran creed and undoubtedly it fell to the Bishop as the responsible English representative to curb the German hopes. It is difficult to account for Nicholas Heath's popularity in Germany, for in

[26] *L.P.*, VII [1534], No. 21, pp. 10-11.
[27] *Corpus Reformatorum*, III, No. 1397, p. 37 (*L.P.*, X [1536], No. 266).
[28] Chapuys, the Imperial Ambassador, considered both Edward Fox and Richard Sampson as favorable to the imperial alliance. *L.P.*, XI [1536], No. 359. See also *L.P.*, X [1536], No. 447.

later life he proved himself a determined adversary of every form of Protestantism. Just what his function was on this mission is unknown, but it is highly probable that he was instructed to ingratiate himself with the Germans and exaggerate their hopes, since his words could always be dismissed as those of an irresponsible minion. If so, he proved himself a master of deception and won for himself the sincere praise of the Lutheran ministers.

Wolsey demanded of his servants accurate and honest reporting of foreign events, and they quickly became trained observers who could see behind the finely polished words of their diplomatic rivals, and penetrate the veil of arguments and subterfuge which surrounded the meetings of foreign ministers. They were expected to be as Edmund Bonner once described Thomas Thirlby, men "of truth, singular good wit, and learning" who could "with all good dexterity and wisdom" complete the tasks assigned them.[29] John Clerk, for instance, justified himself as a faithful observer at the Roman court and as an accurate judge of the men who were responsible for the spiritual policy of Christendom. In 1522 he wrote his superior, Thomas Wolsey, marveling that the Lord Chancellor should ever covet the office of the Papacy, for, he said, it "is in such disorder, ruin, and decay, and every day shall be more and more, except God help and Christian Princes set their hands. It should be too long to write unto your Grace of the reported chiding, brawling, and scolding between these cardinals, and of their great schism, dissension, their malicious, unfaithful, and uncharitable demeanor, [which] every day increased while they were in the Conclave."[30] John Clerk had no doubt as to what was wrong with the spiritual center of Europe and he had little respect for the saintly but incompetent Cardinal of St. Clements, one of the candidates for the papal

[29] *St. P.*, IX, No. DCCLIX, p. 124 (*L.P.*, XVII [1542], No. 609).
[30] Ellis, *Original Letters*, 3rd Ser., vol. I, No. CXII, p. 308 (*L.P.*, III, pt. ii [1522], No. 1960).

chair during the election of 1522. The Cardinal, he reported, was "meet to be Pope in some other time, when the Church should have need to care for nothing, but only for the spiritualities."[31] What the Church of Rome required was not an evangelist, but an honest and broadminded bureaucrat who could extricate the Papal See from the mire of bankruptcy and sordid Italian politics into which it had fallen. The man to head the church, he suggested, was some one who could rule and who would not become a puppet manipulated by a host of nephews and sycophants. Wolsey undoubtedly felt the same way in this case, but not all honest and objective reporting was received with approval. Edmund Bonner fell into considerable difficulty for mentioning in a letter from Spain in 1543 that the Emperor and his ministers seemed unreasonably slow in signing the proposed treaty of alliance between the two governments. Unfortunately, knowledge of the Bishop's words leaked out, and the Council was acutely embarrassed to have the imperialists know that the English were dissatisfied with their new allies or doubted their veracity, and as a result Bonner was recalled in disgrace.[32] William Knight, likewise, risked his personal safety for the sake of keeping the government well informed. When Henry went to war in 1512 against France, he sent to the Continent an army composed primarily of raw recruits, led by court favorites with little military experience, and badly equipped and provisioned. The travesty of Henry's first plunge into the European military arena was soon played out: the army, with little to do but indulge itself on Spanish wines, was almost exterminated by dysentery and the remainder mutinied and crept home to the safety of England. Throughout this ill-fated campaign, Knight, as Wolsey's commissioner and personal informer, soon gained the enmity of the military leaders who were most reluctant that the extent of their own incompetence and the disgraceful condition

---

[31] B.M., Vit. B. v, f. 3 (5) (*L.P.*, III, pt. ii [1522], No. 1932).
[32] *L.P.*, XVIII, pt. i [1543], No. 684.

of the army should be known by the government in London. The unfortunate Knight asked Wolsey for his recall but begged him to keep it a secret, for, he warned, his letters were opened and his life endangered.[33] It speaks well for the integrity of these ecclesiastics that they did not hesitate to report the news from foreign lands and distant parts of England exactly as they saw it despite the possible consequences of such honesty. The correspondence of such men is filled with unwelcome news and sometimes even more unwelcome advice. When Roland Lee, for example, wrote from Wales to his friend Thomas Cromwell in the fall of 1534 that the subjugation of that unruly area would be costly, but if "the King wishes to have this country reformed, he must not stick at a 100 pounds or so," he was merely stating what he knew to be true.[34]

The duties of the bishops in government service were vast and unspecified. Not only were they required to represent their country in Rome, Paris, Nuremberg, and Madrid, but as royal councillors and clerics they were expected to hear cases in the Court of the Star Chamber, decide marriage disputes among the more important personages of the land, and collect the subsidies wrung from a reluctant church. Richard Sampson, Robert Aldridge, and Thomas Thirlby, were appointed in 1539 with a number of the Barons of the Exchequer to examine and determine the petitions of debtors imprisoned at Ludgate who desired to compound with their creditors.[35] John Stokesley, besides proving himself a cunning negotiator at Padua by collecting a majority opinion in favor of Henry's divorce under the noses of the Imperial representatives, was also an able and experienced administrator of the King's ecclesiastical revenues, and it was he who collected the subsidies and tenths from his episcopal colleagues.[36] Nicholas Heath

[33] *L.P.*, I [1512], 3356.   [34] *L.P.*, VII [1534], No. 1571.
[35] *L.P.*, XIV, pt. i [1539], No. 403, grant 1.
[36] *L.P.*, IV, pt. iii [1530], No. 6514; XII, pt. ii [1537], No. 1134.

and Thomas Thirlby were first sworn into the royal council for the sole purpose of hearing cases in the Star Chamber in 1540,[37] while Edward Lee, then Archbishop of York, was one of the regents in charge of the kingdom when Henry left for his meeting with Francis on the Cloth of Gold.[38] Thomas Aldridge, John Bell, John Clerk, Edward Fox, Richard Sampson, Thomas Thirlby, not to mention Edward Lee and Stephen Gardiner, were at one time or another members of the King's Council. Cuthbert Tunstal was president of the Council of the North, while John Voysey and later Roland Lee were presidents of the Council of Wales. John Stokesley, Edward Lee, Edward Fox, Thomas Aldridge, John Skip and Nicholas Heath, held the position of Almoner to the King, a post which, though primarily a stepping stone and a sinecure, involved considerable financial responsibility, since the Almoner and his assistants administered, on behalf of the poor, lands confiscated from persons convicted of felony or who had committed suicide.

Such were their varied services to the crown, for which they received their clerical preferments as reward. But philanthropy was not one of the outstanding virtues of the Tudor monarchs, and though they were liberal rewarders of devotion and service, they found it expedient and economical to be so with the benefices of the church and not with those of the crown. Thomas Holgate, Bishop of Llandaff, had been President of the Council of the North since July of 1538, and when Edward Lee, Archbishop of York, died in September 1544, the Earl of Shrewsbury and others of the Council wrote to the government in London suggesting that the King "bestow that benefice upon the Bishop of Llandaff" for in so doing he would promote an honest and diligent man and save the charge of the president's diets, amounting to almost 1,000 pounds yearly, besides having the first fruits and gift of

[37] *L.P.*, xvi [1540], No. 114.   [38] *L.P.*, v [1532], No. 1421.

Llandaff.[39] Henry needed no prompting, for it had long been a cardinal policy of the Tudor monarchs that wherever possible the church should share the burdens and expense of the royal coffers. The spiritual calibre of the church might suffer, but the state would gain "an honest and painstaking man," and accordingly, Robert Holgate was promoted to the See of York while his salary as Lord President was cut to 300 pounds.[40] Reasons of economy and the desire to reward faithful service, however, were not the sole causes for high ecclesiastical appointments. The government often found it politically expedient to use bishops as foreign negotiators for reasons of protocol and prestige. A royal secretary might be a far more influential person in England than many of the bishops, but abroad the episcopal badge was still of recognized importance, and many of the Continental sovereigns considered it disrespectful to send an untitled person as ambassador to their courts. In 1520, when Emperor Charles heard that the English intended to send William Knight, who was then merely a royal chaplain, as ambassador to his court, he let it be known that he considered it an open slight to his imperial dignity to send a "mean person to be resident with him . . . especially considering that he had appointed a worshipful prelate to attend the king of England."[41] The practice of using ecclesiastical diplomats was dying out in the sixteenth century, but the government did not hesitate to utilize a bishop if it thought his high clerical status would ease the difficulties of negotiation.

The reward for long, single-hearted service to the state was well-earned, for the work was always exhausting and often dangerous, and many of these royal officials must have felt as William Knight did when he wrote that he had grown "old and my sight faileth" under the strain of his administrative

[39] B.M., Add. 32,655, ff. 188-189 (*L.P.*, XIX, pt. ii [1544], No. 239).
[40] Dickens, "The Marriage and Character of Archbishop Holgate," *EHR*, LII (1937), p. 440.
[41] *L.P.*, III, pt. ii [1521], No. 1777.

duties.[42] But laborious work late at night pondering over the routine of government business was not their only problem. All too often the routine of the smooth institutional machinery was broken by violence and armed rebellion. This contact with the more seamy side of life and the strict discipline of official work was, however, a schooling which the reformers never experienced. It fostered in these conservative clerics the knowledge that the secret of good government lay in attention to details; it convinced them that their fellow man was rarely inspired by high-minded ideals and noble causes, but instead was usually cruel and treacherous; above all, it taught them that no one, not even their superiors, was to be trusted and that the safest policy was the successful policy.

Examples of the hardships of their métier are almost limitless. The presidency of the Council of the North was rarely an enviable position, for such distant counties as Yorkshire, Northumberland, and Durham were far from the centralized control of the court, and the resentment of feudal nobles and religious malcontents fell not upon the King but on his representative, the President of the Council. Cuthbert Tunstal, during the northern rebellion of 1536, was forced to flee to the sanctuary of southern England, while Edward Lee, Archbishop of York, though not even a member of the governing council, was taken prisoner by the rebels. The unfortunate Archbishop found himself in an embarrassing and dangerous position, for not only was his life threatened by the rebels unless he joined their ranks, but also, after the suppression of the revolt, his sovereign grew suspicious that he had compromised himself too willingly to the demands of the insurgents, and the government searched carefully for evidence which might have led to his conviction for treason.[43] In the same year, 1536, Bishop Longland of Lincoln escaped an even more harrowing experience. Happily for the Bishop he was out of

---

[42] *St. P.*, I, p. 261 (*L.P.*, pt. ii [1527], No. 3360).
[43] *L.P.*, XI [1536], No. 1261; XII, pt. i [1537], Nos. 29, 991.

his diocese when the uprising of Lincolnshire occurred, and when a mob of farm hands and reactionary religious fanatics attacked his episcopal palace they found not the Bishop but his unfortunate Chancellor whom they seized and promptly murdered. A far more ghastly episode took place close to the Bishop's residence when a servant of Thomas Cromwell was seized by the infuriated mob, bound and gagged and wrapped in the hide of a newly killed cow, and thus trussed was thrown to a horde of starving dogs.[44] A similar fate would have awaited Cromwell himself had he had the ill luck to have fallen into the power of such men. Even after the Pilgrims of Grace, as these series of rebellions of 1536 were called, had been violently suppressed, discontent and belated plots and uprisings continued to fester, and it was only in the nick of time that Robert Holgate, Tunstal's successor to the presidency of the Council of the North, discovered in 1541 a plot to assassinate him, murder the governors of the northern counties, and seize the royal fortresses.[45]

For those who went on foreign mission, the danger was no less great. Edward Fox was detained at Frankfort while returning from his trip to the Duke of Saxony and others of the German Princes, and it took an imperial command to achieve his freedom.[46] When Richard Sampson began writing appeals to his patron, Thomas Wolsey, to be allowed to return to England and his humanistic studies, he was acting as his master's commissioner and Chancellor to the Flemish bishopric of Tournay. Wolsey's right to the see had long been disputed by a French claimant who was considerably more popular with the Flemish populace than the English nominee, and Sampson won for himself the hatred of the people in his efforts to secure his patron's doubtful and unpopular rights. Thus, when in 1515 he was placed on commission along with Tunstal, More,

---

[44] *L.P.*, XI [1536], No. 714.
[45] *L.P.*, XVI [1541], No. 733, p. 346.
[46] *L.P.*, X [1536], No. 954.

and Knight, to settle the outstanding trade disputes between the Lowlands and England, he discovered that he was being openly cursed in the streets of Bruges and had been excommunicated in all the cities of Flanders. His friend and colleague, Cuthbert Tunstal, considered Sampson's position extremely grave, and wrote Wolsey that were not the Bishop's Chancellor a member of the Royal Mercantile Commission, his life might be in danger.[47] It is little wonder then that Master Sampson desired to return to the security of a scholar's life.

Personal dangers on the road and in connection with their varied duties were not the only difficulties which these men encountered. They carried the heavy responsibilities of delegated power, a burden which was not alleviated by the fact that they were often left in the dark concerning the real nature of their diplomatic missions, and sometimes their instructions were antiquated before they had even reached their destination. Nicholas Heath, on his first journey through Germany, for instance, had been instructed to join the experienced English envoy, Christopher Mont, at Munich. When he arrived at the city in March of 1534, he discovered that his future colleague had left and was not expected to return for a month. The young novice had to decide whether to wait his return or complete the King's business on his own authority. He chose the latter, and wrote hastily to Thomas Cromwell that he profoundly hoped the King would approve his decision.[48] Evidently his royal master did, but other men were not so fortunate. When Edward Lee, the King's Almoner, was sent in 1527 to replace Tunstal and Sampson as resident ambassador at the court of the Emperor, he was unaware of the secret negotiations which Wolsey had been carrying on with France in preparation for military operations against Charles V. The Cardinal had arranged with the French that

---

[47] *L.P.*, II, pt. i [1515], Nos. 672, 679.
[48] B.M., Vit. B. XXI, f. 93 (103) (*L.P.*, VII [1535], No. 395).

their representatives in Spain should make the declaration of war, but unfortunately Lee knew nothing of this, and had only been informed not to cause the French any suspicion of English friendship and on no account to occasion a rupture with Spain. Consequently Lee was horrified when the French delegates at the court of the Emperor approached him about the proposed declaration of war, and for fifteen days he succeeded in delaying its presentation. Both Wolsey and the French ministry were furious with the Almoner, and Wolsey assured the Bishop of Bayonne, the French ambassador in England, that unless Lee could "show a good excuse" for his actions, "his life would answer for it"—not a pleasant prospect to look forward to when the disgraced Almoner returned to England.[49]

The future Archbishop apparently did find a plausible explanation for his actions, for he was promoted to the See of York shortly thereafter, but such men could never be sure that their mistakes would not be disinterred to haunt them in the future. The divorce and the breach with Rome made a naturally wary government even more suspicious of the loyalty of its servants, and the King and council more than once found it convenient to confront bishops with the consequence of actions which had taken place years before. The aged Richard Nix, Bishop of Norwich, for instance, was thrown into prison in 1534 for a technical breach of the Statute of Praemunire which had occurred two years before.[50] It is little wonder then that Stephen Gardiner should have been worried by the reports of his behavior at the religious conference at Ratisbon in the early months of 1541. He and Sir Henry Knyvet had left England in November of 1540 with a splendid train designed to impress the Emperor that the English church, despite rumors to the contrary, had not been stripped of all her wealth. The Bishop had been instructed to act as an observer

[49] *L.P.*, IV, pt. iii [1528], App. 147; Pollard, *Wolsey*, p. 157.
[50] *L.P.*, VII [1534], No. 171, p. 70.

at this last of the Emperor's efforts to bring his Protestant and Catholic subjects together, and to prepare the way for a closer association between England and the Empire. Both the Emperor and Gardiner hoped that the fall of Thomas Cromwell only the year before might be a prelude to a future reconciliation between England and the Holy See, and in connection with this expectation, the Bishop of Winchester received a letter from the Pope which by mistake was delivered to Sir Henry Knyvet. What the epistle contained is unknown, but it was sufficiently serious for Sir Henry to report the occurrence to the King. James Muller puts it down to unfounded rumor that Gardiner returned home in fear of his life for having tried too hard for a reconciliation with Rome, and he is undoubtedly correct in saying that Henry was fully aware of what his delegates were doing at Ratisbon, but rumors are often founded on a smattering of truth and certainly Wily Winchester lived to have his actions of this year charged against him at his trial in 1551.[51] The most casual slip, the most innocent mistake, was never so slight that it might not be used against a man at some future date. Stephen Gardiner probably expressed a universal sentiment among these conservative statesmen when he remarked to Thomas Thirlby that he had "sundry times told him that he would go with the King's Highness, and so far as He, but he would never go before, nor enter any dangerous matters, not knowing certain by himself, whether His Grace would after allow him, or no."[52] Unfortunately for Gardiner and the other high officials of Henry's government, the King's honesty and consistency were slender reeds on which to stake one's political life, for Bluff King Hal had more than once given evidence of his unscrupulousness in condemning the actions of royal servants when he himself had been a silent partner to their machinations.

[51] Muller, *Stephen Gardiner*, ch. XIV "A Letter from the Pope."
[52] *St. P.*, VIII, No. DII, p. 51.

Not all the complaints voiced by these ambassadors and state officials, however, were peculiar to the sixteenth century. Speed was often so essential that they had to forsake their trains and travel via post, while the plea for money was a constant and urgent demand. Edward Lee attempted to explain to a reluctant and impoverished government that the presence of the Emperor's court in any city increased prices alarmingly and that his diets were insufficient to maintain the dignity and splendor of an English ambassador.[53] Richard Sampson was even more outspoken about conditions in Spain, and wrote Wolsey that foreign and Spanish lords alike were reduced to the universal practice of borrowing money at exorbitant rates of interest, a practice which he said was little better than "cloaked usury."[54] The high cost of living in foreign lands, the long and fatiguing hours spent on horseback, and the general discomforts of travel were rarely balanced by the pleasures of sightseeing or the lavish welcome occasionally organized upon the arrival of an important English representative. It is true that on Gardiner's first mission to Europe the young royal secretary described in extravagant terms to a friend at home the spontaneous reception he and Edward Fox had met at the little Italian town of Luca. The citizens, he wrote, had presented them with "marvelous goodly presents," brought by "fifty personages, with trumpets of the town, and all manner of instruments. . . . There were 20 great pikes . . . and sundry other fish, brought on four men's heads in basins of silver, decked and trimmed with laurel, and oranges, . . . four basins full of comfits . . . garnished with the King's arms, . . . four basins great and full of bread. . . ." And in addition to these "goodly presents" there were "two dozen torches of white virgin wax and gold." No wonder Gardiner concluded his letter with the final burst of praise that he "could be content to dwell here at Luca, a city of marvelous

[53] *L.P.*, IV, pt. i [1526], No. 2097.
[54] P.R.O., S.P. I, vol. 32, f. 157 (*L.P.*, IV, pt. i [1524], No. 827).

quietness."[55] Unfortunately such unstinted acclaim was exceptional, and a far more usual theme was the plea to return
home to the peace and quietness of English life. Such en-
treaties, however, were rarely heeded, for Henry's ambassadors were expected to remain in foreign lands till their missions were completed or until a better use could be found for
their talents. In fact, Master Gardiner was to sing a very different tune before the mission which had brought him to Luca
was completed. He and Edward Fox had been sent in 1527 to
Italy to entice from a reluctant and frightened Pope a commission to Wolsey to institute a court of last appeals in England in order to settle the question of Henry's divorce from
Catherine. Fox returned to England the moment the coveted
document was signed, but Gardiner remained behind to collect
the aging and gout-ridden Cardinal Campeggio, who was des-
ignated along with Wolsey to decide the case. Unfortunately
for Gardiner, this was more easily planned than accomplished,
for the Cardinal procrastinated and dallied, complaining of
his gout and ill health, while back in London the impatient
Henry fumed. The future Bishop must have been a worried
man when he received from his friend and colleague, Edward
Fox, word that the English court tacitly imputed some of the
blame for delay to the young secretary, and that Gardiner was
expected to accompany the Cardinal until he was safely across
the Alps. Also, Fox said, should the elderly Cardinal-legate
fail to arrive in England, Gardiner was never to return home.[56]
With such a threat, one may imagine that the youthful ambassador redoubled his efforts to fulfill his delicate mission.

Moreover, if the novice statesman were ignorant of the
language of the country to which he was sent, he was expected to learn it, unless, of course, Latin was spoken on both
sides. Edward Lee complained bitterly that the Emperor re-

[55] *St. P.*, VII, No. CXCIX, p. 60, n. 1 (*L.P.*, IV, pt. ii [1528], No. 4078).
[56] Pocock, *Records of the Reformation*, I, No. LIV, p. 158 (*L.P.*, IV, pt.
ii [1528], No. 4290).

fused to help him out of his language difficulties, for though Charles understood Latin, he refused to speak it, and instead forced the English ambassador to carry on his business in very faulty French.[57] Thomas Thirlby also had his troubles and lamented that he was very discouraged with his efforts to learn the Gallic tongue. Like many after him, he was puzzled by the fact that he could understand his own countrymen, such as Bishop Gardiner and Francis Brian, but was completely unable to comprehend the French King when he spoke his native tongue.[58] It must have been a rude shock to many of the young diplomats to discover that their schoolroom French or German was of little use to them when speaking to a native.

It was during these years that the seeds of division between the conservatives and reformers were fostered, that the common basis of their Cambridge lives fell apart, creating a deep abyss between them. The study of law as contrasted to that of divinity, the appreciation of humanistic interests as opposed to the absorbed preoccupation in religion, were not in themselves sufficient to produce the antagonism which existed between their respective modes of thought and living. These were primarily the unseen influences of their early training which attracted the ones to the court, the others to the academic life. This, of course, does not mean that all the reformers were university dons or somber-clad monks, and all the conservatives were government administrators. Personal friendships could and did bridge the gulf of divergent backgrounds and experiences, while the line of demarcation between a conservative bureaucrat and a radical divine was far from being clear. The conservatives, John Skip and George Day, were masters of their respective colleges at Cambridge; William Rugge was Abbot of St. Benet's; Robert Aldridge was Provost of Eton; and John Stokesley, Edward Fox, Edward Lee and Nicholas Heath were all trained in divinity. But these

[57] *L.P.*, IV, pt. i [1526], No. 2095, p. 940.
[58] *L.P.*, XIII, pt. i [1538], No. 977.

last four were drawn early into the orbit of the court life, and by the time they reached the Episcopal Bench, they had grown wise in the ways of the world. On the other hand, certain of the reformers had training in diplomacy and administration. Robert Holgate, though originally a monk and a protégé of the reformer, John Hilsey, Bishop of Rochester, proved himself an able and competent state servant when as Bishop of Llandaff he was placed on the Council of the North.[59] William Barlow, Thomas Goodrich, and Thomas Cranmer had each some knowledge of diplomatic intrigue,[60] but the future Archbishop could hardly expect to bring to his episcopal office the breadth of experience and wide knowledge of human affairs which most of the conservatives had to offer, for he was a man of forty before he even came to the notice of the King in 1529, and for nearly ten years had been instructing at Jesus College in problems of divinity. Though a few of the reformers undoubtedly had administrative training, the figures in regard to the conservatives are impressive evidence of the growing split between the two parties: of the twenty-two conservatives, only two, William Rugge and

[59] Robert Holgate owed his advancement to John Hilsey's influence with Thomas Cromwell; see P.R.O., S.P. 1, vol. 105, ff. 200 and 271 (*L.P.*, XI [1536], Nos. 188, 260). He proved himself a valuable and able aid to Tunstal and won from him words of high esteem. B.M., Harl. 283, f. 164 (*L.P.*, XIII, pt. i [1538], No. 397).

[60] William Barlow was sent to Scotland in 1535 and may have had diplomatic experience before that date, see ch. IV, pp. 107-108; Rupp, *English Protestant Tradition*, pp. 68-72. Thomas Goodrich was sent to France concerning the divorce issue in 1533, was a councilor under Edward VI, and was Lord Chancellor in 1551; *DNB*, Art. "Thomas Goodrich." Thomas Cranmer was attached to the mission of Edward Lee and John Stokesley when they were sent to the Imperial and Papal courts in late January of 1530. He was not, however, an accredited ambassador, going along solely in order to gather the opinions of the European universities on the problem of Henry's divorce. He returned to England in the fall of the same year, but was again sent to Europe in 1532 as ambassador to the Emperor in Germany where he seems to have been luckier at love than at diplomacy, for it was at Nuremberg that he secretly married his second wife, Margaret. Finally, late in October of 1532 he returned to England as the newly appointed Archbishop of Canterbury. Pollard, *Thomas Cranmer*, pp. 42-52.

George Day, never held important government offices under Henry VIII.

Though the peripheral elements of both groups may have overlapped, the central core of the opposing parties was far apart in the nature of its background and the consequent manner of its thinking. The world of Edmund Bonner, Cuthbert Tunstal, Thomas Thirlby, and Roland Lee was the glitter of the court and the wary caution of the conference table, not the quiet of a university town or the introverted meditation of a monastic cloister; their schooling was in the art of cajoling flattery and persuasive deceit, not in the dusty mysteries of divinity; their knowledge was based on experience and observation, not on the rigorous hypothecation of the schoolmen or the evangelical faith of the reformers. The hardships of their métier, the vicarious nature of their profession, created a bond between them which an outsider could never hope to penetrate. Stephen Gardiner may have misjudged the character of his erstwhile friend and old pupil, William Paget, when he wrote him that "we ambassadors . . . must hold [one] with another,"[61] but he was correct in assuming that common interests and mutual experiences had produced a veritable community of bureaucrats. His words were the tacit acknowledgment that neither he nor his colleagues could hope to escape the consequences of their worldly preoccupation or the patterns of thought to which such a training enchained them. Cambridge students might theorize, as the Bishop of Winchester jokingly remarked, that the "increase of worldly things make men poor and not rich, because every worldly thing hath a need annexed unto it," but the wily Bishop had learned from experience the truth of this maxim.[62] Roland Lee might well have seconded the Bishop's observation when, as the new President of the Council of Wales, he discovered that he was expected to maintain a retinue of some two hun-

[61] Gardiner, *Letters*, No. 101, p. 220 (*L.P.*, XXI, pt. i [1546], No. 74).
[62] *Ibid.*, No. 91, p. 198 (*L.P.*, XX, pt. ii [1545], No. 831, pp. 400-401).

[93]

dred persons, and it was not many years after his promotion in 1534 that he wrote to his patron, Thomas Cromwell, that he had just heard of the report that Edward Fox was being groomed as his replacement, and that he would be delighted to have Fox or any other man assume the many responsibilities of his office.[63] There was no escape, however, from the burdens of his official duties, and he died in January of 1543 still President of the Council.

The liabilities of wealth, the problems of practical politics, and the training of their long migrations across the length and breadth of Europe exerted their influence over these men, and determined in large measure their reaction to the coming religious storm. Edward Lee, Richard Sampson, John Clerk, Cuthbert Tunstal, Edmund Bonner, Stephen Gardiner, and Thomas Thirlby had all been to Germany during the course of their diplomatic perambulations, and each had had occasion to view for himself the course of the Lutheran revolution and the civil strife which it precipitated. Tunstal had been at Worms in January of 1521 and had observed at first-hand the course of the growing religious conflict. A hundred thousand Germans, he reported, were on the threshold of civil war, and he begged his sovereign to ban the importation of all Lutheran books into England "lest thereby might ensue great trouble to the realm and church of England as is now here" in Germany.[64] Edward Lee likewise described the shocking state of the German nations in 1523, and was adamant in his opposition to the introduction of Tyndale's Bible into his own country.[65] The example of Germany was constantly before their eyes, and Richard Sampson in 1535, then Dean of the Chapel Royal, is said to have "prayed unto God, that we [in

[63] *L.P.,* VII [1534], No. 967; P.R.O., S.P. 1, vol. 126, f. 22 (*L.P.,* XII, pt. ii [1537], No. 986).

[64] B.M., Vit. B. xx, ff. 218-220 (not calendared in the *L.P.,* but printed in Sturge, *Cuthbert Tunstal,* App. X, p. 361).

[65] Ellis, *Original Letters,* 3rd ser., vol. II, p. 72 (*L.P.,* IV, pt. i [1525], No. 1803).

England] were not scourged as they were in Germany," but he added significantly that he very much feared that these innovations would shortly lead to civil strife in England.[66]

The conservatives were quick to perceive the dangers of the Lutheran revolt not only for Germany itself but for the whole of Europe, and they recognized the fact that both the *bellum civile rusticorum* and the *bellum civile nobilium* were in large part caused by the indiscriminate tampering with religion by inexperienced men. Nor were they blind to history, for they fully appreciated the lesson which the Hussite Rebellion of a previous century afforded them. As administrators to whom "order was as dear as life itself," they could not easily forget the moral of Bohemia, that insignificant religious reforms may lead to social revolution and civil war. "Let the Hussitanian Heresie evince," declaimed John Clerk in his oration to the Pope in 1522, "which though contented at first with small beginnings, yet through the neglect of superiors, increased to such a height, that at last it turned, not only cities and people, but also that most populous kingdom of Bohemia from the Christian Faith, reducing it to that misery under which it now languishes."[67] The conservatives, could they have had their way, would never have been accused of such negligence, for the lesson of John Huss and the example of Luther were to have a lasting effect on their attitude to ecclesiastical problems when they were later confronted with an indigenous religious upheaval.

Though Tunstal and Gardiner, Heath and Bonner and the others of their party, were early aware of the anarchistic implications of Lutheranism, though these men were realists who judged their fellow men by the standards of this world and not the next, and though they were individuals to whom order was a paramount virtue, these bureaucrats and lawyers had

---

[66] P.R.O., S.P. 1, vol. 92, f. 81 (*L.P.*, VIII [1535], No. 603).

[67] John Clerk, "Oration," printed as a preface to Henry VIII, *Assertio Septem Sacramentorum*, fifth page.

serious limitations. In the sphere of religion they were blind to the consequences of their own actions, and not until it was too late did they realize the result of their policy towards the Papacy. They were well acquainted with the secular interests of His Holiness, the moral laxity of the College of Cardinals, and with what Ranke has described as the "intellectual sensualism" which pervaded and corrupted the Rock of Peter. The conservatives were not men of a deeply pious nature, and they recognized in the Pope and his court the same moral elasticity which they themselves at times did not hesitate to utilize. "I had almost forgotten," Thomas Thirlby wrote Secretary Paget in 1546, "to tell my gladness of your tidings of the Cardinal of Scotland. It is half a wonder here that ye dare be so bold to kill a cardinal."[68] Cardinal Beaton was a dangerous threat to the English interests in Scotland and the government found it expedient to have him removed by paid assassins. To modern ears it is appalling to hear a bishop rejoicing over the murder of a fellow prelate and cardinal, but Thirlby and his colleagues were bishops by patronage alone, and in most cases they judged correctly when they assumed that Pope and cardinals alike had earned their offices through simony and political astuteness. The worldly corruption of the Papal See and the secular character of Clement VII could hardly have been lost on Edmund Bonner when he reported that the Pope "interpreteth his words for his own commodity or pleasure, or else that a man cannot believe such [words as] here shall be spoken."[69]

In fact, it was difficult to see in the terrified and shaken Clement the spiritual leader of Christendom. When Edward Fox and Stephen Gardiner visited the Pope at Orvieto in March of 1528, Clement was housed in a ruined and decayed castle, sparsely furnished, with the roof in immediate need of repair, while the papal entourage consisted of some "thirty

---

[68] *St. P.*, XI, p. 219 (*L.P.*, XXI, pt. i [1546], No. 1070, p. 532).
[69] B.M., Vit. B. XIV, f. 42 (40) (*L.P.*, VI [1533], No. 886).

persons, rif raf and other, standing in the chambers for a garnishment. And as for the Pope's bed-chamber, all the apparel in it was not worth twenty nobles, bed and all."[70] The Pope's Holiness was pictured by the two English delegates as a perplexed and trembling old man—hardly the perfect image of the inheritor of Peter's chair. It is not difficult to appreciate the scornful remarks of the English ambassadors if we imagine Clement, as Edmund Bonner saw him, journeying from Rome to Bologna with a small company of cardinals, who, as Bonner sardonically said, were "not all good saints." The weather was rainy and the roads a sea of mud; the Pope was forced to go on foot for several miles through the rain and slush, and that night his company of lordly cardinals were "compelled to lie in the straw," where, the unsympathetic Englishman commented, "if I had been harbinger, I would other have caused them to lie on the boards with sorrow, or else have set fire in the straw."[71] Of course, the future Bishop of London was writing for the benefit of Thomas Cromwell, but even so he must have had little respect for either Pope or cardinal. To those who had visited the Vatican and done business with the Pope, Clement was little more than an Italian princeling, a man to be cheated and deceived in the game of diplomacy. When the breach with Rome occurred, there was little sympathy for such a man, and it took Tunstal, Gardiner, Day, and Heath almost a lifetime to realize that the office of the Pope was worth fighting for even if the man was not; that it was impossible to maintain the unity of Christendom or even safeguard Catholicism in England without the unifying link of Saint Peter's chair.

Innocent trust and naive faith were not the virtues bred in these bishops, and it was at the Papal court and elsewhere in Europe that so many of the conservatives learned to view

---

[70] Pocock, *Records of the Reformation*, I, No. XLVI, p. 89 (*L.P.*, IV, pt. ii [1528], No. 4090).

[71] P.R.O., S.P. I, vol. 72, f. 172 (*L.P.*, V [1532], No. 1658).

with skeptical caution the solemn oaths of these "most politi-
kist fellows in all the land." They learned to tread their way
nimbly through the labyrinth of diplomacy, looking for the
innuendo which might conceal a hidden meaning. Thomas
Thirlby voiced what was probably the guiding principle of
their schooling and profession when he remarked of the Spanish ambassador that "I never trusted him so well that I will
put my finger in his mouth."[72] The same skepticism was involved in their relations with their own sovereign as well as
with visiting dignitaries, and the Bishop of Durham, Cuthbert
Tunstal, was once pictured by one of his underlings as being
too wary an ecclesiastic to accept the post of Vicar-general in
December of 1539 when Cromwell was showing signs of im-
minent eclipse, for, as the minion observed, "my lord, my master, is too good a lawyer, knowing by his book the inconsistency
of princes, where there is a text that says: Lubricus est primus
locus apud reges."[73]

Cautious skepticism was no doubt a valuable aid to their
vocation, but it often led them into believing that every
casual remark concealed a veiled threat. When confronted
with Protestant fanaticism, they were never quite able to
believe that the reformers were actually so naive as they appeared, nor could they ever be sure that the passionate words
of a Protestant divine were not, in effect, the clever deception
of a man who aims at personal gain. Tunstal, despite his wide
learning, completely misjudged the character of the Protestant
opposition when he gave Sir Thomas More license to keep
and read heretical books. His reasons for doing so were, he
said, to allow More a chance to "understand in what lurking
places these twisting snakes hide themselves, and by what
wrigglings they seek to slip away again when they are caught.
For it is a great help to victory to have tracked out the plans

[72] *St. P.*, x, p. 596 (*L.P.*, xx, pt. ii [1545], No. 436, p. 191).
[73] Sturge, *Cuthbert Tunstal*, App. xvi, sec. B, p. 372 (*L.P.*, xiv, pt. ii
[1539], No. 750).

of one's foes, to know their thoughts fully, and at what they are aiming."[74] Stephen Gardiner likewise perceived in Protestantism a vast and insidious campaign working from within the structure of society, deliberately designed to foster social discontent, and strategically organized so as to appeal to the widest section of society. He viewed the movement in terms of cloaked conspirators and carefully planned tactics, controlled by clever and unscrupulous men whose avowed policy of social and religious reform was a veil behind which they concealed their ultimate aim of seizing control of the country for their own advantage. In deriding the writings of George Joye, he clearly indicates his fears and suspicions as to the fundamental nature of the Protestant movement. "And ye flatter the world with licentious doctrine," he wrote, "and offer them to pull from their necks all such yokes as ye think did at any time let or impeach them either in thought or deed. Ye promise them liberty of all things. And then to rid them out of debt, ye translate Saint Paul thus: that we owe nothing to no man but love. Ye flatter the covetous master with pulling away holy days, that he may have the more work done him for his year's wages. Ye flatter again the servant with pulling away all opinion of fast by abstinence from any meat either in Lent or otherwise. Ye offer priests wives to wed and they can win them to you. . . . Ye take away distinction and difference of apparel, days, times and places." These were the allurements with which Bishop Gardiner thought the reformers planned to make England theirs. As for the men who opposed their cunning, and gave evidence against their machinations, "them," he claimed, "ye deprave and blaspheme with all kinds of villainy wherewith to destroy their credit in so much as among you, a bishop or a priest hath a new sense in English, to signify a knave."[75] All this has an alarmingly modern flavor, but actually Winchester overrated

---

[74] *Ibid.*, App. XI, p. 363; Foxe, IV, p. 697.
[75] Gardiner, *A Declaration of true Articles* (1546), ff. cli-cliii.

his evangelical enemies, for he was attributing to the Protestants the experience of his own life, the subtlety of his own
reasoning. He was judging them as he would judge the representatives of a foreign land, but Protestantism was not a
planned campaign, its disciples were not consciously appealing
to the riffraff of society by advocating a world in which men
would "owe nothing to no man but love."

It was a grave error on the part of the conservatives to assume that Protestantism was a rational and diabolical movement aimed at materialistic gain. Gardiner and Tunstal never
fully appreciated that the spirit which inspired Ridley and
Hooper, Cranmer and Latimer, was not logical, not calculated,
but was founded on the passionate emotionalism of religious
faith. They tended to forget that they were not dealing with
traitors but fanatics, not rationalists but idealists, and they
would have done well to remember the ancient adage that
"the blood of the martyrs is the seed of the gospel."[76]

The secular careers of these conservative bishops produced
still another weakness besides their failure to appreciate the
importance of the Papacy and their inability to recognize the
basic motives of the Reformation leaders. It also led them
to compromise many of the chief tenets of their faith for the
sake of national unity. The legal education and the detailed
training in administration of these men gave them a profound
feeling for law and order, and magnified in their eyes the
importance of internal unity. They could never appreciate the
introverted egotism of a Protestant divine who did not consider himself bound by the "ungodly" decisions of the community. The individual at all costs was expected to accept the
decisions of his superiors and his government. In defending
the policy of persecution under Queen Mary, Edmund Bonner expressed the opinion of most governing officials when
he said: "In matters of State, individuals were not to be so

[76] This saying was quoted by an unknown reformer in a vitriolic and
anonymous letter to Bishop Bonner in 1555(?). B.M., Harl. 416, f. 76.

much regarded as the whole body of the citizens."[77] Stephen
Gardiner voiced the same sentiment but in more constitutional
terms when he wrote in 1550 that "living in a commonwealth,
men must conform themselves to the more part in authority.
. . ."[78] These doctrines, however, were to prove a serious obstacle to the conservatives' ability to combat heretical opinions. Much as they feared and dreaded the consequences of
religious reform, they felt obliged to maintain the image if
not the fact of unity, and as we shall see, Edward Fox and
Thomas Thirlby, Nicholas Heath and Stephen Gardiner, all
compromised their principles in religion in order to retain the
appearance of unity and uphold the principle of majority
rule.[79] It was only as a last extreme that they retreated to
the uncompromising stand of open disobedience.

Though their background bred in these men serious flaws,
flaws which in the end were to be fatal for their religious cause,
the study of law and the experience of diplomacy and administration taught them one fundamental political principle:
that government was the result of power, not ideas, and that
the greatest danger to the state lay not in Protestantism itself
but in its corollary, social revolution. Deep as their respect
for law was, they were not so idealistic as to believe that law
without force could achieve order. A man like John Clerk had
little faith in the ultimate effectiveness of his sovereign's book
against Martin Luther, and in 1524 he wrote Cardinal Wolsey
that if he really desired to prevent the growth of Lutheranism
in Germany and please the Pope, he would do better to
threaten "the heads of Steeds and of that fellowship in London" (i.e. the Hanseatic merchants) with loss of their privileges unless they extirpated the Lutheran heresy from their
cities.[80] The sword was deemed by Bishop Clerk a far more

---

[77] Sanders, "Report to Cardinal Moroni on the change of religion in
1558-59," *Catholic Record Society*, I (1904-1905), p. 39.
[78] Gardiner, *Letters*, No. 125, p. 350.
[79] See ch. IX, pp. 260-264.
[80] B.M., Vit. B. VI, f. 42 (*L.P.*, IV, pt. i [1524], No. 320, p. 134).

effective weapon than the pen. John Longland expressed a similar opinion when he wrote Wolsey concerning the Government's decision to ban Lutheran books in England and the severe punishment proposed for its infringement. He thought that harsh secular discipline was the only way to ensure the enforcement of such an edict and assured the Cardinal that most men had more fear of the long arm of temporal authority than the vitiated power of the church to excommunicate.[81] Law and order were based on power which in turn was predicated upon wealth, and these conservatives could well appreciate the annoyance of Thomas Wolsey when the imprudent Robert Barnes suggested that he sell his "pillars and pole axes and other ceremonies, which, no doubt, be but trifles and things of naught." The Cardinal queried Barnes about this statement and asked him whether it were "better for me (being in the honor and dignity that I am) to coin my pillars and pole axes and to give the money to five or six beggars, than for to maintain the commonwealth by them as I do? Do you not reckon the commonwealth better than five or six beggars?" Barnes had the nerve to reply that he thought the commonwealth was not worth such a price and that the Cardinal might conceivably save his soul if he did as the self-assured friar suggested.[82] But to Wolsey and his disciples "Power is present. Holiness hereafter" and they were not concerned with the salvation of their souls.

Cardinal Wolsey may have failed in his efforts to extirpate heresy through "good learning" at his new college at Oxford, but in the greatest of all his schools, his own court and household, he was supremely successful in disseminating the doctrine of human prudence. Tunstal, Gardiner, Sampson, Fox, Clerk, Bonner and the two Lees, Edward and Roland, had all had their apprenticeship in Wolsey's retinue, the college which could claim more justly than Trinity Hall the motto:

[81] B.M., Vit. B. v, f. 9 (12) (*L.P.*, IV, pt. i [1525], No. 995).
[82] Barnes, *Supplication*, pp. 214-215; Foxe, V, pp. 416-417.

learning "for the advantage, rule, and direction of the commonwealth." Like master, like pupil, they discovered that Protestantism was not the innocent dabbling of university students, but was a revolutionary movement with vast social and political implications. The Legate's young disciples did not hear the aged and disgraced Cardinal's last warning, the final exposition of his doctrines, but their later actions and writings are eloquent testimony that they remembered his teachings. The deathbed speech of England's last great clerical administrator is a long one, but it is worth giving in full for it anticipates almost everything which his protégés were to say themselves in later years. These are Wolsey's words as reported by his friend and biographer, George Cavendish:

I request his Grace, in God's name, that he have a vigilant eye to depress this new pernicious sect of Lutheranism, that it do not increase within his dominions through his negligence, in such a sort, as that he shall be fain at length to put harness upon his back to subdue them; as the King of Bohemia did, who had good game, to see his rude commons (then infected with Wickliffe's heresies) to spoil and murder the spiritual men and religious persons of his realm; the which fled to the king and his nobles for succour against their fanatic rage; of whom they could get no help of defense or refuge, but they laughed them to scorn, having good game at their spoil and consumption, not regarding their duties nor their own defense. And when these erroneous heretics had subdued all the clergy and spiritual persons, taking the spoil of their riches, both of churches, monastaries, and all other spiritual things, having no more to spoil, they caught such a courage of their former liberty that then they disdained their prince and sovereign lord with all other noble personages, and the head governors of the country, and began to fall in hand with the temporal lords to slay and spoil them, without pity or mercy, most cruelly. Insomuch that the king and other his nobles were constrained to put harness upon their backs, to resist the ungodly powers of those traitorous heretics, and to defend their lives and liberties, who pitched a field royal against them; in which field these traitors so stoutly encountered, the party of them was so cruel and vehement, that in fine they were victors, and slew the king, the lords, and all the gentlemen of the realm, leaving not one person that bare the name or post of a gentleman alive, or any person that had any rule or authority in the common-weal. By means of which slaughter they have lived ever since in great misery and poverty without a head or governor, living all in common like wild beasts abhorred of all Christian nations. Let this be to him an evident example to avoid the like danger, I pray you . . . there is no trust in routs, or unlawful assemblies of the common people; for when the riotous multitude be assembled, there is among them no mercy or consideration of their bounden duty; as in the history of King Richard the Second, one of his noble progenitors, which lived in that same time of Wickliffe's seditious opinions. Did not the commons, I pray you, rise against the king and the nobles of the realm of England; whereof some they apprehended, whom they without mercy or justice put to death? and did they not fall to spoiling and robbing, to the intent they might bring all things in common; and at the last, without discretion or reverence, spared not in their rage to take the king's most royal person out of the Tower of London, and carried him about the city most presumptuously, causing him, for the preservation of his life, to be agreeable to their lewd proclamations? Did not also the traitorous heretic Sir John Oldcastle, pitch a field against King Henry the Fifth, against whom the king was constrained to encounter in his royal person, to whom God gave victory? Alas, . . . if these be not plain precedents, and sufficient persuasions to admonish a prince to be circumspect against the sembable mischief; and if he be so negligent, then will God strike and take from him his power, and diminish his regality, taking from him his prudent counsellors and valiant captains, and leave us in our own hands without his help or aid; and then will ensue mischief upon mischief, inconvenience upon inconvenience, barrenness and scarcity of all things for lack of good order in the commonwealth, to the utter destruction and desolation of this noble realm, from the which mischief God of his tender mercy defend us."[83]

Ridley and Hooper and the other reformers never had occasion to learn the lesson which the aged Cardinal and Chancellor had to offer. For them the terms of the coming conflict were simple, a battle between Christ and Anti-Christ, between good and evil. But for the graduates of Wolsey's

[83] Cavendish, *Wolsey*, pp. 251-253.

school, the sagacious ministers of state, the most powerful of all fears, that of social revolution, was to cloud the clear air of religious controversy. Their human prudence and political expediency, predicated upon fear of the social consequences of meddling with religious tradition, were to become the doctrines against which the reformers cried out, and which led the conservative bishops into the false paradise of believing that the *status quo* could and should be retained.

CHAPTER IV

THE RELIGIOUS IDEALISTS

𝒯HE party of reform, grouping together such divergent characters as Latimer and Thomas Cranmer, Nicholas Ridley and John Hooper, William Barlow and Nicholas Ferrar gives rise to difficulties and problems which are conspicuously absent when dealing with the conservatives. For the most part they were relatively obscure men and the legions of historical events of the first two decades of Henry's reign passed them by untouched. As scholars still working for their advanced degrees in divinity and instructing younger men in the fundamentals of theology, or later as professors, university preachers, and masters of their colleges, they lived in a closed world, an atmosphere alien to that of the fast moving and vivacious life of the court. Many were monks or friars who, once they had completed their education at the monastic houses established in the two university towns, moved away to some distant foundation where not even the brief records of a college register lighten the obscurity of their early lives for us. John Wakeman, for instance, was a Benedictine monk who probably studied at Gloucester Hall, a collegiate organization founded at Oxford by his order. He received the degree of Bachelor of Divinity in February 1511, but from that date until his promotion to the See of Gloucester in September of 1541, almost nothing is known about him except that he suddenly appeared as abbot of the wealthy monastery of Tewkesbury in 1532,[1] and that he probably owed that position to the patronage of Thomas Cromwell.[2] How he incurred that favor, what

[1] *DNB*, Art. "John Wakeman."
[2] He sent Cromwell five pounds as a gift to buy a new saddle. *L.P.*, IX [1535], No. 677.

he had done to come to the notice of the court, remains a mystery.

The early years of William Barlow are almost as baffling. Not only is his college career unrecorded, but six important years, 1528 to 1534, are completely unaccounted for. Although there have been several theories offered to explain these missing years, none of them has been satisfactorily proved.[3] Presumedly he became Prior of Bromehill in Norfolk shortly after leaving the university, but in 1528 that small foundation was dissolved by Cardinal Wolsey and the disgruntled prior disappeared into the limbo of unrecorded history. It seems unlikely that Wolsey would have left Master Barlow unrecompensed, and he may be the unnamed Barlow who was the Legate's chaplain and is mentioned as carrying diplomatic dispatches between England and the Continent in June of 1528.[4] He also may have been the "William Barlow, councillor" who in December of that year delivered letters to Henry's sister, Queen Margaret of Scotland.[5] To substantiate such a theory, it can be shown that the Bishop's sister was a lady-in-waiting to the Scottish Queen, and it is quite natural that her brother should have been used as a courier between the royal brother and sister.[6] Unfortunately, however, there are two William Barlows, cousins to one another. One, of course, was the future bishop, the other was a Bachelor of Law from Cambridge whose sister married Lord Gray.[7] To add to the confusion, moreover, the Bishop's brother, John, was chaplain to Sir Thomas Boleyn, father to the future queen, and during the early years of the divorce was constantly used by the Boleyn family as their personal representative in Eu-

---

[3] The most thorough research done on Barlow is by Rupp, *English Protestant Tradition*, ch. IV "The Early Career of William Barlow." See also *DNB*, Art. *"William Barlow"*; *N. and Q.* Ser. 6, vol. VIII (1883), pp. 33-34, and vol. CLXXXIII (1942), p. 327.

[4] *L.P.*, IV, pt. ii [1528], Nos. 4379, 4647.

[5] *L.P.*, VII [1534], Nos. 1528-1529.

[6] Rupp, *English Protestant Tradition*, p. 63.

[7] *Ibid.*, p. 65.

rope. On the other hand, William may very well have entered the large monastic foundation of St. Bartholomew, and have been rescued only by his brother's influence with Queen Anne.[8] Whatever his career was during these uncertain years, he reappeared in 1535 as Prior in the Queen's Lordship of Pembroke and under her patronage as Prior of Haverfordwest.[9] In the same year his position as a rising figure among the Boleyn clientele was confirmed by his appointment as one of the ambassadors to Scotland,[10] and in the following year by his promotion to the diocese of St. David's.

Nor is the baffling and scanty evidence relating to these two men exceptional. It is true that we can trace the major events in the lives of many of the reformers, their promotion in academic circles, their appointment as chaplains to noble lords and high ecclesiastics, and occasionally their actions as suffragan bishops or court preachers, but this is hardly comparable to the knowledge which we have of their conservative colleagues whose deeds and letters fill so large a part of the extant documents of Henry's reign. Even the records of the professional days of Thomas Cranmer, the future Archbishop of Canterbury, are but a bare skeleton of his life during these important and formative years. We know, for instance, that he was elected a fellow of Jesus College in 1512, and that he was obliged to resign that position when he married his first wife, a young girl who lived with an innkeeper's family. On losing his fellowship, he was immediately appointed "common reader" at Buckingham College,[11] and when his young bride died in childbirth, he was honored by being reinstated at his old college. He became a university preacher in 1526 and three years later had taken on the task of tutor and schoolmaster to two young pupils.[12] There in a few short sentences

[8] *Ibid.*, p. 69.   [9] *L.P.*, IX [1535], No. 1091.
[10] *Ibid.*, No. 527.
[11] Buckingham College is now known as Magdalen College.
[12] These details are all taken from Pollard, *Thomas Cranmer*, pp. 17-18, 22-23.

is the recorded life of the Archbishop for some seventeen years. No clue is given in these meagre facts to his character or even to how far he had proceeded in the direction of Protestantism. All we can be reasonably sure of is that by 1525 he had begun privately to pray for the abolition of the Papacy,[13] but other than this there is no evidence of his increasingly unorthodox opinions.

Occasionally personal bits of information are available. Robert Ferrar incurred the suspicion of the authorities as early as 1528, and was forced to recant his heretical opinions,[14] while the story of Hugh Latimer's encounter with the aged and cautious Bishop West has been preserved in detail.[15] As Latimer confessed himself, until Thomas Bilney called him to the light of God, he was "as obstinate a papist as any was in England." In 1524 he "began to smell the word of God, and forsook the school-doctors and such fooleries,"[16] and by the following year his reputation was such that the Bishop of Ely deemed it wise to pay him an unannounced and unexpected visit. He arrived when the young university preacher was about to commence his sermon. On seeing the aged ecclesiastical administrator enter the church, Latimer prudently decided to change his subject but had the audacity to announce, by way of introducing his extempore sermon, that "a new auditory . . . requireth a new theme. . . . Therefore it behoveth me now to divert from mine intended purpose, and somewhat to entreat of the honorable estate of a bishop." The ensuing sermon was hardly flattering to the ears of a man who had little time or interest for the "innumerable souls" of his diocese, but the Bishop took it in good part and afterwards complimented the imprudent Cantab, and requested him to use his oratorical powers against Martin Luther. Lati-

[13] *Ibid.*, p. 21.
[14] *DNB*, Art. "Robert Ferrar."
[15] B.M., Harl. 422, Art. 12, f. 84; Latimer, *Sermons and Remains*, "Latimer's first conversion at Cambridge," pp. xxvii-xxxi.
[16] Latimer, *Sermons*, "First Sermon on the Lord's Prayer" (1552), p. 278.

mer evaded the request with the provocative answer that he could hardly be expected to refute what he had been prohibited by law from reading. The worldly prelate undoubtedly had the worst of this verbal duel, but is said to have remarked upon leaving: "Well, well, Mr. Latimer, I perceive that you somewhat smell of the pan; you will repent this gear one day."[17] The Bishop never lived to see his prophecy realized, for it was not until thirty years later that this newly made Bachelor of Divinity was burnt at the stake for his heretical doctrines.

Although the knowledge of the early years of these reformers is meagre, the recorded history of their careers follows a common pattern. Of the twenty-four men who cannot be accounted as conservatives, twenty-two had degrees in divinity, while the status of William Barlow is unknown and John Hooper seems only to have had his Bachelor of Arts.[18] Sixteen were monks or friars while the remaining eight rose to important academic positions.[19] Cranmer, Shaxton, and Latimer became university preachers; Goodrich was a Doctor of Theology and university proctor; Taylor and Ridley were masters of St. John's and Pembroke Hall respectively, while Harley was master of Magdalen School, and John Poynet was Dean of Queen's College.

Again the reader must be warned against statistics. The fact that two-thirds of the reformers belonged to the regular clergy may not be coincidence, but it does not necessarily prove that the monastic environment of these men determined their Protestant leanings. Not only has Geoffrey Baskerville pointed out that a large proportion of the monks clung to the faith of their fathers, but also many of the monkish bishops were appointed to their sees for reasons of economy.[20] They were men who had become abbots and priors of their houses and had proved themselves willing advocates of the Royal Su-

---

[17] *Ibid., Sermons and Remains*, pp. xxviii-xxix.
[18] See App. IV.   [19] See App. IV.
[20] Baskerville, *English Monks and the Monasteries*, pp. 247, 258.

premacy; after the dissolution of the larger monastic orders in 1538-39 they were given bishoprics by a government which was anxious to escape the financial drain of paying their yearly pensions.[21] Moreover, many of them lived comfortably through three reigns, retaining a discreet silence throughout the bitter conflict, and it is impossible to be sure whether their true complexion appears under Protestant Edward or Catholic Mary. Anthony Kitchen, Abbot of Eynsham, was certainly no open reformer in his early days as proctor to his monastic order at Cambridge, but he lived through four reigns and was the only member of the Marian episcopate to retain his see under Elizabeth.[22] John Chambers, Abbot of Peterborough, retained a foothold in both camps throughout Henry's life by his friendship with Edward Lee, Archbishop of York, and his connections with the Parr family, while he accepted the religious changes under the two following reigns.[23] Robert Warton, Abbot of St. Saviour's, Bermondsey, was created Bishop of St. Asaph's in 1536; he retained that post throughout Edward's rule and was finally promoted to the far wealthier bishopric of Hereford by Queen Mary.

On the other hand, the position of some of the other monks is clear. Robert Ferrar and John Hooper both died for their faith under Mary, and one was an Austin canon, the other a

---

[21] They were William Barlow, Bp. of St. David's (1536), Bath and Wells (1558); John Bird, Bp. of Bangor (1539), Chester (1541); Paul Bush, Bp. of Bristol (1542); John Chambers, Bp. of Peterborough (1541); John Hilsey, Bp. of Rochester (1535); Henry Holbeach, Bp. of Rochester (1538), Lincoln (1547); Robert Holgate, Bp. of Llandaff (1537), York (1545); Robert King, Bp. of Oxford (1545); Anthony Kitchen, Bp. of Llandaff (1545); William Rugge, Bp. of Norwich (1536); John Salcot, Bp. of Bangor (1534), Salisbury (1539); John Wakeman, Bp. of Gloucester (1541); Robert Warton, Bp. of St. Asaph (1536), Hereford (1554). Coverdale, Ferrar, Hooper, and Scory, though they were monks or friars, did not receive their bishoprics until the reign of Edward VI.

[22] Foxe, v, p. 425; *DNB*, Art. "Anthony Kitchen"; Whitebrook, *The Consecration of Matthew Parker*, pp. 19-22.

[23] *L.P.*, VI [1533], No. 399; B.M., Add. Ms. 5828, "Ms. notes of Bishop Kennett and Mr. Thomas Baker on Mr. Gunston's *History of Peterborough*," p. 150; B.M., Cleo. E. IV, f. 205; *DNB*, Art. "John Chambers."

Cistercian monk. Henry Holbeach was a Benedictine and Prior of St. Mary's, Worcester. He was a friend of Hugh Latimer and his suffragan bishop, and owed his promotion to the See of Rochester in 1544 not only to Henry's desire to escape from paying his pension, but also to Thomas Cranmer's patronage.[24] John Bird and Miles Coverdale were both friars and sincere reformers, the one as the Henrician Bishop of Chester, the other as the Edwardian Bishop of Exeter. Both were deprived of their sees under Mary, but while Coverdale escaped abroad, Bird remained at home, apparently deciding it was more prudent to bend with the times and accept the return of Catholicism than to risk imprisonment and possible death.[25]

There was one thing, however, which all these men had in common; both university professor and monk were innocent in the ways of government administration and diplomatic maneuvering. It is true that individual reformers on occasion proved themselves competent administrators, even able diplomats and statesmen, but as a group they lacked the experience and training which could aid them in their new positions of responsibility as episcopal officers, or in the flattery and subtlety necessary for a successful career at court. Dislike of court life was not necessarily an attitude peculiar to the reformers, but was the product of a lifetime spent in a totally different environment. When William Buckmaster, the conservative and cautious Vice-Chancellor of Cambridge, went up to London on business connected with the University's decision concerning the royal divorce, he returned home as soon as he could,

[24] *L.P.*, IX [1535], No. 97; XII, pt. ii [1537], Nos. 587, 1044; XIII, pt. ii [1538], No. 1133.

[25] John Bird, Bishop of Chester, was deprived in March 1554 because of his marriage. He renounced his wife and returned to Catholicism, and became Rector of Great Dunmow in Essex and Bishop Bonner's suffragan. He had originally begun his ecclesiastical career under the patronage of John Hilsey, Bishop of Rochester and Robert Holgate, Bishop of Llandaff whose suffragan he became in 1537. *L.P.*, XII, pt. i [1537], No. 726; Willis, *History of the Cathedral Church of Chester*, pp. 31-32.

gratefully remarking that he was "out of the court, where, as I both heard and perceived, many men did wonder on me."[26] The quiet doctor was not at home in the glitter of London or the intrigue of the royal retinue, and there must have been many men like him, products of a university atmosphere, who found the duties of a royal councillor and the social responsibilities of an episcopal position exacting and vexing work. Thomas Cranmer, after his advancement to the See of Canterbury, rarely turned up at the meetings of the Royal Council, and as Professor Pollard has noted, he was "little interested in the political aspect of affairs."[27] Hugh Latimer, it is said, skipped with joy when he was deprived of his bishopric,[28] while John Hooper was disgusted with the vice and corruption of the court, and with majestic wrath demanded that "These gentlemen that liveth upon dicing, carding, idleness, or with other men's goods, must be also admonished," and, if unrepenting, "cast . . . into the sea."[29] The moral self-righteousness of a puritan and the elastic conscience of a courtier and diplomat are rarely compatible, and the reformers did not hesitate to denounce what they considered a "carnal cluster of corruption and wickedness."

When the conservatives were rewarded with bishoprics, they discovered that their episcopal burdens were merely a remunerative extension of their other duties, but for the reformers the plunge into an active ecclesiastical life was a completely new experience. They brought to their positions a vast fund of reforming fervor, but singularly little urbanity or business acumen, and many of them shortly came to blows with the canons of their cathedral chapters or with the municipal authorities of their cathedral towns. From the moment that William Barlow became Bishop of St. David's, he ran into

---

[26] *L.P.,* IV, pt. iii [1530], No. 6325.
[27] Pollard, *Thomas Cranmer,* p. 119.
[28] *DNB,* Art. "Hugh Latimer."
[29] Hooper, *Early Writings,* "The third sermon upon Jonas" (1550), p. 481.

trouble with his canons, who reported to Roland Lee, the Lord President of the Marches of Wales, that their bishop had preached against purgatory, against confession, and that he had claimed that when two or three persons, even "cobblers and weavers were in company, and elected, in the name of God, that there was the true Church of God."[30] Lee sent the petition on to Cromwell who evidently decided to ignore it, but a year later, in 1537, the President of the Council of Wales was again requested to deal with the results of the Bishop's tactless behavior. Barlow had apparently lost patience with one of the "chaunters" of his cathedral and had imprisoned him. When the affair was reported to the Council, Roland Lee investigated the charges and ordered the Bishop to restore to the prisoner his house and property on pain of a five hundred pound fine. This Barlow peremptorily refused to do.[31] What steps were taken thereafter are unknown, but the Bishop of Coventry and Lichfield must have been thoroughly annoyed with his undiplomatic colleague at St. David's. Nor was this the end of the chronic dispute which raged in the bishopric. Barlow, claiming that he had discovered "anti-Christian superstition" of a detestable nature, tried to move his cathedral seat away from St. David's to Caermarthen in order to escape the control of "barbarous rural persons."[32] This, of course, infuriated not only the canons but also the populace of the cathedral town. The canons not unnaturally refused to be reformed or moved, and were reluctant to accept the Bishop as the head of their chapter, stating that no bishop had ever claimed so much before, a statement which the Bishop's brother avowed to be quite true, for, he said, "no bishop dwelt so long among them as my brother hath,

---

[30] B.M., Cleo. E. v, f. 414 (382); printed in Strype, *Ecc. Mem.*, I, pt. ii, No. LXXVII.

[31] P.R.O., S.P. I, vol. 241, f. 73 (*L.P.*, Add. [1537], No. 1225).

[32] Wright, *Suppression of Monasteries*, Cam. Soc. XXVI (1843), No. XCIII, p. 183.

and intendeth to do." Here indeed was zeal but extraordinarily little discretion.[33]

Nicholas Shaxton had similar troubles in his diocese of Salisbury, but in this case not with his canons but with his city of Sarum. The conflict grew out of the actions of the Bishop's under-bailiff, an uncompromising Protestant named Goodall whose zeal won the hatred of most of the city authorities, especially of the mayor. In an effort to be rid of the under-bailiff, the city claimed that it was the King's city and not the Bishop's and that the Bishop's delegates had no authority. This led to a particularly unsavory dispute in which the city fathers denounced Shaxton as a heretic whom they would gladly see hung, while the Bishop labeled them reactionary and bigoted fools. The controversy was brought to the attention of Thomas Cromwell, who ordered the Bishop to drop the entire affair and not to bother him with it again. He remarked of Shaxton's autocratic and uncompromising behavior that he had "a stomach more meet for an emperor than for a bishop," and he should learn a little patience and tact.[34]

This, of course, is not to say that some of the reforming bishops were not capable administrators, but there are too many incidents of disputes and minor controversies, too many cases of inability to pay the clerical subsidies and tenths through mismanagement, which indicate that as a group they lacked the necessary training for their posts.[35] Today their spiritual zeal and energy would be highly esteemed, but the

[33] P.R.O., S.P. 1, vol. 140, f. 175 (*L.P.*, XIII, pt. ii [1538], No. 1132).

[34] *Ibid.*, vol. 126, ff. 186-187 (*L.P.*, XII, pt. ii [1537], No. 1114).

[35] The government's attitude toward the fervent idealism and energy of the evangelical bishops is exemplified by a remark of Hugh Latimer when he was describing the occasion of his deprivation in 1539. "When I was in trouble," he said, "it was objected and said unto me, that I was singular; that no man thought as I thought; that I loved a singularity in all that I did; and that I took a way contrary to the King and the whole Parliament; and that I travailed with them that had better wits than I, that I was contrary to them all." *Sermons*, p. 116.

Church of Tudor England was considerably more than a matter of spiritual cures and solely religious problems. It was a vast administrative machine which was expected to function smoothly, for the church was a social and political as well as a spiritual organization.

The faith that moved these reformers was deep and esoteric, their moral fortitude was rigid and uncompromising, and their aim was to return to the ethical austerity of the primitive church. Their passionate belief in predestination and their profound faith that he who believed would be saved was a strange mixture of intellectualism and mysticism every bit as aristocratic and far more dogmatic than the humanism of the conservatives. Their early training in scholasticism and prolonged study of divinity led them to investigate the deepest mysteries of God and man, producing a theology as rigidly rational and intolerantly dogmatic as any dialectical philosophy. Their logical thinking, joined to a profound preoccupation with the omnipotence of God, created in the minds of some of the conservatives the awe-inspiring image of a Jehovah who damns the many to everlasting torment in order to vindicate his justice and saves the few to prove his mercy. Their faith supported them in the sublime conviction that they alone in a depraved and corrupt world were the "elect" of God's creatures. They were scornful of the plebeian who found solace in the beauty of a religious ceremony and received aid in the appreciation and understanding of the unknown from the symbolism of a stained-glass window. "What Jewish and dull Pharisees are these," William Turner asked in answer to Gardiner's argument that most men prefer to recall Christ by "all the gates of our senses," "that either will not or cannot be content with the holy word of Christ and his Sacraments to bring Christ to their memories that they may think on him except they smell something to remember him and taste something also to remember him thereby?"[36] Such men did not need the

---

[36] Turner, *The Rescuynge of the Romishe Fox* (1545), sig. G IIII.

daily props which the church afforded the average man, and they were quick to point out that many of these rites and usages had lost their original symbolic nature and had acquired certain attributes of supernatural power. The ringing of bells, John Hooper once wrote, has long since ceased to signify merely the calling together of men for religious prayers and services, and has now "come to that point, that people think God to be highly honored by the sound of bells," while others "say that the sound can drive away the devil, and cease all tempests."[37] While the conservatives regarded misuse and abuse as mere foolishness, the reformers saw in them the inevitable path to eternal perdition. An omnipotent Godhead could not sanction any encroachment upon his divinity, and though saints and relics might be venerated as symbols of human virtue, of patience, of obedience and humility, they were "not to be prayed unto, nor to be as God." There could be no mediator between God and man other than Christ himself for it was faith and faith alone which could justify man in the eyes of God, and guide him along the tortuous path to salvation.

It was this profound faith, this overwhelming belief, which transformed predestination from an engine of vengeance into one of mercy, but at the same time it blinded them to the importance of human law and the daily considerations of government, leading them to assume that nothing had value unless it had Scriptural sanction. It fortified their rigid morality and puritanical instincts, causing them to see sin where only weakness existed, leading them to behold evil where only folly was evident. Such men demanded of their lesser followers the same conviction, the same burning interest in religion and salvation as inspired their own acts and thoughts. "Let no man make excuse," expostulated Thomas Cranmer in his preface to the Bible, "and say, saith he, 'I am busied about matters of the commonwealth'; 'I bear this office or that'; 'I am a crafts-

[37] Hooper, *Early Writings*, p. 197.

man, I must apply mine occupation'; 'I have a wife, my children must be fed, my household must I provide for.' Briefly, 'I am a man of the world, it is not for me to read the scriptures, that belongeth to them that have bidden the world farewell. . . .' " An interest in the affairs of man was all the more reason to turn to the Gospel, for, said the Archbishop, men are "in the midst of the sea of worldly wickedness, and therefore thou needest the more of ghostly succour and comfort."[38] Only by the complete spiritualization of this world could man hope to escape the retribution of the next, and had the Primate had his wish, all men would have spent their days in reading the Scriptures, for, he concluded, "if it were possible so to live, I would think it good for a man to spend all his life in that, and to do no other thing."[39] Passive acceptance of religion was not enough, for the Son of God did not reside in any church "made of lime and stone by man's hands, but only in heaven above, and in man's heart in earth."[40] For the lukewarm supporter of their creed, Bishop Hooper had little sympathy. It was not sufficient to abhor the Pope and cavil against idolatry and superstition; to the man who demanded the "joyes that the gospel promised" merely on such conditions, the Bishop exclaimed: "No! it shall be said unto him, Depart in the devil's name, thou wicked person, to eternal pain; for all thy religion was in the tongue: no man can possess the joys promised in the gospel, but such as study with all diligence to live after the gospel, as God gives us all grace to do!"[41] Here indeed was the spirit that generations before had led men into the monasteries, and which was to make martyrs of many of these reforming bishops, martyrs

[38] Cranmer, *Works*, "Preface to the Bible" (1540), p. 119.

[39] *Ibid.*, p. 123.

[40] These words were spoken by John Bale, Bishop of Ossory, and recorded by William Broman. B.M., Cleo. E. v, f. 397 (365) (*L.P.*, IX [1535], No. 230).

[41] Hooper, *Early Writings*, p. 247.

who faced death in this world rather than jeopardize their salvation in the next.

As bishops on the Episcopal Bench, the hard core of the reformers were widely separated from their conservative brethren not only in matters of religious belief but also in the attitude they took in regard to the affairs of state and the considerations of government. Men who felt close upon them the dangers of sin, whose eyes were turned heavenwards and not earthwards, and whose moral convictions demanded that they control life, not countenance it, were unwilling to accept the cautious policy of the conservatives, predicated as it was upon the exigencies of human life and respect for mortal law. The man who could write as Bishop Hooper did that the less men "feel the danger of eternal damnation, the nearer they be unto eternal pain, and have already one foot in hell . . . ," was not ready to hold the unity of the nation in high esteem if the cost involved placing one foot in hell.[42] Nor would he bow to the will of the majority if in so doing he was risking his chances of salvation. Divine law was their guide, and they considered the controls of men petty compared to the majesty of divine jurisdiction. "God forbid," prayed one divine, "that for the cause of any mortal man I should condemn the law of my Lord God."[43]

The reformers considered themselves to be the "elect" of God, and they constantly warned against the dangers of majority rule. Nicholas Ridley, when he was confronted with the Marian reaction preferred his own interpretation of the Scriptures, and cautioned against the tyranny of the majority. "It is a known thing," he wrote, "and a common proverb, 'Oftentimes the greater part overcometh the better.' "[44] This, of course, was written after Ridley had been deprived of his episcopal status, but Hooper expressed the same opinion un-

[42] *Ibid.*, "The third sermon upon Jonas" (1550), p. 495.
[43] Pocock, *Records of the Reformation*, II, No. cccxx, "A glasse of the truth," p. 411.
[44] Foxe, VII, p. 415.

der Edward when his own party was in control of the government. "Fear neither," he urged in a treatise written in 1547 and dedicated to the young King, "of the ordinary power or succession of bishops, nor of the greater part. For if either the authority of bishops, or the greater part, should have power to interpret the scripture, the sentence of the Pharisees should have been preferred before the sentence of Zachary. . . . Consider, that many times the true church is but a small congregation. . . . Therefore . . . the interpretation of the scripture [is not] obligated unto an ordinary power, nor [to] the most part. . . ."[45] Such men had little regard for the ideal of unity which moved so many of the conservatives, and when Gardiner accused William Turner of failing to call the King supreme head of the church which, the Bishop claimed, he ought to have done because "the whole realm hath given it unto him," Turner answered that if Henry "be therefore lawfully head of the Church of England and Ireland because the whole realm hath agreed there to, then when all the whole realm consented that the Pope should be called the head of the Church of England, he was lawfully called the head of the Church of England. If it be a good argument to say the whole realm do it, ergo it must needs be true. A little before ye have builded the King's supremacy upon the Pope's traditions, and here ye build it upon a multitude of men. Have ye no better foundation for it?"[46]

"And, to say the truth, better it were to have a deformity in preaching, so that some would preach the truth of God, and that which is to be preached, without cauponation and adulteration of the word . . . than to have such a uniformity, that the silly people should be thereby occasioned to continue still in their lamentable ignorance, corrupt judgment, superstition, and idolatry, and esteem things, as they do all prepos-

[45] Hooper, *Early Writings*, "A Declaration of Christ and his office" (1547), p. 84.
[46] Turner, *The Rescuynge of the Romishe Fox* (1545), sig. C II.

terously. . . ."[47] These are the words of Hugh Latimer before
he became Bishop of Worcester in 1534, and they are a remarkable omen of his future behavior as a government official
and bishop, for Latimer was never a man to bend to the will
of the majority, or jeopardize his doctrines in order to preserve
national unity. John Hooper likewise was adamant in his refusal to compromise his faith in order to reach a temporary
solution agreeable to all. "Some [people]," he exclaimed,
"prescribe laws for the conscience of men for a time, until it
may be farther deliberated upon or approved good by a general council. These men grievously offend themselves, and
causeth others to do the same. In case the law made for the
time seem not good unto such as shall at a more leisure have
the examination thereof, the law for the mean time shall be
condemned as heretical and pernicious. Then put the case, that
many, or at the least some, of those that led their conscience
after the law made for the mean time die: how standeth then
the case with these departed souls that were deceived while
they lived by false doctrine? They doubtless are lost for ever
and without time, if they died in any error of the catholic
faith. . . ."[48] Hooper could never have understood the words
of Edmund Bonner when he said "In matters of state, individuals were not to be so much regarded as the whole body
of the citizens."[49]

Many of the reformers were loud in their protest against
unpreaching prelates who regarded the mundane affairs of
the world as the proper milieu for their talents and interests.
Hugh Latimer danced with rage when he observed the lavish
living and princely behavior of bishops who left their spiritual
duties to suffragans and underlings. In his famous "Sermon

[47] Latimer, *Sermons and Remains*, No. VII, "Latimer to Sir Edw. Bayn-
ston" (1531-1532), p. 347.
[48] Hooper, *Early Writings*, "A Declaration of the Ten Commandments
of Almighty God" (1550), pp. 276-277.
[49] Sanders, "Report to Cardinal Moroni on the change of religion in
1558-59," *Catholic Record Society*, I (1904-1905), p. 39.

of the Plough" he denounced the faults of such men in pithy and sarcastic language. "But now for the fault of unpreaching prelates," he accused, "methink I could guess what might be said for excusing of them. They are so troubled with lordly living, they be so placed in palaces, couched in courts, ruffling in their rents, dancing in their dominions, burdened with ambassages, pampering of their paunches, like a monk that maketh his jubilee; munching in their mangers, and moiling in their gay manors and mansions, and so troubled with loitering in their lordships, that they cannot attend it. They are otherwise occupied, some in the King's matters, some are ambassadors, some of the privy council, some to furnish the court, some are lords of the parliament, some are presidents, and comptrollers of mints."[50] To the fiery preacher these were not the occupations for a bishop, for a priest who had the cure of souls. Those who preferred such posts to their ecclesiastical obligations, Latimer condemned as the devil's disciples.

In their desire to reform life, these reformers had but small regard for the social and political consequences of their actions. For them there was no middle ground between right and wrong, good and evil. They considered as diabolical the elastic morality and pragmatic philosophy of men such as Thirlby, Heath, and Gardiner, whose words and actions were mutable and varied with circumstance. "When I call to remembrance . . . the state of those that for fear of trouble, either for loss of goods, will do in the sight of the world those things that they know and are assured are contrary to the will of God, I can do no less but lament their case, being assured the end thereof will be so pitiful . . . that I tremble and fear to have it in remembrance." Such was the answer of Bishop Nicholas Ridley to the compromising expediency of the conservatives.[51] The reformers had no desire to adapt their creed to all tastes,

---

[50] Latimer, *Sermons*, "Sermon of the Plough" (1548), pp. 61-62.
[51] Foxe, VII, "A letter of Ridley, sent to a cousin of his," p. 425; Ridley, *Works*, No. XXIX, p. 385.

or, as the Archbishop wrote his friend, John à Lasco, to "deal in ambiguities."[52]

Hugh Latimer was equally critical of those whose criterion of action was one of human prudence and political consideration. While in prison, he argued that "in civil or politic matters, often times the magistrates do tolerate a less evil for avoiding of a greater, as they which have this saying oft in their mouths: 'Better an inconvenience than a mischief.' And 'It is the property of a wise man,' saith one, 'to dissemble many things; and he that cannot dissemble, cannot rule.' In which sayings they betray themselves, that they do not earnestly weigh what is just, what is not. Wherefore forasmuch as man's laws, if it be but in this respect only, that they be derived by men, are not able to bring anything to perfection, but are enforced of necessity to suffer many things out of square, and are compelled sometimes to wink at the worst things: seeming they know not how to maintain the common peace and quiet otherwise, they do ordain that the more part shall take place."[53] The worthy divine had no understanding of the workings of parliamentary government even as it functioned under Tudor despotism. He was sublimely ignorant of the daily problems of government, the very essence of which is compromise. He was unable to appreciate the skill and subtlety of diplomacy, the basis of which is dissembling. He misunderstood the nature of law which aims not at perfection but at the enforcement of order. The old controversy between the "more part" and the "better part" had been thrashed out long before, but in sixteenth-century England it reappeared in the guise of the "elect" of God—strengthened by the fanatical conviction of the reformers in the justice of their cause and the burning zeal of their religion. It is little wonder then that Stephen Gardiner, a past master of practices and chicanery, summed up the attitude of his episcopal opponents by saying

---

[52] *Original Letters*, I, No. IX, p. 17.
[53] Foxe, VII, "A conference between Ridley and Latimer," p. 417.

that they "would have the old house pulled down ere the new be framed."[54] Here, in fact, is the core of the dispute between the two parties, the gulf which since time immemorial has divided the idealistic seeker of truth and the cautious conservative; there could be little compromise between such widely divergent opinions.

To the reformers, however, religion included something more than salvation, for they tended to view society as an essentially theocratic structure. The social obligations of the corporate state were the temporal reflections of divine will, and though salvation was basically a religious problem, it included many social manifestations as well. Poverty was looked upon not as a social but as a spiritual evil; avarice and greed were condemned not because they were harmful to the state, but because they involved a loss of grace which was tantamount to everlasting torment and damnation; deceit, murder, and breach of contract were only secondarily a violation of human law, for, as Bishop Hooper was careful to emphasize, "it is not the magistrate that pulleth them [the criminals] to execution, but God, whose minister they be"; and "it is God that sendeth to hell, that hangeth for transgression upon the gallows. . . ."[55]

Cranmer and Latimer, Ridley and Ferrar, sincerely believed that by making men more godly they were also making them better citizens. The mere reading of the Scriptures, they thought, could not help but transform the vagrant into a worthy member of society, make the criminal virtuous, the corrupt pure. Thomas Cranmer was passionate in his belief that ignorance of the Gospel was the key to civil disorder and perversion, for "that is the thing," he claimed, "that bringeth in heresies; that is it that causeth all corrupt and perverse liv-

[54] Gardiner, *A Discussion of Mr. Hoper's Oversight* (1550), P.R.O., S.P. 10, vol. 12, f. 48.

[55] Hooper, *Early Writings*, "The fourth sermon upon Jonas" (1550), p. 495.

ing; that is it that bringeth all things out of good order."[56] John Hooper was even more sweeping in his faith in the salutary effect of the spread of the Bible, and he tried to impress upon his royal audience that "Among all other most noble and famous deeds of kings and princes, none is more godly, commendable, nor profitable to the commonwealth, than to promote and set forth unto their subjects the pure and sincere religion of the eternal God, King of all kings, and Lord of all lords. Then shall justice, peace, and concord reign, the door of idolatry be shut up, by the which hath entered all evil. . . ."[57] Wealth and power, order and security were consequent to a godly life, and, predicted the Bishop, mankind would not only find "grace at God's hand, but also more health and soberness of body, more riches in the coffers, more plenty in the realm,"[58] if they would only follow the gospel in their lives. It was gluttony and idleness, avarice and slander, deceit and ignorance which were the seeds of social discord, and only through the purging light of the Testament could man and his society be saved. They aimed not at transforming things, but peoples, not governments but individuals. Theirs was a magnificent dream, the hope that the assurance of salvation for all men would bring heaven to earth, and make of this "carnal cluster" of worldliness a paradise of saints. Their faith was religious, not social, their methods spiritual, not material.

However, in attacking the moral degeneration of society and in holding up the foibles of men to the standards of a community of saints, they aggravated a host of social and economic problems, giving added impetus to the current of social unrest which ran through Tudor England. For many of

[56] Cranmer, *Works*, p. 121.

[57] Hooper, *Early Writings*, "An Oversight and Deliberation upon the Holy Prophete Jonas," "The Epistle" (1550), p. 435.

[58] Quoted in Janelle, *Obedience in Church and State*, p. lxvii, from Hooper, *An Oversight and Deliberation upon the Holy Prophete Jonas*, B.M. (call number G. 11850), f. clvii b.

the conservatives, the line between ethical rejuvenation and social revolution was a thin one, and they turned their backs on religious reform for fear of the social consequences. Festering sores of social discontent were chronic throughout the sixteenth century; enclosures were upsetting time-honored methods of production, depriving thousands of their livelihood, and producing an army of vagrants and paupers. The machinery of Tudor despotism weighed heavily upon the yeoman and peasant, while it fostered the breakdown of those social inhibitions which had contributed to the stability of the medieval economy. Upstarts and pedigreed nobles rubbed shoulders together at court, and one could no longer discern a gentleman by dress alone. The disparity between rich and poor, if not more real than in the past, had become more apparent, as luxury and wealth began to rival birth and breeding in importance. To old sores was now added the bitter salt of religious controversy, and the advocates of religious radicalism quickly united with the partisans of social amelioration in a sweeping indictment of the entire social, economic and religious fabric of Tudor society. Moreover, the pious dreams of the reforming bishops that the ability to recite scriptural verses would ease the existing social tensions proved to be a mirage, while the biblical ideal of religious communism merely aggravated the claims of the disciples of revolution.

As we have already pointed out, the reformers did not consciously stir up the embers of the age-old conflict between the "haves" and the "have-nots," but as one author has remarked of the social-religious literature of the era: "It is not surprising that to churchmen, probably in the main the spokesmen for this tradition, the issue of religious reform should have seemed the more urgent, but it is likely that to the masses of the people, the hope of the social betterment to be won from religious changes was of at least equal interest and perhaps of even greater immediate attractiveness."[59] In spread-

---

[59] White, *Social Criticism*, p. 82.

ing the knowledge of the Scriptures, in contrasting the cupidity and evilness of this world with the Biblical standards of what ought to be, they opened a Pandora's box of dissension and discontent. When Hugh Latimer denounced enclosure, he was not merely reflecting the interests of his own class, but sincerely believed that the yeomen were the backbone of Christ's religion. His wrath was directed not only against the economic cupidity of the new landed gentry, but also against their immorality, when he declared "if ye bring it to pass that the yeomanry be not able to put their sons to school . . . and that they be not able to marry their daughters to the avoiding of whoredom; I say, ye pluck salvation from the people, and utterly destroy the realm. For by yeoman's sons the faith of Christ is and hath been maintained chiefly."[60] Whether or not Latimer was sincere, his words gave religious sanction to the poverty-stricken peasants in their claims against landlords who were enclosing their lands. When John Hooper preached against the grasping noble who "hath enough given him from God, yet is not content therewith" and who "in vain glory and pride of the mammon of the world . . . will condemn and disdain the very image of God in the poor," his underprivileged listeners forgot that the worthy divine's pontifications were not directed alone against the rapacity of the nobility.[61] His angry words were pointed equally towards the common people who, he said, "live idle, and will not labor" and who "examine all apart, and prove: the nobility make unprofitable expenses, more than their ability can or is able to sustain. . . ."[62] It made but slight difference to the advocates of class strife that Hooper was condemning vices universal to all men, that he abhorred idleness and dicing, drunkenness and gaming, in rich and poor alike.

Such remarks as these gave added impetus to the demands of the poor since they could now claim that they alone were

[60] Latimer, *Sermons*, "First sermon preached before Edward VI" (1549), p. 86.
[61] Hooper, *Early Writings*, "Third sermon upon Jonas" (1550), p. 466.
[62] *Ibid.*, p. 459.

the children of God, and that the rich by being rich were bringing upon themselves the wrath of God. The danger was explicit when William Turner, whether consciously or not, raised the spectre of class warfare by deriding the worldly ecclesiastics as "ye lordly bishops and ye clean fingered gentlemen of the clergy."[63] When Latimer preached that "the poorest ploughman is in Christ equal with the greatest prince that is,"[64] he was reiterating the essential philosophy of Christianity, the equality of all men in the eyes of God, but, for his audience, it was easy to omit the qualifying assumption that this equality exists only in God, and to translate religious idealism into social program. The reformers preached that wealth involved a moral responsibility and that the riches of this world were the gift of divine benevolence, not the reward of human initiative. Thus the individual who abused this godly favor won for himself and his family the full lash of divine wrath, for, said Bishop Hooper, "What availeth great riches in a realm, and neither the head nor the greatest part of the members to be the better for it?"[65] It was not difficult to argue from this that the man who misused his wealth did not deserve to keep his riches—a dangerous weapon indeed in the hands of penniless vagrants and overburdened peasants.

Common knowledge of the Bible produced a host of amateur theologians who expounded the meaning of the Scriptures at street corners and in beerhouses, stirring up religious ferment and spreading questionable social theories in regard to the proper behavior of a Christian man. The leaders of the Protestant religious movement, the bishops of the Episcopal Bench, however, refused to see the undermining and unsettling effect that this spread of the gospel might have upon society and the enforcement of law and order, and they were

---

[63] Turner, *The Rescuynge of the Romishe Fox* (1545), sig. C v.

[64] Latimer, *Sermons*, "Last sermon preached before Edward VI" (1550), p. 215.

[65] Tytler, *England under the Reigns of Edward VI and Mary*, I, "Hooper to Cecil" (April 1551), p. 365.

scornful of the growing alarm of their conservative, secularly trained, colleagues. The reformers considered with a certain amount of reason that the worried fear of the conservatives was primarily a trick to maintain the pernicious creed of popery, and contended that even the smallest abuse warranted immediate reform, for the failure to do so meant inevitable damnation. " 'It is but a little abuse,' say they," ridiculed Latimer, " 'and it may be easily amended. But it should not be taken in hand at the first, for fear of trouble or further inconveniences. The people will not bear sudden alterations; an insurrection may be made after sudden mutation, which may be to the great harm and loss of the realm.' " The men who argued in these terms Latimer considered as "blanchers, that hitherto have stopped the word of God, and hindered the true setting forth of the same." The future martyr deeply lamented these "put-offs, so many put-byes, so many respects and considerations of worldly wisdom," and vehemently urged that the actions of the Old Testament figure, King Hezekiah, should be a lesson to the disciples of secular considerations. "Good King Hezekiah," he praised, "was not moved with the worldly respects, with these prudent considerations, with these policies: He feared not insurrections of the people. . . ." No, the Hebrew monarch refused to be poisoned with the "dreams of men's imagination" and, according to Master Latimer, he won for himself and his people the bliss of everlasting salvation.[66]

Unfortunately for the future purity of the Protestant creed, religious radicalism and social revolution did walk hand in hand. It made small difference that sixteenth-century communism looked backward to the imaginary days of the Apos-

[66] Latimer, *Sermons*, "Sermon of the Plough" (1548), pp. 69-70. Gasquet and Bishop, p. 251, n. 2, say that "Latimer . . . had warned the government of a popular rising," and give the above quotation as a reference. Unfortunately the authors have forgotten the use of quotation marks. Latimer was not warning the government but instead urging it not to heed the "ungodly" advice of the conservatives.

tles when all was held in common, and not forward to some future materialistic utopia on earth. It was still dangerous and the exponents of the *status quo* had reason to regard its growth with alarm. This is not the place to discuss varied doctrines of the social reformers,[67] but the fact that such religious sects as Sacramentarians and Anabaptists advocated a form of communism which they piously believed and abortively practiced, and that these revolutionary ideas were regarded with growing alarm by people who held a stake in society, is eloquently expressed in the words of one worried reformer, Robert Crowley. After the prophecy of the conservatives had been realized during the riots and insurrections of the summer of 1549, Crowley wrote of these "greedy cormerauntes" that they "know no obedience, they regard no laws, they would have no gentlemen, they would have all men like themselves, they would have all things common. They would not have us master of that which is our own."[68] Reform was one thing, revolution quite another, and Crowley is here voicing the deep concern of all Englishmen who owned property and had a position in society, or who were responsible for the administering of law and justice. The doctrine of the Anabaptists, with its anarchistic principles of the abolition of law, of class, and of property, struck deep into the social sensitivities of Tudor England. It was this image, the appalling picture of social revolution, the destruction of law, property, and reasoned government in the wake of the bitter wrath of the "common sort" which haunted the minds of the conservative bishops. As bureaucrats and administrators, as lawyers and statesmen, they could not condone a philosophy which implied such consequences, and long before their fears were realized in the uprisings of 1549, they were preaching a policy of cau-

[67] See Tawney, *The Agrarian Problem in the Sixteenth Century*, and White, *Social Criticism in Popular Religious Literature of the Sixteenth Century.*

[68] Quoted in White, *Social Criticism*, p. 118.

tion and human prudence. They were quick to perceive the connection between religious radicalism and social disorder, and it fortified them in their faith in the old religion; it convinced them in their opposition to their radical colleagues on the Episcopal Bench; and it led them to the tragic renunciation of their early tolerant attitude toward reform, causing them to forsake their humanistic training. The issue at stake was no longer merely ecclesiastical reform but was soon to become social revolution.

CHAPTER V

THE RIVAL PARTIES

ꝚN the course of this study, the words reformer and conservative have been carefully left undefined, and no attempt has been made to express the exact connotation of the two terms when applied to religious classifications. The explanation for this may be stated in a negative form: that the use of Catholic and Protestant as a means of cataloguing religious sentiment is so unsatisfactory that some broader and less biased description had to be found. The difficulty grows out of the fact that it is almost impossible to give a rigid and exact definition to such words. If, for instance, we define Protestantism as meaning the renunciation of the papal authority, then Gardiner, Bonner, Thirlby, and Heath were Protestants. If, on the other hand, we say that Catholicism is the belief in the Real Presence in the Mass, then Thomas Cranmer must be included among the Catholic ranks at least until 1540,[1] while Richard Sampson, in holding to a strange and rather muddled belief in what he called "transmutation," must be classified as a Protestant. However, Sampson was loud in his denial that his disavowal of transubstantiation which "he thought ever that could not be" was tantamount to his acceptance of the Mass as a memorial and purely symbolic ceremony.[2]

If the problem of resolving the Catholic creed into an accurate yet universally accepted dogma is difficult for the modern historian, it was even more precarious for the men of the sixteenth century. For those who lived before the long series

---

[1] Cranmer, *Works*, No. CXCIII, p. 343 (*L.P.*, xv, No. 137). The *L.P.* date this letter in 1540, the Parker Society in 1537.

[2] B.M., Royal 17 B XXXIX, printed in Gasquet and Bishop, App. v, pp. 407, 415, 439.

of meetings known as the Council of Trent, there was no sure rock of Catholic interpretation on which to build their faith, and the individual was required to wade through the mire of intellectual and historical confusion as best he could. The Renaissance Papacy was far from being the divinely inspired organ of infallibility which it later became in the nineteenth century. The disturbing schism of the previous century had seriously weakened the prestige of the See of Rome, while the quick succession of councils following the schism had merely resulted in giving authoritative recognition to the fact that two fundamentally opposed schools of thought existed concerning the limits and nature of papal power.[3] Though More reiterated his belief in the divine origins of Saint Peter's chair,[4] it took him seven years to assure himself that there was not some truth in the argument of those who claimed that the authority of the Roman Pontiff was "derived from human law, and not standing upon a divine prescription."[5] The new study of the classics, the origins of Christianity, and the primitive church had cast the whole question of papal supremacy into doubt, and even Erasmus, though never questioning the existing spiritual preëminence of the Papacy, wondered whether St. Jerome would have sanctioned such a concentration of divinity.[6] For many pious men the Papacy was essentially an historic phenomenon and political necessity, but not necessarily a divine institution, and, as Professor Janelle has pointed out, there is no evidence to believe that Stephen Gardiner, in returning to communion with Rome under Catholic Mary, ever recognized the papal claim to be the Vicar of Christ. His motives were those of human prudence and political expediency.[7]

---

[3] Constant, I, pp. 383-384; Messenger, *The Reformation, the Mass and the Priesthood*, I, p. 237.

[4] More, *Correspondence*, No. 199, p. 499.

[5] Quoted in Constant, I, pp. 385-386.

[6] *Ibid.*, p. 385.

[7] Janelle, *Obedience in Church and State*, p. lix.

If we add to the controversy over the divine status of the Roman Pontiff the fact that the popes of the sixteenth century were behaving more like petty Italian princes than the spiritual leaders of Christendom, and that their waning prestige was unscrupulously utilized in the interests of the national and dynastic policies of rival sovereigns, it is not surprising that many learned divines lent their support to the breach with Rome. But in so doing they cut themselves off from the one source of authority which could unequivocally interpret the faith of Christian men. Catholicism had never been solely based on scriptural verses, but owed as much to a thousand years of growth. The church fathers had added their interpretation of the Bible to the vast fund of knowledge which was the common heritage of western Europe, while custom had compromised the original severity of the Primitive Church, adapting it to the needs of a growing society. When, under the impetus of the "New Learning," the ancient doctors were reread in their original texts, when the Gospel was retranslated and purged of centuries of impurities and corruptions, when, in brief, the Church of Rome was compared to the austerity of the days of the Apostles and the Christian creed was held up to scriptural proof, it was impossible to prove the divine origin of many ecclesiastical institutions or the "gospel" truth of many time-honored customs and beliefs. As one historian has observed, the application of intellectual agility meant that now "any man could find arguments to prove the rightness of the things he desired."[8] When, for instance, the issue of auricular confession arose, even the arch-conservative, William Rugge, was forced to admit that he could not find confession expressly enjoined in the word of God, but he and many others regarded it as "very requisite and expedient."[9] Nor was the papal decision that communion should be celebrated only in one kind a universally accepted

---

[8] Powicke, *The Reformation in England*, pp. 16-17.

[9] P.R.O., S.P. 1, vol. 152, f. 19 (*L.P.*, XIV, pt. i [1539], No. 1065, sec. 3).

principle, and even under Queen Mary, George Day, who in the previous reign had been deprived of his see for disobedience, confessed to the heretic, John Bradford, that he wished "the church would define again, that they might have" communion in two kinds once more.[10]

There was no consistent tradition of theological interpretation on which to fall back, for even such an important doctrine as transubstantiation had been queried by many distinguished churchmen. Both Duns Scotus and William of Occam doubted whether it was conclusively proved by Scriptures apart from tradition and church authority, but these men accepted transubstantiation even while questioning its divinity, for the criterion of acceptance was not predicated solely upon Scriptures but was equally based on centuries of tradition and the supremacy of the authority of Rome.[11] Unfortunately, however, in the sixteenth century Christendom lacked both unity and authority, and though there were many men like Edmund Bonner who believed that if a custom were good it was worthy of being kept regardless of its origins,[12] there were others who held the Bible as the sole rule of godliness. To such men a particular custom or institution had to be explicitly sanctioned by Scripture or else be discarded as the devil's creed. The burden of proof was placed upon the Catholics to find scriptural verification for such ancient customs as clerical chastity, images, and communion in one kind; unimpeachable evidence was naturally difficult to discover. Moreover, there was no longer a universally esteemed authority to interpret the Scriptures, and the very basis of Biblical proof collapsed since there was no common ground from which a decision could be reached. The Marian Bishop of Coventry and Lichfield, Ralph Bayne, was quick to perceive this dilemma, and refused even to attempt to settle the outstanding theological con-

[10] Foxe, VII, p. 178.
[11] Messenger, *The Reformation, the Mass and the Priesthood*, I, pp. 100-102.
[12] Bonner, *Homilies*, f. 39.

troversies between the Catholics and Protestants when Elizabeth first succeeded to the throne, for, he said, "those about to dispute must at least agree on some points. There can never be a well regulated debate with one who denies everything."[13] This, of course, was said after the fires of Smithfield had darkened the religious air with the smoke of burning martyrs, but years before, under Henry VIII, Stephen Gardiner had already recognized the futility of arriving at any definite scriptural proof. In his theological dispute with Martin Bucer at Ratisbon in 1541 he scornfully turned aside the German's opinion that scriptural authority could be used as a common basis of debate, for, said the Bishop, each side would then apply "their own interpretation and therein stand obstinately."[14]

Lacking the final authority of the Pope, with the Bible open to a multitude of interpretations by a host of amateur theologians, and with no clear tradition on which to depend, the opponents of religious change were placed in the position of defending a creed which was far from explicit in its meaning or clear in its origins by the unsatisfactory argument that what has been accepted as the law of God is the law of God. The Bishop of Winchester stated the question which was uppermost in the minds of the conservative party when he asked: "Shall we, after XVC years, begin to inquire whether the state of our religion be established in mere idolatry as they do nowadays term it blasphemously?"[15] The Bishop may have reached the ultimate heights to which a liberal sentiment can attain when he later confessed that he believed that "what so ever is good spoken, or used by any man is of God,"[16] but it was a difficult premise to maintain in the face of men who worshiped a god who was willing to damn ten generations of mortals because

---

[13] Sanders, "Report to Cardinal Moroni on the change in religion, 1558-59," *Catholic Record Society*, I (1904-1905), p. 30.

[14] Quoted in Muller, *Stephen Gardiner*, p. 98.

[15] Gardiner, *A Declaration of the Devils Sophistrie* (1546), f. cxxv.

[16] Quoted from Gardiner's lost book in Turner, *The Rescuynge of the Romishe Fox* (1545), sig. E II.

they were ignorant of his will. To divines such as Hooper, who believed that the man who died under "the law of the meantime" would be cast into hell, ignorance of the law did little to mitigate the final consequence of divine wrath.

In the midst of this intellectual confusion the actions of many of the conservative bishops approach the point of servile compliance. For example, George Day, Bishop of Chichester, who had previously been "a vehement affirmer of Transubstantiation" reversed his opinion and publicly voiced his renunciation of the ancient doctrine in a sermon preached at Westminster in April of 1549.[17] This may have been the action of a man who offered his conscience to the highest bidder, but the Bishop in the following year preferred to lose his see and face imprisonment rather than consent to the government's order to replace the altars of his diocese with tables.[18] It was quite possible for Day to question the divine origin of transubstantiation and still never doubt the miraculous nature of the Mass. Many of the same men who wrote against the use of communion in both kinds in the questionnaire sent to the bishops in 1539 voted in favor of double communion in 1547.[19] Undoubtedly they found it prudent to do so under the compulsion of a Protestant government, but there was no clear evidence that the cup should not be presented to the laity, and many must have approved the new order of communion for the same reasons as the Bishop of Winchester, who wrote that "it was well done of the Parliament, for moving the people more and more with devotion, to ordain that this sacrament should be received in both kinds."[20] An even more startling example of theological uncertainty can be found in

[17] Burnet, IV, "The Journal of King Edward's Reign," p. 207.
[18] See ch. IX, pp. 268-270.
[19] L.P., XIV, pt. i [1539], No. 1065, sec. 1 and 3; *Lords' Journal*, I, p. 306. The vote took place on 10 December, 1547. Although present at the session, neither the name of Tunstal nor Aldridge appears on the list of those who dissented.
[20] Foxe, VI, "The sermon of Stephen Gardiner," p. 89.

the doubt surrounding the question of clerical chastity. John Voysey as a young man had pointed to clerical marriages as an illustration of his belief that "no positive ecclesiastical law binds any but those who receive it," for, he said, the Greeks had never recognized the papal decree of chastity and no one denounced them for what might appear to be adultery.[21] For men like Gardiner and Voysey who believed that universal acceptance and good usage were nine-tenths of the law of God, it was difficult to crystallize their opposition to those who favored the legality of ecclesiastical nuptials. In fact, the uncertainty surrounding the question involved both parties, for in the debate in the House of Lords in February 1549, the two reformers, Paul Bush and Anthony Kitchen, voted against the bill to legalize marriage of the clergy, while the three conservatives, Thomas Thirlby, John Skip, and Richard Sampson refused to go along with the rest of their party in registering their dissent in the Journal of the Lords.[22]

There was considerable truth in the words of Edward Lee, Archbishop of York, when he argued with an obstinate monk that "as it is allowable to die for the truth when the cause is good and the ground sure, so it is folly to die, the cause being evil and the ground unsure."[23] These men, the conservative bishops, were not martyrs who died without questioning the foundations of their faith. Eventually they preferred loss of preferment and the threat of death rather than the renunciation of their faith in the miraculous nature of the Catholic Mass, but the decision was the result of a lifetime of bitter

[21] Ogle, *The Tragedy of the Lollards' Tower*, p. 150; *L.P.*, II, pt. i [1515], No. 1313, p. 352.

[22] *Lords' Journal*, I, p. 343. Though Paul Bush voted against the marriage of the clergy, he evidently changed his mind, for shortly afterwards he married Edith Ashely, who fortunately died three months after the accession of Queen Mary. However, the Bishop was deprived of his see for his violation of the Catholic laws of chastity and retired to the rectory of Winterbourne, near Bristol where he died on 11 October, 1558. *DNB*, Art. "Paul Bush."

[23] B.M., Cleo. E. VI, f. 234 (238) (*L.P.*, X [1536], No. 99).

experience, and long before the final stand was taken, a large part of the ancient creed had been swept away. The core of their religion remained firm, but around it were many ceremonies, rites, doctrines, and customs, which were difficult to prove and were uncertain reeds on which to stake one's life.

Most of the conservatives had gone "with the world" because they were essentially products of the world, and many of these bishops were to feel the sharp barb of John Fisher's accusation against his chaplain, George Day, when the Catholic martyr wrote: "I blame neither George Day nor any other man for favoring the King's cause. But I remember having said, when I heard that he followed neither opinion, that I was not pleased with him because he studied to obtain the goodwill of both sides."[24] Perhaps the conservatives did "curry fauvell back and side" but it was dangerous not to do so. At one time or another almost all the bishops, both reformers and conservatives, were faced with lingering death in a dungeon or a fiery test of their convictions at the stake. Both sides were caught by the unexpected aftermath of their past actions, by the consequences of forgotten weaknesses. When Thomas Cranmer, after much soul-searching and recanting, chose to die a martyr to his religious faith, he was not merely choosing between life and death; the issue was far more complex, for he had been deeply involved in the Northumberland plot to place Lady Jane Grey on the throne against the legitimate claims of Catholic Mary. Had he not died a heretic, in all probability he would have been executed as a traitor. When Stephen Gardiner was first imprisoned under Edward, the decision was made not so much because Gardiner had been a vigorous and outspoken opponent of the administration's religious policy, but because the wily Bishop was too dangerous an antagonist to be allowed his freedom. Gardiner was not only the leader of the opposition party, but he controlled seats in the House of Commons, and his influence and ability, it was

[24] *L.P.*, VIII [1535], No. 859, sec. 4, Art. 23, p. 336.

feared, might have swung the undecided members of both Houses of Parliament.[25] Fear, confusion, politics and personal gain, all joined to sully the clear air of religious faith, and it is almost impossible to decide whether the particular action of an individual was the result of sincere belief or motivated by fear and thoughtful prudence. In a word, the conflicting events of their lives is an uncertain premise on which to predicate their religious beliefs. Though the overall pattern of their careers may well be a valid indication of their religious faith, it is impossible to state categorically the religious motive behind a specific action. Cranmer, Ridley, Hooper, and Ferrar paid the ultimate price for their religion, but who can say exactly when these men lost their Catholic and inherited beliefs and became Protestants. Thomas Cranmer renounced the Pope as early as 1525, but he still believed in the Catholic Mass as late as 1540. Nicholas Shaxton missed burning at the stake by one day through a timely recantation and disavowal of the Protestant concept of the Sacrament of the Altar, but he died a Catholic under Mary and suffragan bishop to Thomas Thirlby.[26] His life falls into two halves, half seemingly Protestant, half avowedly Catholic; how then does one classify such a man?

The truth about a man's convictions sometimes came as a surprise to his contemporaries themselves, and when the pliable and agreeable Bishop Thirlby returned from Europe for the discussion on the First Prayer Book in 1548-49, no one was more astonished than Protector Somerset at his opposition to the new religious policy advocated by the government. John Burcher has preserved the story of the Duke's surprise: in writing to Henry Bullinger he remarked "When the disputation was ended, the Protector accosted the King with an expression of his surprise, saying, 'How very much the Bishop

[25] Muller, *Stephen Gardiner*, p. 170; Gardiner, *Letters*, No. 132, p. 410.
[26] *DNB*, Art. "Nicholas Shaxton"; B.M., Add. Ms. 5828, "Thirlby's Episcopal Register" (October 1555), f. 15.

of Westminster has deceived my expectation.' 'Your expectation,' the King replied, 'he might deceive, but not mine.' When the Protector further inquired the reason, 'I expected,' said the King, 'nothing else but that he, who has been so long time with the Emperor as ambassador, should smell of the *Interim.*' "[27] Apparently the worldly Bishop of Westminster had deemed it prudent to keep his convictions to himself until forced into the open, and though Thirlby was eventually forced into open disobedience under Queen Elizabeth, there were many bishops, holders of lesser sees, who rarely came to court, and lived peacefully through three reigns, dying without ever disclosing their religious preferences. It is impossible, for instance, to say whether John Chambers or Henry Wakeman, Robert King or Anthony Kitchen were Catholic or Protestant, and it is mere guesswork to fit them into the far less exacting classification of conservative and reformer.

There is one thing, however, that all the bishops had in common: each had his patron. One might assume from this that the political and religious complexion of the patron might give a fair premise for presuming the opinions of their clients. Unfortunately these bishops were not minions who voted as they were ordered, for they held high ecclesiastical and governmental positions in which they were required to lay down policy, not merely to vote on it. Responsibilities of office, fear, and political caution were far more influential in determining their behavior than was any loyalty that they might have felt toward their patrons, for gratitude was not a lasting sentiment in the midst of religious debate. Moreover, should we use patronage as a criterion of classification, we are confronted with the baffling picture of Edmund Bonner owing his promotion in the episcopal hierarchy exclusively to the influence of Thomas Cromwell.[28] Were the Bishop of London the only

---

[27] *Original Letters*, II, No. CCXCIX "John Burcher to Henry Bullinger" (1549), p. 646.
[28] Foxe, V, p. 150; *L.P.*, VI [1533], No. 1299; VII [1534], No. 257.

conservative who was indebted to the patronage of the Vicar-
general, it might be possible to accept the explanation of the
religious historian, Bishop Gilbert Burnet, who dismisses the
Bishop as a hypocritical and ambitious state servant whose
sole talent was his nimbleness at fitting his political and religious complexion to the prevailing color of the court.[29] However, both Richard Sampson and Thomas Thirlby were indebted to Cromwell for their dioceses.[30] Sampson had been
working in close connection with his patron since 1532, and
when the octogenarian Bishop of Chichester, Robert Sher-
burn, resigned his see in 1536, the Bishop wrote Cromwell
that he would do what he could to gratify "this Master Dean,
your friend."[31] Evidently the valued Dean of the Chapel
Royal was thoroughly gratified, for Richard Sampson became
Bishop of Chichester the moment the formalities of Sher-
burn's resignation were completed. But the newly installed
Bishop, like his colleague Edmund Bonner, proved himself
ungrateful and hypocritical, for, as we shall see in the following chapter, he began to associate with Cuthbert Tunstal and
John Stokesley, the religious and political opponents of the
Vicar-general, and by 1540 had so antagonized his late patron
that he was committed to prison on the charge of high treason.
As for Thomas Thirlby he was a close friend of the Archbishop of Canterbury, having been Cranmer's household chaplain,[32] and as early as 1534 Thomas Cromwell was jotting
down memoranda "to remember Mr. Thirlby for some promotion."[33] Thus it was through the efforts of his two power-

---

[29] Burnet, III, p. 226.

[30] Even Edward Lee owed his promotion to the See of York to Thomas
Cromwell. *L.P.*, V [1531], No. 367.

[31] *L.P.*, X [1536], Nos. 818, 1146-47.

[32] Thirlby was working for Cranmer as early as May 1534, and at that
time he evidently incurred the Prelate's displeasure, for Cranmer wrote
him criticizing him for his "negligence" and "imprudence." (Cranmer,
Works, No. CXIX, p. 292). This, however, did not destroy the friendship
which existed between the two men (Foxe, VIII, pp. 71-72).

[33] *L.P.*, VII [1534], No. 257.

ful friends that the young law graduate was elevated to the post of Bishop of Westminster in June of 1540, just a month before the Vicar-general's fall from power;[34] but Thirlby, like so many others, was unfaithful to his early patrons and he lived to vote against the Prayer Book of 1549 and was finally deprived of his see under Elizabeth.

Roland Lee was another conservative who not only owed his promotion to Cromwell but was probably the Vicar-general's closest friend,[35] but the Bishop of Coventry and Lichfield did not lose his post of President of the Marches of Wales when his patron was imprisoned and executed. Likewise, the three conservatives, John Skip, George Day, and Nicholas Heath were closely associated with the party of reform. Skip was almoner to Anne Boleyn and a friend of Hugh Rawlyn, Bishop Latimer's chaplain, and he received his bishopric of Hereford on the promotion of Cromwell's factotum, Edmund Bonner, to the See of London in the fall of 1539.[36] Nicholas Heath was consecrated Bishop of Rochester in April 1540, at the same time that Bonner was officially installed as Bishop of London, and though some historians have attempted to construe these appointments as being in opposition to the Vicar-general's interests, all the evidence seems to indicate that Cromwell himself engineered the election of both men.[37] Only the year before Bonner had written

---

[34] Thirlby's elevation to the See of Westminster was closely related to the political upheaval which took place during the spring of 1540 and was a direct consequence of Richard Sampson's deprivation and imprisonment. See ch. VII, pp. 216-218.

[35] *L.P.*, IV, pt. iii [1530], No. 6212; VI [1533], Nos. 337, 1226.

[36] *L.P.*, VIII [1535], No. 632, grant 9; XIV, pt. ii [1539], No. 255.

[37] Both A. F. Pollard and the Abbé Constant claim that "the changes on the episcopal bench in 1539-1540 were all in their [the conservatives'] favour" (Pollard, *Thomas Cranmer*, p. 135; Constant, I, p. 380). However, with the possible exception of John Bell, Bishop of Worcester, all the episcopal nominations of 1539-1540 seem to have been in the interests of the party of reform. The fact that these appointments preceded the Vicar-general's fall by only a few months and that in later life most of these men proved themselves to be determined opponents of Protestantism, conceals the fact that Bonner, Heath, and Skip, at the time of their eleva-

to Cromwell to thank him in lavish terms for his favor in promoting him to the See of Hereford, and it was while he was still in France that Bonner received the royal consent to his elevation to the Bishopric of London in March of 1540, and as far as his patron knew, Bonner's friendship and political affiliations had not changed.[38] As for Nicholas Heath, his relations to the Cromwell-Cranmer party were even closer. In December 1539, the Archbishop wrote the Vicar-general that when he had first been created Primate of England, he had given Heath the Deanery of South Mallying at the request of the Earl of Wiltshire, Queen Anne's father. Cranmer then went on to remind Cromwell that the Vicar-general had asked Cranmer for the living and consequently Heath had been obliged to give up the Deanery, but now that the benefice was again vacant, Cranmer said that he would like to return it to his friend, Master Nicholas, for "I consider how necessary it were for your lordship to plant your friends about those parties, forasmuch as you have now so much land there; and therefore I would very fain satisfy your request herein: but I trust surely that you can put in that deanery no man that shall be more assured unto you, and do you better service, than

---

tion, were regarded as being in the Cromwellian camp, and that their promotions were determined by Cromwell's shaken but still considerable influence. As for Bishop Bell, it is impossible to say who engineered his appointment, and he may already have been considered a member of the Gardiner-Tunstal faction. However, since the other promotions were arranged by Cromwell, it seems unlikely that Bell's advancement was opposed by the Vicar-general who had known him when they were both working for Wolsey. If Salcot was a reactionary, his career certainly does not indicate it. He was a friend of Wriothesley who was closely allied with Cromwell (*L.P.*, XIII, pt. ii [1538], No. 636), and he owed his bishopric of Bangor in 1533 to Cromwell. Moreover, he was regarded by Chapuys as one of Anne Boleyn's party (*L.P.*, VI [1533], Nos. 1067, 1460). Later under Edward VI he acquiesced in the Protestant religious changes and his only overtly Catholic action seems to have been to return to Rome under Queen Mary, a step which he shared with Bush, Bird, Holgate, and Shaxton.

[38] *L.P.*, XV [1540], Nos. 388, 436, grant 82; Foxe, V, p. 150.

Mr. Heath shall do."[39] As for George Day he did not attain episcopal status until 1543 when Richard Sampson was elevated to the See of Coventry and Lichfield on the death of Roland Lee, but Master Day had been suggested as early as April 1540 as a worthy candidate to fill the proposed See of Dunstable when Cromwell's authority, though shaken, was still sufficiently great to cause the imprisonment of Richard Sampson and the selection of such men as Thomas Thirlby and Nicholas Heath as episcopal figures.[40]

It is difficult to believe that all these men were time-servers and political sycophants who discarded their patron at the moment of his fall, and overnight lost their mildly radical proclivities. If they were all as Burnet has described Edmund Bonner, it would be impossible to explain the fact that these same men brought upon themselves the wrath of the Edwardian government by refusing to approve the religious changes of the reign and that three of them lost their sees for open disobedience.[41] The explanation lies in the fact that Cromwell's death signaled a change in opinion, a shift which had been gradually taking place throughout the decade of the thirties. As we shall see in the following chapter, many of the men who had started their careers in full approval of the religious reforms under Cromwell had by 1540 become alarmed by the revolutionary implications of reform, and the social consequences of religious meddling. Thus the execution of the Vicar-general for combined treason and heresy was primarily the political reflection of a fundamental change in opinions.

Though patronage and internal evidence merely add to the difficulties of classification, there is one event which can be

---

[39] Cranmer, *Works*, No. CCLXVI, p. 399 (*L.P.*, XIV, pt. ii [1539], No. 699). In February 1536 Heath was recommended to Osiandes by Vitus Theodorus as a friend of Thomas Cranmer. *L.P.*, X [1536], No. 289.

[40] P.R.O., S.P. 1, vol. 243, f. 50 (*L.P.*, Add. [1540], No. 1457); *ibid.*, vol. 131, f. 73 (*L.P.*, XIII, pt. i [1538], No. 718).

[41] They were George Day, Edmund Bonner, and Nicholas Heath.

used as a convenient and reasonably valid measurement of the religious beliefs of many of these bishops. On January 15, 1549, the vote in the House of Lords on the first Edwardian Prayer Book took place. By then most of the peripheral doctrines of the Catholic faith had already been discarded or substantially modified. The monasteries and the chantry and cathedral colleges had been dissolved; communion was now legally practiced in both kinds; marriage of the clergy was officially recognized; and the radical attitude toward the veneration of saints and images prevailed. The issue at stake in 1549 involved the fundamental creed of the ancient faith, the concept of the Mass as a miraculous and sacrificial ceremony capable of bestowing grace upon the communer. Though the Prayer Book was undoubtedly still capable of a mildly Catholic interpretation, the issue of the Mass was clearly recognized by both parties, as the Abbé Constant has pointed out.[42] Both Professor Messenger and Cardinal Gasquet have used the vote as recorded in the Journal of the House of Lords as a method of differentiating the two opposing parties on the Episcopal Bench,[43] and certainly the names of those who dissented from the majority decision is a clear indication of their religious leanings. Unfortunately, however, both scholars have presumed that those who did not dissent in writing voted for the bill. There is no clear proof of this, however, for our knowledge of the parliamentary machinery of the Upper House is extremely scanty. The Lords do not seem to have voted as a unit, as did the Lower House where all those in favor shouted "yes" and those opposed shouted "no."[44] In the words of Sir Thomas Smith, the members of the House of Lords gave their dissent or consent "each man severally and by himself . . . saying only content or not content without

[42] Constant, II, p. 87.
[43] Gasquet and Bishop, pp. 171-172; Messenger, *The Reformation, the Mass and the Priesthood*, I, pp. 330-339, 404-407.
[44] Smith, *De Republica Anglorum*, p. 56.

further reasoning or replying."[45] However, this does not mean that the clerk necessarily wrote down in his Journal the names of the affirmative and negative votes. In fact, the scanty evidence indicates the contrary. In 1641 four members of the House of Lords dissented from a majority decision of the Upper House and "demanded their right of protestation and leave to enter their dissents" in the clerk's Journal. Moreover, on the same day, the Lords instituted a standing order that "such Lords as shall make protestation or enter their dissents to any votes of this House shall make their said protestation or give directions to have their dissents entered into the Clerk's Book the next sitting day of this House or else the said protestation or dissent is to be void and of none effect."[46] This, of course, is a hundred years after the time of Edward VI, but parliamentary usages are usually of ancient origin and it seems likely that the privilege of recording one's opposition to a given bill was a "right" of long standing which was for the first time being codified into the written rules of the House. If this were the case, it would appear that only those who felt sufficiently strongly against the Prayer Book went to the trouble of having their names officially recorded in the Journal as being opposed to the will of the majority, and, therefore, the list would not mean that only the eight bishops listed voiced a dissent when the vote was actually taken.

Moreover, there is considerable internal testimony to support this conclusion. Neither the name of Richard Sampson nor of John Chambers appears in the Lords' Journal as among those who opposed the bill.[47] But Sampson was a confirmed conservative who had been thrown into the Tower back in 1540 for papal affection, and was a strong supporter of the conservative party during the colloquy held on the Prayer Book just a month before the final vote.[48] If John Chambers voted for the bill, it is difficult to reconcile this with the fact

[45] *Ibid.*, p. 51.
[47] *Ibid.*, I, p. 331.
[46] *Lords' Journal*, IV, p. 628.
[48] Gasquet and Bishop, App. V, p. 439.

[147]

that two days after the crucial decision he returned to his see giving his proxy to Edmund Bonner and Nicholas Heath, two men whose attitude was transparently clear since they had taken the trouble to place their names in the Lords' Journal.[49] Proxies, however, are hardly a satisfactory basis on which to judge a man's personal convictions, especially since there is little known concerning the manner or extent of their use.[50] Cardinal Gasquet has attempted to place those who were absent at this Parliament by their proxies, but unfortunately there is no evidence to show that these absentees knew what was being voted upon, and they certainly had no chance to read the Prayer Book before they gave their proxies.[51] The book was probably drawn up sometime in September of 1548 and at that time received the sanction of all the conservative bishops present except George Day. But between the time of the original draft and the final presentation in Parliament, the Prayer Book was substantially modified without the knowledge of most of the bishops.[52] Thus, even had the bishops of outlying sees who were absent during the parliamentary colloquy heard of the original Prayer Book as it was first composed and supported by both groups of the Episcopal Bench, they certainly could have had no idea that it had been sufficiently changed to induce at least eight of the original sup-

[49] *Lords' Journal*, I, p. 332.

[50] The only occasion that I have discovered on which a proxy, if not actually used, was at least given in the expectation of use, was Bishop Tunstal's proxy to the Bishop of Ely. Accompanying the proxy, Tunstal sent a letter explicitly laying down the manner of voting and instructing his colleague that he could in his "own name say what you will, and what God putteth in your mind; but I desire you . . . never in my name to consent to any such thing proposed, either harmful or prejudicial to the marriage. . . ." Burnet, *History of the Reformation*, ed. N. Pocock, 7 vols. Oxford, 1865, vol. III, p. 206. Burnet states that this letter is in the Bodleian Library but the editor notes that it has vanished.

[51] Gasquet and Bishop, p. 172.

[52] *Ibid.*, p. 179 and App. V, p. 405. Bishop Thirlby pointed out during the discussion that several essential words had been deleted from the original copy including the important word "oblation."

porters to change their minds and oppose the Prayer Book in Parliament.

While the vote on the First Prayer Book gives us the names of those who were most bitterly opposed to the religious changes of the period, it does not necessarily present us with a clear division between the two parties. The vote was as follows:

Opposed: Bonner, Tunstal, Heath, Thirlby, Rugge, Aldridge, Day, Skip.

Those not listed but present: Cranmer, Holbeach, Goodrich, Ridley, Barlow, Holgate, Bush, Salcot, Sampson, Chambers, Kitchen, Ferrar.

Absent: Gardiner, King, Wharton, Bird, Voysey, Wakeman, Bulkeley.[53]

To the list of those in opposition we can add the names of Stephen Gardiner who was absent on compulsion, being in prison during the entire session of Parliament; John Voysey who was induced to resign his bishopric of Exeter under Edward but who was reinstated by Mary; Richard Sampson for reasons already given; and Arthur Bulkeley. Bulkeley has been variously classified as "neutral" by Cardinal Gasquet and "opportunist" by Professor Messenger, but a man who was attainted for treason and papal affection in 1544 can hardly be called a neutral or opportunist,[54] though he may

---

[53] *Lords' Journal*, I, p. 331. Gasquet and Bishop, p. 172, say that Robert Ferrar and Anthony Kitchen were absent on the day of the vote, 15 January, 1549. However, Kitchen was present at the colloquy on the Prayer Book on Wednesday, 18 December, 1548 (Gasquet and Bishop, App. v, p. 429) and was again heard from on 19 February, 1549 when he voted against the bill allowing the marriage of the clergy (*Lords' Journal*, I, p. 343). Though the Clerk of the House was not always accurate, he does not list either Ferrar or Kitchen as being absent during the period from the 7th to the 21st of January (*Ibid.*, pp. 327-337). Moreover, no proxy appears for either man during the entire session. Accordingly, it would appear that both men were present and voted on the bill. As for John Wakeman, Gasquet and Bishop, p. 172, state that "nothing is known." However, his proxy appears late, not arriving until "Ultimo," February 1549, and was given to Bonner and Heath (*Lords' Journal*, I, p. 347).

[54] *L.P.*, XIX, pt. i [1544], No. 1035, grant 140.

well have learned from experience the need for discretion in expressing his real sentiments.

If we are to appreciate the strength of the conservative party as it existed between 1536 and 1550 we must include in the list the names of ten conservatives who died before 1548.[55] This would bring the number of the conservatives to twenty-two bishops, and though the inclusion of John Kite and William Knight is open to some argument since they never seem to have divulged their religious preferences, there are only two men, Fox and Lee, whose careers are sufficiently controversial to warrant detailed treatment. Most historians have grouped Edward Fox with the main body of the reformers and Thomas Fuller has gone so far as to describe him as the "principal Pillar of the Reformation."[56] The proof of such a classification is primarily based on the opinion of Martin Bucer, Edward Barnes, and John Foxe, and the fact that the Bishop was the patron of such radicals as William Turner and George Joye. It is true that Martin Bucer did classify Fox along with Hugh Latimer as one of the promoters of Cranmer's "godly designs" in 1537,[57] and that Robert Barnes wrote Cromwell from Germany in 1535 referring to Fox by the quaint expression that he was "in a great love with him by cause he hath used himself so honorably."[58] Moreover, the Bishop did patronize the two vitriolic reformers, Turner and Joye, for both men were in his service in 1535-36.[59] On the

---

[55] These men were: John Bell, Bp. of Worcester, resigned 17 November, 1543; John Clerk, Bp. of Bath and Wells, died January 1541; Edward Fox, Bp. of Hereford, died May 1538; John Kite, Bp. of Carlisle, died 1537; William Knight, Bp. of Bath and Wells, died September 1547; Edward Lee, Archbp. of York, died September 1544; Roland Lee, Bp. of Coventry and Lichfield, died January 1543; John Longland, Bp. of Lincoln, died May 1547; Robert Sherborn, Bp. of Chichester, died August 1536; John Stokesley, Bp. of London, died September 1539.

[56] Fuller, *Worthies*, p. 205.

[57] *Original Letters*, II, No. CCXLIV, p. 520 (*L.P.*, XII, pt. ii [1537], No. 969).

[58] B.M., Vit. B XXI, f. 114 (124) (*L.P.*, IX [1535], No. 1030).

[59] P.R.O., S.P. 1, vol. 93, f. 21 (*L.P.*, VIII [1535], No. 823); *ibid.*, vol. 103, ff. 116-117 (*L.P.*, X [1536], No. 654).

other hand, with the exception of Bucer, most of the reports
from Germany are highly critical of the Bishop of Hereford,
and while Nicholas Heath was covered with praise, Fox was
accused of having the bearing of a prelate and was described
by Melanchthon as not having "tasted our philosophy or
sweetness."[60] When Friar Barnes wrote his eulogy of the
Bishop to Thomas Cromwell, he was careful to qualify his
"love" by adding that "though he and I do not agree in
omnibus articulis religionis, but I trust at length so to use him
that there shall be no great variance, for he is gentle, and
more abide all manner of honest communication, wherefore I
doubt not but to draw him at length to me through God's
grace."[61] There is no indication whatsoever to assume that
Barnes ever succeeded in drawing the subtle Bishop to him.
Certainly in the year that Barnes wrote of his plans, Fox was
still a convinced believer in the Catholic concept of the Mass,
for George Joye won his continued friendship only by promising never again to attack the orthodox belief concerning the
Sacrament of the Altar.[62] The Bishop of Hereford was undoubtedly affiliated with the party of reform, but then so
were Thirlby, Heath, Skip, and Bonner. Moreover, he had
been associated with the pseudo-Protestant and early martyr,
John Firth. When Firth was burnt in 1533, Germain Gardiner, the Bishop's nephew, wrote Fox a long and interesting
account of the execution and remarked during the course of
it that Firth had been the friend and disciple of Fox's protégé,
George Joye "at whose name," Gardiner said, "I am sure ye
sigh, seeing yourself to have been so deluded with the hope
which once ye conceived of him. . . ." Whether or not Fox
was deluded by the actions of such men as Firth and Joye is
not recorded, but it is interesting to note that his friend and
future Catholic martyr should have assumed as much.[63]

[60] *Corpus Reformatorum*, III, No. 1396, p. 35 (*L.P.*, x [1536], No. 265).
[61] B.M., Vit. B XXI, f. 114 (124) (*L.P.*, IX [1535], No. 1030).
[62] P.R.O., S.P. 1, vol. 93, f. 21 (*L.P.*, VIII [1535], No. 823).
[63] This letter is printed in Gairdner, *Lollardy*, I, p. 406.

Though Edward Fox was certainly a liberal man and was possibly tainted with the "New Learning," he had little respect for the violent indiscretions of Hugh Latimer, and his reactions on hearing that Latimer was stirring up trouble at Cambridge in 1530 were those of the trained administrator who dislikes extremism wherever he finds it. When these "shameful contentions in sermons between Latimer and certain of St. John's College" were reported to him, he requested the Vice-Chancellor of the university to order both sides to silence. Not for one moment did the future bishop believe the rumor which was current at court that this quarrel had been caused because Latimer favored the King's cause. "On the contrary," he said, "Latimer, perhaps, is more vehement than becomes the very evangelist of Christ, and purposely speaks paradoxes to offend and slander people. . . ." Master Fox was a keen judge of character and prudently concluded his letter by warning the university authorities that such behavior was dangerous at any time, and especially now that the whole question of the King's divorce was threatening the unity of the country.[64] Moreover, Fox was a close friend of Stephen Gardiner,[65] and, as we shall see in a future chapter, he was far more interested in national unity than in religious purity. During the religious debates in 1537 over the formation of the Bishop's Book, he was one of the strongest advocates of compromise even though he disagreed with Bishop Stokesley over the theological meaning of a sacrament.[66] Exactly what he would have done had he lived beyond 1539 it is impossible to say, but he has most of the earmarks of a conservative administrator and it is likely that he would have taken up his position along with his friend Stephen Gardiner when it became apparent that religious reform was leading to social revolution.[67]

[64] *L.P.*, IV, pt. iii [1530], No. 6162.
[65] Muller, *Stephen Gardiner*, p. 11.
[66] See ch. VII, pp. 194-195.
[67] Janelle, *Obedience in Church and State*, p. xxiv, says: "Those whom

The case of Roland Lee is equally perplexing because of his close personal friendship with Thomas Cromwell, and the tradition preserved by Nicholas Harpsfield that he was the ecclesiastic who married Henry VIII and Anne Boleyn. The story of Lee's consecration of the royal marriage accomplished secretly at Whitehall is difficult to prove, but the details of the scene are strikingly in character, for the young Archdeacon of Cornwall was a strict legalist, and as Harpsfield tells the story, he refused to perform his clerical duties until he had been shown proof of the papal license sanctioning the union. The evidence, of course, was not forthcoming, but the King swore on his royal honor that it existed but was not obtainable at the moment.[68] Under the circumstances, Lee could have done little else but obey the King. The Bishop's friendship with Cromwell, however, is supported by a vast body of testimony, for Lee was a tireless correspondent and constantly referred to the Vicar-general in such endearing terms as "My loving friend."[69] The Bishop's connection with Cromwell was no fair-weather affair, for the two men had been old and devoted friends during their service with their mutual patron, Cardinal Wolsey. In later years Cromwell selected Lee as the tutor and guardian of his young son Gregory—an appointment which speaks highly for the faith which Cromwell placed in the Bishop's friendship.[70] The fondness and respect which existed between the two men seems to have transcended the latent conflict between their religious views, and Stephen Vaughan in writing to Cromwell in 1533 was unable to conceal his horror at the Secretary's promotion of his friend to

---

he [Henry VIII] chose as defenders of his supreme headship, from 1534 to 1539, were conservatives who, like Gardiner, were making the best of an unwelcome situation, and who, after feebly struggling for a time, had let themselves be pressed into his service. Such was the case of Edward Fox, Bishop of Hereford. . . . Such was also the case of Richard Sampson, Dean of the Chapel Royal."

[68] Harpsfield, *The Pretended Divorce*, Cam. Soc. XXI (1878), p. 235.

[69] *L.P.*, IV, pt. iii [1530], No. 6212; VI [1533], No. 1226.

[70] *L.P.*, VII [1534], Nos. 940, 968.

the bishopric of Coventry and Lichfield. I cannot keep silence on this matter, he lamented. "You have lately holpen an earthly beast, a mole, and an enemy to all godly learning, into the office of his damnation—a papist, an idolater, and a fleshly priest unto a bishop of Chester." Then with true evangelical if misplaced advice, Vaughan goes on to admonish Cromwell's leniency. "Remember God in all your facts," he added, and "let none affections of persons lead you to condescend or work so evil a deed. You cannot undo that [which] you have done. . . . Who knoweth more of the bishops' iniquities than you? Who knoweth more their tyranny, falsed and untrouthe, against God, prince and man than you? And should you help in this time especially to increase the number of wicked men where there is a lack and so great a need of good and virtuous men?"[71] Vaughan had nothing to gain by writing this letter and a great deal to lose, and we may reasonably assume that it represents what he calls his "most trusty and friendly mind," and that his judgment, though hardly an unbiased one, is probably close to the truth. Lee was primarily an administrator who was given his diocese so that the Government could afford to maintain him as Lord President of the Marches of Wales. He proved himself a just if severe dispenser of justice, and a man who had little sympathy for the evangelical spirit of his brother bishop of St. David's. When word of the bitter fight between William Barlow and the canons of his cathedral chapter was reported to Lee, he sent the information on to Cromwell saying that he was sorry to hear about the controversy but he felt it his duty to "intimate the same to your lordship, for that further inconveniences do not ensue." And he advised his friend to order the Bishop to more tactful behavior, for then "the common people

---

[71] P.R.O., S.P. 1, vol. 80, f. 80 (*L.P.*, VI [1533], No. 1385). The bishopric of Coventry and Lichfield was often referred to by its ancient name of Chester. It was not until 1541 that a diocese by the name of Chester was created.

would the better be content."[72] Like Edward Fox, the Bishop of Coventry and Lichfield died before the conservatives were driven into open disobedience.[73] He does not seem to have been particularly partial to any religious doctrine, being entirely absorbed with secular interests. Though he might not have voted against the Prayer Book of 1549 for religious scruples, he almost certainly would have done so from political and social motives.

In turning to the reformers, we are confronted with the problem of separating the sheep from the goats, for many of the erstwhile supporters of reform found it expedient to return to the faith of their fathers as soon as Catholic Mary was installed on the throne. There are not many men like Nicholas Ridley, who could eat a hearty meal on the night before his martyrdom and joyfully announce that he was celebrating his spiritual "marriage," presumedly with God.[74] There was a deep ring of conviction when Ridley turned to Hugh Latimer as both were being bound to the stake and encouraged his aged friend by saying: "Be of good heart, brother, for God will either assuage the fury of the flame, or else strengthen us to abide it."[75] Such faith deserves the intervention of the supernatural and we can only hope that the torments of the flames were assuaged by divine ordinance. But our respect for Ridley and Latimer, Cranmer, Ferrar and Hooper, must not destroy our sympathy for the lesser men who preferred conformity to martyrdom, for as Erasmus himself once confessed: "Every man has not the courage to be a martyr. I am afraid if I were put to the trial, I should be like Peter."[76] Weakness and fear are no criteria on which to accuse a man of insincerity and opportunism. That John Bird and Robert Holgate returned to Rome under Mary makes them no less reformers than those who died for their faith. They lacked strength, but we can

---

[72] B.M., Cleo. E. v, f. 414 (*L.P.*, XII, pt. i [1537], No. 93).
[73] Roland Lee died 24 January, 1543.
[74] Foxe, VII, p. 547.   [75] *Ibid.*, p. 548.
[76] Quoted in Beckett, *The English Reformation*, p. 113.

hardly say that they were secret Catholics under Henry and Edward and warmly accepted the Marian reaction. The evidence is to the contrary, for it was infinitely easier to be a conservative under Henry and his son than to be a Protestant under Mary. To the small list of reforming or Protestant martyrs, we must add, therefore, William Barlow, who recanted and then fled to Germany after the death of Edward; Robert Holgate and John Bird, both of whom conformed under the Marian government; and finally Henry Holbeach and Thomas Goodrich whose timely deaths saved them from the consequences of their past lives.[77] We must also include the lesser Edwardian appointments: Coverdale of Exeter, Harley of Hereford, Poynet of Winchester, Scory of Chichester, and Taylor of Lincoln. Finally there is Nicholas Shaxton, who preferred to risk the problematical torments of the soul rather than face the painful and immediate consumption of the body in the fire of the stake. But until his recantation in 1546 he was an avowed reformer and must be grouped with his more stalwart brethren.

This leaves the doubtful, the unknown, and the opportunists who have many of the characteristics of the reformers in being divines and monks and who certainly did not receive their episcopal promotions for their secular services to the crown. The story of their lives is either so contradictory or the evidence so scanty that it is impossible to catalog them except by arbitrary pigeonholing. I have usually grouped these bishops with the reformers since they environmentally belong with that class, but it would probably be more just to say that intellectually they constituted a substantial middle group whose silent history and equivocal lives are evidence that they maintained a discreet neutrality between the opposing parties.

The final classification including the academic and monastic standing of the bishops is given in Appendix IV. In some

---

[77] Holbeach died 2 August, 1551, and Goodrich on 10 May, 1554.

cases the listing may seem rigorously arbitrary, but it must be remembered that we are not dealing in terms of Catholic and Protestant but in the much looser terminology of conservative and reformer. It might be pointed out, of course, that the reformers of the early sixteenth century were conservative compared to the Puritans of the following century, but the terms are relative to time and space. Edmund Bonner was described as a Lutheran in Spain but he was considered a conservative in England.[78] Edward Fox was condemned by the German divines for stubborn blindness toward the light of God, but across the channel he was pictured by some as "among the most perfect Lutherans in the world."[79] Thomas Cranmer was cautious and methodical in his retreat from the Catholic creed, renouncing the Real Presence only after years of thoughtful study, and even in 1549 he was regarded by his radical brethren as a weakhearted supporter of their doctrines.[80] Nicholas Heath was deeply committed to Cranmer and the reform party both in sympathy and in ecclesiastical preferment, yet he lived to be Lord Chancellor of England under Catholic Mary. We are not dealing with concrete divisions but with degrees of opinion which were constantly fluctuating, and what was radical for one decade was often conservative for the following. The political complexion of the Episcopal Bench cannot be painted in the violent hues of scarlet and navy blue, but rather must be portrayed in varying shades of purple, tones which differed with individuals and times.

The political-religious coloring of the conservative bishops moved from a mild pink to a more conservative purple during the decade of the 1530's, and it is the history of this

[78] *L.P.*, XIII, pt. ii [1538], No. 59.
[79] Quoted in *DNB*, Art. "Edward Fox."
[80] John ab Ulmis wrote Henry Bullinger in August 1548 that "this Thomas has fallen into so heavy a slumber, that we entertain but a very cold hope that he will be aroused even by your most learned letter." *Original Letters*, II, No. CLXXXV, pp. 380-381; Pollard, *Thomas Cranmer*, p. 22.

gradual change which we must narrate in the following chapter. The change is essentially the history of the Reformation throughout these years, but it is a story of a distinctly limited character. The picture of these years as presented in the next few pages is darkened by religious prejudice and blurred by the mental myopia which hinders most contemporaries in attempting to interpret and appreciate the events of their own age. The conservatives lacked the hindsight which is so valuable and often so misleading to modern historians of the Reformation years, and their causal reasoning was often grotesque to the point of absurdity. It remains an essential task of this narrative, however, to picture the Reformation as the conservatives saw it, for only then can we explain the philosophy which they developed and preached in an effort to preserve and maintain what they considered to be the essential elements of society and religion.

CHAPTER VI

RELIGION AND REACTION

$\mathcal{F}$ROM the commencement of the Reformation in the early 1530's to the death of Edward VI in July of 1553 a fundamental change took place within the conservative party, for it was during these years that Gardiner and Bonner, Heath and Day, Tunstal and Thirlby began to renounce many of the ideals which as youthful humanists they had so ardently supported. In a word, they finally perceived that the Reformation was in fact a revolution, both theologically and socially. The history of the crystallization of this conservative opposition to the policies of their reforming colleagues is important, not only because it helps to explain why so many of the bishops under Edward VI were ready to face imprisonment and deprivation of their sees rather than sanction a religious program which ran counter to their conscience, but also because it establishes the necessary background for the gospel of human prudence, the plea for caution and retrenchment which was preached by the conservative party after they came to power in 1540. The development of this reaction is a progressive one, and only in part lends itself to a chronological treatment. Although it is possible to trace the slow deterioration of Catholicism in England during the first years of the Reformation, it must be remembered that this is essentially the history of the Reformation as the conservatives viewed it, and that much of the evidence for such a narrative was written only after the full implications and dangers of the new creed had been realized.

One of the first men to warn of the dangers of abolishing the pernicious authority of the Pope in England and of banishing from the realm that "painted whore of Babylon,"

euphuistically known to the Protestants as Mistress Rose of
Rome, was Sir Thomas More. "Since all Christendom is one
corps," he said to Thomas Cromwell in 1534, "I cannot perceive how any member thereof may, without the common assent of the body, depart from the common head. . . . As for
the general council assembled lawfully, I never could perceive, but that, in the declaration of the truth, to be believed
and to be standen to, the authority thereof ought to be taken
for indubitable, for else were there in nothing no certainty,
but through Christendom, upon every man's affectionate reason, all things might be brought, from day to day, to continual ruffle and confusion. . . ."[1]

Many years later another Lord Chancellor was to reëcho
these sentiments on the floor of Parliament, when Nicholas
Heath, Archbishop of York and Chancellor under Queen
Mary, warned of the consequences of a second Act of Supremacy and the renewal of the fatal schism of Henry's reign.
"Saint Cyprian," he exclaimed, ". . . saith, *That the unity of
the church of Christ doth depend upon the unity of Peter's
authority*; therefore by our leaping out of Peter's ship, we
must needs be overwhelmed with the waters of schism, sects
and divisions, when the same holy martyr saint Cyprian saith
. . . that all heresies, sects, and schisms do spring only, for
that men will not be obedient unto the head bishop of God. . . .
And how true this saying of Cyprian is, it is apparent to all
men that listeth to see by the example of the Germans, and
by the inhabitants of this realm."[2] Heath was just over thirty
years of age when his predecessor on the Woolsack urged
obedience to the Papal See for the sake of security and "certainty," and when he rose to voice the same warning in Elizabeth's first Parliament, he was speaking with the lesson of a

---

[1] B.M., Cleo. E. vi, f. 156 (More, *Correspondence*, No. 197, pp. 498-
499).
[2] Strype, *Annals of the Reformation*, I, pt. ii, App. vi, "Hethe, Archbishop
of Yorke, his Oration made in the Parliament House, 1559, against the
Bill of the Queen's Supremacye," pp. 403-404.

quarter of a century on which to draw.[3] What was obscure to most men in 1534 was by 1559 terribly apparent—that Catholicism was a vast arch of institutional and religious authority stretching from Poland to the British Isles, and its very existence depended upon the permanency of the papal supremacy, the keystone of the entire structure. Once Saint Peter's chair was destroyed, only the mortar of custom and tradition maintained the anomaly of an arch without a center, and within a generation the Catholic ecclesia in England was a crumbling heap of masonry, its mortar weakened by the blast of Protestant controversy. Stephen Gardiner, Cuthbert Tunstal, and Nicholas Heath lacked the prophetic gift and stoic strength of More, but the course of succeeding years was to convince them of the truth of his warning and the value of his death, for it was soon clear that they could not maintain the Catholic creed without the Roman Pope.

The dilemma of the conservative position was only too evident, for was not the Pope's doctrine the Pope? Was not all that had been sanctioned and exploited by the Papal See corrupted and desecrated by that association? If the Pope for all these years had been preaching a false and diabolical creed in regard to his supremacy, how could Englishmen be sure that this Anti-Christ had not also led men to damnation by preaching a false belief in purgatory, in the sacrificial nature of the Mass, in the worship of images, and in the spiritual value of monasteries? The reformers were quick to exploit the weakness of the conservative stand and to condemn the Catholic faith as the "strange voice" of the Bishop of Rome. "The Pope's doctrine is the Pope," wrote William Turner to Stephen Gardiner, "and ye hold still the Pope's doctrine, ergo ye hold still the Pope."[4] The connection may be false,

---

[3] Heath was not the only bishop who learned the lesson of the Reformation years. With the exception of Kitchen, the entire Marian Episcopate including Tunstal, Bonner, and Thirlby, refused to accept the new Act of Supremacy, and as a consequence were deprived of their sees and imprisoned.

[4] Turner, *The Rescuynge of the Romishe Fox* (1545), sig. C VIII.

the argument specious, but it was difficult to refute and to lay ears the efforts of the conservatives to differentiate between the Pope's authority and the Catholic creed was of little weight. In vain Gardiner attempted to point out that it was ridiculous to believe "that all that which was taught either by the Bishop of Rome or under his authority was his own doctrine and [was] to be cast away," and it availed the Bishop little to say that "only that which was worthily to maintain his authority [was] to be rejected with him; and that which was good [was] to be retained and kept, not because it was his, but because it is good." And he asked: "Shall not we confess Christ the Son of God because the devil said the same?"[5] Unfortunately the Protestants refused to admit that the Pope acknowledged Christ to be the Son of God, and Hugh Latimer was quite convinced that "the devil, by the help of that Italian bishop yonder, his chaplain, hath laboured by all means that he might to frustrate the death of Christ and the merits of his passion. And they have devised for that purpose to make us believe in other vain things by his pardons: as to have remission of sins for praying on hallowed beads. . . ."[6]

On all sides the conservatives were confronted with the spectacle of ancient customs, old traditions, being condemned as the decrees of "that stinking whore of Babylon" who for generations had fed all nations with "the cup of her drunkenness and poison." Everywhere the cry was going up to "get rid of the poison with the author."[7] "Our King," lamented Bishop Hooper to Henry Bullinger, "has destroyed the Pope, but not popery."[8] Pardons, pilgrimages, purgatory, and "fained religious foundations of monasteries," were associated by Doctor Crome with Peter's pence and other monetary exactions of the Pope. That "bold valiant, sturdy beggar," the

---

[5] Gardiner, *Letters*, App. 2, "Gardiner's Lost Tract against William Turner" (1544?), p. 482.

[6] Latimer, *Sermons*, "Sermon of the Plough" (1548), p. 68.

[7] *L.P.*, XIV, pt. i [1539], No. 631, p. 245.

[8] *Original Letters*, I, No. XXI, "Hooper to Bullinger" (1546), p. 36.

Bishop of Rome, is cast out of the realm, exclaimed the impassioned divine. "Yea, the King's Majesty with his high court of Parliament has taken this beggar by the head and whorled him quite out of this realm like an idle beggar. But alack, this bold beggar's staff hath this beggar of Rome left here behind him which staff beateth both the bodies and souls of men."[9] The Protestants had keen eyes in detecting the "bold beggar's staff" which weighed so heavily upon their consciences, and the Convocation of 1536 was induced to complain to the King that amateur theologians were canvassing the land saying that "the hallowed oil is not better than the Bishop of Rome's grease or butter" and that "the stole about the priest's neck is nothing else but the Bishop of Rome's rope."[10] The hard shell of Catholic security had been penetrated and it was not difficult to continue the undermining of the ancient structure, if only through association with the Papacy. As Cranmer once attempted to impress upon his sovereign, Henry had renounced the papal supremacy and logically he should also discard all doctrines which had for their foundation the pernicious authority of papal pontification.[11] If it was now treason to advocate the papal authority, why was it not also treason and heresy to hold the Pope's doctrines?

Not only did the reformers try to bring upon the Catholic creed of the Mass, purgatory, pilgrimages and monasteries, the stigma of papism and to arouse patriotic sentiment against any decree which stemmed from Rome, but they also realized that the abolition of the Papacy was an implied threat to all time-honored institutions and customs. For a thousand years the Bishop of Rome had been accepted as the Vicar of Christ, and now it was openly denied by the laws of the realm. Might

[9] B.M., Harl. 425, "Certain notes of a sermon made at Pauls Cross by Doctor Crome" (May 1541), ff. 65-66 (*L.P.*, xvi [1541], No. 814).
[10] Strype, *Ecc. Mem.*, I, pt. ii, No. LXXIII, "The Protestation of the Clargie of the Lower House within the Province of Canterbury," p. 262.
[11] Burnet, I, pp. 282-283.

not other equally sacred and ancient rites also be proved false?
"But the Pope and his papists are false prophets and refute
the truth, ergo, all their precepts, ceremonies, and doctrines
are to be banished out of the church."[12] This was the logic
of one reformer whose inductive methods of reasoning are far
from unimpeachable, but whose point, nevertheless, was well
made. The implication was only too obvious. If the Pope for
so many generations had been teaching a false doctrine in regard to his supremacy, what assurance did any Englishman
have that many other principles were not also untrue? Thomas
Cranmer placed his finger on the weakest point of the Catholic
position when he wrote that "variety in opinions have been
occasion of the opening of many verities heretofore taken for
heresy . . . as namely the usurped authority of the Bishop of
Rome hath by that occasion come into light, with effusion of
the blood not of a few, such as were the first stirrers up
thereof."[13] Stephen Gardiner might scoff at William Turner,
saying that never before was "any man so mad [that in] ex-
pelling a tyrant [he] would cast away with him both that
which was good and that which was evil also,"[14] but who was
going to vouch for the goodness or evilness of time-honored
customs, now that the very source of Christian authority had
been called in question and its divine sanction and authority
found to be false? If the head was the devil's disciple, might
not all else prove equally diabolical? Once the inherited and
cultivated methods of thinking had been exposed to doubt,
there was no escape from the Chancellor's prediction that the
final solution would rest upon "every man's affectionate reason."

The collapse of the Papacy posed issues which were fundamental if not immediately apparent to the religious faith of

[12] Turner, *The Rescuynge of the Romishe Fox* (1545), sig. D v.
[13] Cranmer, *Works*, App. vi, "Some considerations offered to the King
to induce him to proceed to further Reformation," p. 466.
[14] Turner, *The Rescuynge of the Romishe Fox* (1545), sig. E iii. This
is William Turner quoting from Gardiner's lost book.

all English Catholics, and it created in the minds of many
of the conservatives the spectre of the inevitable collapse and
decay of all they held to be paramount in the maintenance of
order, certainty, and security. As the pattern of history un-
rolled, they became convinced that Satanic powers of darkness
were manipulating the course of human affairs through a
causal chain of events which had its commencement in the
royal divorce and the consequent denial of the papal authority. The conservative bishops were unable to escape the conclusion to be drawn from the chronological events of Henry's
reign that the course which the Reformation had taken was
apodictic. The breach with Rome had followed upon the heels
of the divorce; the annihilation of the monasteries was closely
associated with the constitutional quarrel with the Pope, for
these monastic orders were regarded as the final stronghold of
popery in England, and the banishment of the Bishop of
Rome from English soil now added the voice of political
necessity to the demands of those who desired their dissolution for reasons of avarice and economic gain. The destruction
of the religious foundations in turn had seriously weakened
the concept of purgatory and the worship of saints and images;
finally, if the belief in purgatory was discarded and the concept of an intermediate world between heaven and hell was
denied, then there was little excuse for the offering of private
masses for souls departed. So the process evolved until the
foundation of the Catholic faith itself, the sacrificial Mass, was
exposed to direct attack. Nicholas Harpsfield, Archdeacon of
Canterbury and contemporary Catholic raconteur of the English Reformation, was keenly aware of this sense of inevitabil-
ity when he wrote that once Henry VIII had renounced "first
his true marriage and then his obedience to the See Apostolic,
and took upon him St. Peter's authority and suffered the
people, or rather compelled them, to a schism and to some
heresies, he could no more stay and bridle them from other
heresies that they were inclined unto than it is possible for a

man to roll [down] a millstone from the top of a high hill
and afterward to stay it in the midst of its course. He was like,
I say, to one that would throw down a man headlong from
the top of a high tower and bid him stay when he was half
way down."[15]

Such a philosophy of history was undoubtedly tortured, its
perspective warped and its reasoning over-simplified. The
conservatives were blind to the fact that the monasteries
would never have been dissolved had not the ascetic spirit
of Christendom been profaned and at times grossly abused,
and had not public opinion, if not welcoming the change, been
on the whole apathetic to their fate.[16] The concept of purgatory, the saying of private mass, and the worship of images
might never have been abolished had they not often been corrupted by superstition and their use become stereotyped and
mechanistic. Beneath the political and religious events of
Henry's reign were vast and undefined social forces consequent to a changing economic order and intellectual outlook.
Had not enclosures, the rising importance of the wool in-
dustry, and the increasing cost of land become dominant social issues, the monasteries might never have been abolished
and their wealth and property been absorbed by the land-
hungry gentry. Again, had not the old nobility lost its power
and influence in a bureaucratic machine run by middle-class
lawyers and social upstarts who owed all but their souls to
their sovereign, the course of the Reformation might have
been very different. Finally, the conservatives forgot that personal decisions, individual emotions, chance, and even blunders
were essential ingredients of what they fondly regarded as an
inevitable evolution. In a word, their concept was wrong, but
their position was not altogether an unreasonable one, for in
outward appearances at least the Reformation did follow the
course which they so clearly discerned.

[15] Harpsfield, *The Pretended Divorce*, Cam. Soc. XXI (1878), p. 297.
[16] Constant, I, p. 155.

When Bishop Bonner wrote in his *Book of Homilies* in 1555 warning the people of the many sinful consequences of "this late schism," such as the pulling down of abbeys, the robbing of churches, and the destruction of colleges and chantries, he was convinced that "all these surely, with many more, have come upon us because we have been out of the house of God."[17] The Bishop may have been simplifying, but he was not fabricating one of the causes of the dissolution of the monastic orders. The legal recognition of the Royal Supremacy undoubtedly did place the monastic foundations in an enigmatic position. Being essentially international organizations, they were an anomaly in a national church, and as Lord Herbert has noted, they were generally regarded as "a seminary of factious persons" who recognized an authority above that of the crown.[18] During 1535 the abbeys and priories reluctantly accepted the oath of supremacy, but their silent disapproval won for them the suspicion of a still uncertain government, and Cromwell, for one, openly considered them equivalent to the "spies of the Pope."[19] As James Gairdner has said, "the monasteries, without outspoken opposition, were a far greater obstacle than the bishops and Convocations" to the royal claims to the Supreme Headship of the English church.[20] It makes but small difference whether their fall was occasioned by political advisability or whether, as Pollard has claimed, their dissolution was in effect "a gigantic bribe to the laity to induce them to acquiesce in the revolution effected by Henry VIII,"[21] for the argument remains valid that the break with the See Apostolic did determine their fate. The denial of the papal supremacy and the ensuing claims of national independence did "place the monastic wealth within the King's

---

[17] Bonner, *Homilies*, f. 42.
[18] Herbert, *The Life and Raigne of King Henry VIII*, p. 398.
[19] Quoted in Gasquet, *Henry VIII and the English Monasteries*, I, p. 249.
[20] Gairdner, *Lollardy*, II, p. 45.
[21] Pollard, *Henry VIII*, p. 341.

reach," and in this sense their destruction was, if not inevitable, directly related to the legal breach with Rome.[22]

The slow process of deterioration did not stop with the fall of the monastic orders, but was, in fact, accelerated by their collapse. The government, as Baskerville has said, was well aware of the intimate association between the religious houses and the doctrines of purgatory, of private mass and the worship of images, and when Katherine Bulkeley, Abbess of Godstow, wrote to Cromwell in 1538 to "be assured there is neither Pope, purgatory, images nor pilgrimage, nor praying to dead saints used amongst us," she was, in effect, denying one of the cardinal reasons for the existence of her abbey.[23] Nor were the reformers slow to appreciate the strength of the argument that the fall of the monasteries was a tacit disavowal of the existence of purgatory. "The founding of monasteries," wrote Bishop Latimer, "argued purgatory to be; so the pulling of them down argueth it not to be. What uncharitableness and cruelness seemeth it to be to destroy monasteries, if purgatory be!"[24] The doctrine of the existence of an unknown limbo suspended between the bliss of heaven and the torments of hell was retained throughout Henry's reign, but it was so far watered down that in the *King's Book* of 1543 the authorities hesitated to call it by its ancient name and contented themselves with naming the section on purgatory an "Article of prayer for souls departed." They pointed out that little was known about conditions after death, and men could do little more than commend the multitude of souls to the boundless mercy of God.[25] But five years later, in 1547, the Edwardian government officially denounced the belief as superstitious. The step, of course, was taken in order to give

---

[22] Constant, I, p. 140.

[23] Baskerville, *English Monks and the Monasteries*, pp. 21-22.

[24] Latimer, *Sermons and Remains*, "Bishop Latimer's Arguments against Purgatory" (1537), p. 249 (*L.P.*, XII, pt. i [1537], No. 1312).

[25] Lloyd, *Formularies*, pp. 375-377; Smith, *Henry VIII and the Reformation*, p. 376.

religious sanction to the ensuing destruction of the chantries and collegiate churches whose primary duties were the saying of masses for the benefit of souls in purgatory.[26] The government by Edward's reign had finally accepted the truth of one reformer's logic when he wrote that "as long as praying for souls departed is suffered, the people will think that there is a purgatory, and that in process of time will cause many to think that it is [a] pity that houses of Religion should be decayed whose prayers, as they think, profited much to souls departed. And that thereafter shall cause the King's deed in suppressing of houses of Religion to be thought uncharitable, and that may be hereafter right dangerous as well to the King's supremacy as to his succession. Wherefore it seemeth not good that the matter be any longer winked at, but that it be plainly declared and known whether there be any such place or not, and no man to hold opinion against that declaration."[27]

In other fields also the opening up of the floodgates of heresy and change was more or less directly attributed to the recognition of the Royal Supremacy. The publication of the Bible in English had long been one of the paramount demands of the reformers, but as late as 1530 the government had been reluctant to allow such a dangerous book to be spread about the land in the vulgar tongue. In that year Henry had thought it expedient to issue a proclamation explaining the reasons why the Council thought it unwise to sanction the translation of the Bible into English. The proclamation stated that on the advice of the "Council and the agreement of great learned men, [the King] thinketh . . . that the divulging of this Scripture at this time in English, tongue, to be committed to the people, considering such pestilent books, and so evil opinions as be now spread among them, should rather be to

[26] Constant, II, p. 157.
[27] P.R.O., S.P. 6, vol. 3, No. 20, p. 164 (*L.P.*, XIV, pt. i [1539], No. 376, sec. 4).

their further confusion and destruction than the edification of their souls."[28] The King presumably signed this order on the advice of More, Tunstal, Gardiner, Sampson, and Bell, who were all present at the meeting of the Council and whose opinion outweighed that of the two radical members, Hugh Latimer and Edward Crome. However, within six years Henry was to issue an injunction ordering the clergy to provide an English Bible in every church of the realm, and in 1537 the King licensed the publication of the first English edition. In the meantime the breach with Rome and the recognition of the Royal Supremacy had changed the entire political situation, and what had been "rather to their further confusion and destruction than the edification of their souls" in 1530 was by 1536 a political necessity. As Professor Pollard has said, Henry's reasons were "political rather than religious. The reading of Scriptures, and the growing disbelief in purgatory tended to destroy what hold the Papacy still had over the minds of Englishmen and indirectly to reconcile them to Henry's own supremacy."[29]

The translation of the Bible may have been a political maneuver on the part of the government, but for the Protestant cause it was an important impetus to the spread of their doctrines. Now that the common man could read the Scriptures, the doctrine of religious purity founded upon a literal interpretation of the Bible was no longer restricted to scholarly divines. The "common sort" could view for themselves the contrast between the simplicity of the Bible and the intricate formulae preached by the Catholic church; rites and ceremonies could be held up to Biblical proof by layman and cleric alike, and, if explicit evidence was lacking, could be condemned on the basis of individual scrutiny, as papistic, superstitious, and diabolic. Despite the very real benefits and personal satisfaction which the Bible in English, undoubtedly

[28] Wilkins, *Concilia*, III, p. 736.
[29] Pollard, *Thomas Cranmer*, p. 115.

had, the placing of Scriptures in the hands of each individual in an age when religion was still a vital element of daily life threatened to destroy all organized and authoritarian religious institutions. Well might Stephen Gardiner wonder where the appeal to scriptural purity would end, and in writing Bishop Hooper he posed just this question. If you deny the use of altars, he said, because you say the Apostles had none, then "the fonts by that rule must away also, of which there is no such mention, and the pulpits also taken down, for they be not testified, and much less the churches thus builded of stone in such greatness."[30] The final end, however, was perfectly clear to the reformers, and Thomas Cranmer expressed the aim of most of his followers when he wrote against the Bishop of Winchester in 1550 asking "what availeth it to take away beads, pardons, pilgrimages, and such other like popery, so long as two chief roots remain unpulled up? . . . The rest is but branches and leaves, the cutting away whereof is like topping and lopping of a tree, or cutting down of weeds, leaving the body standing and the roots in the ground; but the very body of the tree, or rather the roots of the weeds is the popish doctrine of Transubstantiation, of the Real Presence of Christ's flesh and blood in the Sacrament of the Altar, and of the sacrifice and oblation of Christ made by the priest for the salvation of the quick and the dead. Which roots if they be suffered to grow in the Lord's vineyard, they will overspread all the ground again with old errors and superstition." The Archbishop was sincerely convinced that such pernicious roots which "no Christian heart can willingly bear" had to be eradicated, and he announced that he had set his "hand and ax with the rest to cut down this tree, and to pluck up the weeds and plants by the roots which our heavenly Father never planted but were grafted and sown in his vineyard by his adversary the devil and antichrist his

[30] P.R.O., S.P. 10, vol. 12, Stephen Gardiner, *A Discussion of Mr. Hoper's Oversight* (1550), f. 65.

minister."[31] It is small wonder then that the conservatives, in looking back over these years of change, came to the conclusion that it was impossible to maintain the old creed without the central authority of the Pope. To quote Bishop Heath again, the Chancellor had little doubt that a renewal of the Royal Supremacy by Elizabeth would force Englishmen to "seek further for another gospel of Christ, other doctrine, faith, and sacraments, than we hitherto have received. Which shall breed such a schism and error in faith, as was never in any Christian realm. . . ."[32]

The philosophy which Nicholas Heath preached, the warning which he voiced at the commencement of a new reign, and the lesson which all the conservative bishops had learned, did not spring fully armed from their Olympian brows. Their appreciation evolved slowly as the historical events at their disposal fell into their allotted place in time. At no point in the evolution did they dare, and in many instances care, to resist the causal chain created by the declaration of royal omnipotence. The laconic but pregnant phrase of the chroniclers: "hung, drawn, and quartered," was a constant threat, and, like the man who fears to turn his head for right behind him a frightful monster treads, they preferred the wary caution of compliance to the brutal consequences of opposition. The Papacy, the monasteries, purgatory, the worship of saints and images by themselves, were not issues worth dying for, and not till Edward's reign were the conservatives of the Episcopal Bench compelled to accept the Reformation in its entirety and sanction the principles on which it rested. It was then and only then that they risked imprisonment and possible death by refusing to compromise their religious ideals. As we shall see, Stephen Gardiner was willing to accept under duress the fact of the Prayer Book of 1549, but refused to approve

[31] Cranmer, *Writings and Disputations*, "An Answer unto a Crafty and Sophistical Cavillation devised by Stephen Gardiner," p. 6.

[32] Strype, *Annals of the Reformation*, I, pt. ii, App. VI, "Hethe . . . his Oration made in the Parliament House, 1559," p. 405.

the theory on which the Protestant doctrines were based by admitting his own faith to be wrong and ungodly.[33] The breach with Rome, the suppression of the monastic orders, and the reform of abuses were judged by these men singly and on their individual merits, and it was long after More's death that they finally acknowledged the justice of his warning that the parts can be viewed only in relationship with their whole.

Terror undoubtedly played its part in determining the extent of conservative compliance, and as Edmund Bonner confessed under Queen Mary, "fear compelled us to bear with the times, for otherwise there had been no way but one."[34] That one way was the way of the Carthusian monks, of More and Fisher, and later of Gardiner's nephew, Germain Gardiner. How truthful the Bishop of London was when he excused his past in terms of forced compliance is difficult to say, for it was more prudent under Mary's reign to admit compulsion based on terror than acceptance through approval. However, the conservatives in many cases approved of particular steps taken by Henry. As exponents of this world and as court officials, they had little sympathy for the monastic ideal, while as humanists and bishops they had excellent reasons for disapproving of the abuses and disliking the independence of the regular clergy. John Longland must have heartily approved of Erasmus' opinion when the latter wrote him in September of 1528 that the Dominicans and Franciscans were victimizing an "innocent man for saying that the expense laid out on a monastery had better been bestowed on the poor" and that it would be better for all concerned if the monasteries were brought more completely under episcopal authority.[35] The Bishop himself had only three years before attempted to reform one of the exempt foundations of his diocese and had written in exasperation to the monks

---

[33] See ch. IX, pp. 265-266.   [34] Foxe, VIII, p. 110.
[35] *L.P.*, IV, pt. ii [1528], No. 4692.

of the Abbey of Thames that "if you won't do your obvious duty and get in a better lot of monks, I shall apply the possessions of the monastery to some use more acceptable to God."[36] Longland had been associated with both Gardiner and Roland Lee in the dissolution of the small orders occasioned by the creation of the Cardinal's new college at Oxford in 1525, and in the following year he tried to persuade the Abbot of Peterborough to contribute money for the building of Wolsey's seat of learning. Evidently the finances of the Abbey were not above reproach, and the Abbot prevaricated to the point where the Bishop, losing his temper, wrote the Cardinal that if this "swerve and warble" in the Abbot's words continues, he ought to be forced to resign.[37]

The secular clergy, on the whole, had little use for their regular brethren, and though the time had long since passed when the person of an Archbishop of Canterbury was actually attacked by a wrathful group of monks who were determined to resist his visitation and inspection of their house, the tradition of animosity still existed.[38] Many of the orders were exempt from episcopal jurisdiction and their independence a constant thorn in a bishop's side, so that when the final dissolution came, the monasteries could expect little support from the Episcopal Bench. Roland Lee, for all his conservatism, did not hesitate to augment his family fortunes by persuading Cromwell to request the Chancellor of Augmentations to give some of the land of the Abbey of Wigmore to his niece.[39] John Stokesley reported to Mr. Thomas Wriothesley his pleasure in suppressing the friars of Caversham and his anticipation in continuing the process with "several other houses of friars in the same manner."[40] When the Parliament of February 1535 gave authority to the King to abolish

---

[36] Quoted in Baskerville, *English Monks and the Monasteries*, p. 92.
[37] B.M., Vit. B. v, f. 78c (92) (*L.P.*, IV, pt. ii [1526], No. 2378).
[38] Stowe, *The Survey of London*, p. 336.
[39] *L.P.*, XIV, pt. i [1539], No. 1289.
[40] B.M., Harl. 604, f. 96.

all orders whose revenues were under three hundred marks (two hundred pounds) a year, the same Bishop rose and is said by the Chronicler, Edward Hall, to have remarked that the lesser houses were merely the thorns "but the great abbotts were putrified old oaks and they must needs follow . . . or many years be passed."[41]

Nor had another conservative bishop a higher opinion of the religious foundations, and as Baskerville has pointed out, Stephen Gardiner had little sympathy for monks.[42] The Bishop in 1539 publicly announced his gratification that these friars "be gone with all their tromperye"[43] while later, in 1546, he wrote Sir William Paget that "it hath pleased the Court of Parliament to give unto the King's Majesty's hands the disposition of all hospitals, chantries, and other houses; whereof I am very glad. . . ."[44] In fact, Gardiner's sole criticism of the spoliation of the monastic houses was the same as that of many reformers, that the wealth had been misused, and that a hundred great houses had been destroyed with nothing to show for the exchange except a single building for "scurvy and lowsy boys."[45]

As the lines between the opposing parties became consolidated, and the conflict between them took on a more militant aspect, many of the more liberal members of the Episcopal Bench discovered that the intermediate middle ground which they had tried to maintain was no longer tenable. They were reluctant, like Reginald Pole, to forsake truth because it involved heresy, to condemn reform because it involved change, and as liberals, they were deeply worried by the superstition and misuse which had crept into the church. Tunstal and Gardiner, Sampson and Aldridge, were the outspoken admirers of Erasmus, and as we have already pointed out,

[41] Hall, *Henry VIII*, II, pp. 267-268.
[42] Baskerville, *English Monks and the Monasteries*, p. 258.
[43] Gardiner, *Letters*, No. 81, "Gardiner to George Joye" (1545), p. 169.
[44] *Ibid.*, No. 101, "Gardiner to Paget" (1546), p. 218.
[45] Muller, *Stephen Gardiner*, p. 232.

these men were not averse to reform. "The best men were desirous of reforms," as Canon Smith has said, "but they hoped to carry them out on old lines."[46] When, in 1538, the government ordered that all images were to be destroyed which had been used in an idolatrous and superstitious manner, there were few men who would have condemned the theory behind the injunction. But who was to decide what was abuse and what was legitimate worship? The final decision rested with the bishop of the diocese, and he could administer the law leniently or harshly as he chose. For men such as Cranmer the law was essentially an excuse to abolish all images, and the Archbishop encountered considerable opposition in his own diocese when his commissioners ordered the removal of several images which the canons of Canterbury claimed had not been abused at all.[47] The problem between the two parties was essentially one of interpretation, and to men such as Thomas Cranmer the meaning of the words *idolum* and *imago* was identical, the one being Greek, the other Latin.[48] On the other hand, Stephen Gardiner and his followers tried to distinguish between the two, and the Bishop endeavored to point out that "when we have images, to call them idols, is a like fault in fond folly as if a man would call *regem* a tyrant, and then bring in old writers to prove that *tyrannus* signified once a king, like as *idolum* signified once an image."[49]

The difficulty confronting the conservative bishops was one of differentiation, of distinguishing between the abuse and the thing abused. John Hilsey, though a reformer himself, was worried by this problem, and in writing to the Chancellor of the See of Worcester concerning the seemingly heretical sermon preached by Hugh Latimer, he said: "I did write unto you of the great division that was (yea and yet is) among

[46] Smith, *Pre-Reformation England*, p. 241.
[47] *L.P.*, XVIII, pt. ii [1543], No. 546, pp. 349, 369.
[48] *Ibid.*, p. 321.
[49] Gardiner, *Letters*, No. 116, "Gardiner to Ridley" (1547), p. 256.

the people in the town of Bristol of the which I wrote unto
you that it came by the preaching of one Master Latimer, a
man not unknown. . . . He spoke of pilgrimages, worshipping
of saints, worshipping of images, [and] of purgatory, in the
which he did vehemently persuade toward the contrary."
Hilsey apparently disapproved of such outspoken words and
lamented the growing dissension which the sermon had precipitated, but, he confessed, he had listened to only one side
of the argument against Latimer and he had changed his mind
after reading the fiery preacher's sermon. "I have heard him
preach and have entitled his sermon, sentence for sentence,"
he said, "and I have perceived that his mind is much more
against the abusing of things than against the things itself,"
and, he concluded, that his conscience had been "for the time
erroneous and deceived for lack of taking heed diligently to
mark and know the abuse of a thing from the thing."[50] Unfortunately, it was almost impossible to maintain this distinction, and when Bishop Bonner asked one youthful heretic
whether he knew what he was talking about when he spoke
of "idols," the young man answered back that "God hath
taught us what they be: for whatsoever is made, graven, or
devised by man's hands, contrary to God's word, the same
is an idol."[51] These words were spoken under Queen Mary
and by then the distinction had collapsed. It was no longer
possible to reform an abuse without endangering the thing
abused.

John Voysey, Bishop of Exeter, was a lawyer and state official, and certainly no reformer, but he had little use for the
multitude of holy days which he considered to be a serious
threat to the economic well-being of the realm. In 1539 the
Bishop issued an injunction to his diocese that the practice
of shoesmiths in ceasing all work and refusing to shoe horses

[50] P.R.O., S.P. 6, vol. 1, No. 19, pp. 162-164 (*L.P.*, VI [1533], No. 433,
sec. III).

[51] Foxe, VII, "The examination of Thomas Haukes" (1555), p. 108.

on Saint Lewis' Day was to cease, and fishermen were ordered back to work when they stopped to celebrate the holy day of their patron saints. The reason for these prohibitions, said the prelate, is because the work of the nation at all costs must continue unimpeded, and he described the labor of the fisherman and shoesmith as being essential trades and "necessary to the use of man." But what is significant in the Bishop's proclamation is that nowhere does Voysey say that holy days are evil or ungodly; they were merely inexpedient to the welfare of the state and abused by overuse.[52] Likewise, John Skip was perfectly willing to admit the need of reform in the church, and even to sanction the removal of certain corrupt ceremonies, but he was never willing to argue from this that all images or relics were evil in themselves. It is well done, he said, to take away evil abuses of ceremonies, and "it is the preacher's part to speak against the abuses of such things, and the King's office is to see the abuses taken away, and not the good things themselves except it so be that the abuses cannot be taken away."[53]

The Bishop of Winchester also admitted that there had been "many images, which be now all taken away, for it was in the liberty of the rulers, for the abuse of them, either to reform them or to take them away: and because it was an easier way to take them away than to bring them to the right use that they were ordained for, they were all clean taken away; and so they might be. 'Yea, sir,' will ye say, 'but ye have maintained and defended them; and have preached against such persons as despised them.' It is truth: I have preached against the despisers of them, and have said, that images might be suffered and used in the church, as laymen's books. Yet I never otherwise defended them, but to be used for such purposes as they were first set up in the church for. But

[52] Wilkins, *Concilia*, III, p. 846 (*L.P.*, XIV, pt. ii [1539], No. 342).
[53] P.R.O., S.P. 6, vol. 1, No. 3, "The sense of the most special and principle part which Master Skyppe brought in his sermon said in the King's Chapel" (1536), p. 19 (*L.P.*, X [1536], No. 615, sec. 4).

now that men be waxed wanton, they are clean taken away; wherein our religion is no more touched than when books were taken away for abusing of them."[54] To Gardiner the abuse might excuse the "taking away" but it did not prove the ungodliness of an ecclesiastical institution. The evilness lay with the people who abused the ceremonies and customs of the church, not with the church itself. But the Bishop forgot that though the discarding of images might not touch his religion, the consequences of the removal had far-reaching effects, for was not the Mass composed of corruptible and mortal elements such as the bread and the wine, and were not these also susceptible to idolatry. In fact, Gardiner was not slow to voice this question, and concluded that the logical answer was that even in the Sacrament of the Altar "there is not God, but it is an idol."[55]

At every step of the way, the conservatives were confronted with the consequences of their liberalism, for under the guise of reform to which even the conservative bishops had given their consent, the reformers were finding excuses to introduce much which was new. What seemed to warrant removal and destruction in the end only led to further dissension. When, for instance, the monastic houses were dissolved, Stephen Gardiner soon discovered that in destroying the institution of monasticism the government had loosed upon the country a swarm of ex-friars and monks who lacked discipline and discretion. It was no longer possible to recall heretical monastics to their foundations or punish their transgressions by exactments instituted by their abbots or priors. Recusant friars were now legally exempt, and it was with considerable truth that the Bishop of Winchester preached from the pulpit that friars had vanished only to return in laymen's garb and were called "by an English name, bretherne, and go apparelled like other men. . . ." The Bishop called upon the King to

---

[54] Foxe, VI, "The sermon of Stephen Gardiner" (1548), p. 92.
[55] Gardiner, *A Detection of the Devils Sophistrie* (1546), f. x.

banish these brethren as exponents of the devil and heresy,
as he had previously banished the friars as advocates of papism.[56] The old Archbishop of York, Edward Lee, likewise
lived to regret the consequences of the destruction of the
monasteries, and soon learned that monks infected with heresy
were much safer under the watchful eye of their abbot than
wandering about contaminating the inhabitants of his bishopric. In 1539 the radical Suffragan Bishop of Dover reported to Cromwell that in the See of York "poor men who
surrendered their houses are hardly ordered by the Bishop's
officers by the Bishop's orders, and not suffered to sing nor
stay in any parish church without showing their letters of orders. . . ."[57] The Archbishop had good cause to be alarmed
by these unlicensed monks who had recently been released
from their monastic vows and had little else to do but wander
about the countryside expounding either the Catholic or Protestant doctrine or sometimes a hybrid belief uniquely their
own.

By the fourth decade of Henry's reign the conservative
bishops had begun to realize where reform was leading, and
that they themselves, in advocating limited change, had paved
the way for religious revolution. By 1546 Gardiner was fully
aware of the course of his surrender when he wrote in his
Detection of the Devils Sophistrie that "in the discussion of
ceremonies, semelynes and orders, the devil frameth his questions by division, and asketh of each thing alone, dissevered
from the rest. As, for example, whether a shaven crown
maketh a priest? Where unto a man must answer . . . Naye.
Well, says the devil, then away with your crown and calleth
it a flesh mark. . . . Then he asketh whether a long gown
maketh a priest? . . . and then it must be answered, Naye. . . .
Then the devil cometh to the ceremonies . . . and asketh of
ceremonies severally alone, where unto as he dissevereth them,

[56] Gardiner, *Letters*, No. 81, "Gardiner to George Joye" (1545), p. 170.
[57] *L.P.*, XIV, pt. i [1539], No. 494.

the answer must be, no. Where upon, he concludeth, ergo, they be nothing requisite." "And so he will peruse all, and by sophistry in division wipe out all, as nothing. . . . Shall [says the devil] forbearing of meats save a man? The answer must be, No, and then, ergo, eat all day long. Doth watching bring a man to heaven? Naye, ergo, sleep and spare not. Is the place cause why a man's prayer is good? The answer must be, Naye, and what needeth thou [to] come to church then, sayeth the devil, unless it be to hear my false teaching set forth."[58]

As early as 1536 the tide of reaction had set in, and John Longland, Bishop of Lincoln, was one of the first to regret his participation in the King's divorce. The Spanish ambassador reported to his master that the Bishop "has said several times since Christmas that he would rather to be the poorest man in the world than ever have been the King's councillor and confessor."[59] But the final words of regret were spoken by the Bishop of Winchester when he warned the Archbishop of Canterbury in 1547 that "this I take to be true, that if the wall of authority, which I accompted established in our last agreement [i.e. *The King's Book* of 1543] be once broken, and new water let in at a little gap, the vehemence of novelty will flow further than your Grace would admit. And when men hear of new gear, every man maketh his request, some new hose, some new coats, some new caps, some new shirts; like as in religion we have seen attempted where the people thought they might prevail. . . ." After delivering this warning, Gardiner went on to state his approval of the "notable act of our late sovereign lord [Henry VIII] to reform and then moderate religion as he did, which he did not without all trouble."[60] The process of moderation which the Bishop mentions began in 1539-40 after almost a decade of change and

---

[58] Gardiner, *A Detection of the Devils Sophistrie* (1546), ff. cxlix-cl.
[59] *L.P.*, VII [1534], No. 14, p. 8.
[60] Gardiner, *Letters*, No. 124, "Gardiner to Cranmer" (1547), p. 308.

reformation. By then the conservatives were fully alarmed by the course of the social and religious dissension which had developed, while Henry himself felt reasonably assured of the safety and permanency of his throne and supremacy. Thus, on the fall of Thomas Cromwell in the early summer of 1540, the King began the laborious process of leashing the forces which his divorce had released, for both the conservative bishops and their sovereign had begun to suspect that the mere demand for reform was undermining the basis of European culture and society, and there are few so conservative as a thoroughly disillusioned liberal.

CHAPTER VII

THE CRISIS AND THE CONSERVATIVE
TRIUMPH (1537-1540)

ℐN the preceding chapter the religious background to the doctrine of human prudence and the history of the slow awaking of the conservative party to the full consequences of the Reformation were described. It remains now to narrate in considerable detail the history of the critical years 1537-40 in order to trace the collapse of the government's religious policy and to set the political stage for the final triumph of the conservatives during the concluding years of Henry's reign.

By the early months of 1537 the need for some sort of religious compromise was glaringly apparent. The transfer of religious supremacy from Rome to London had been accomplished on the whole with surprisingly little opposition, but the price of the "Supreme Headship" was not slow in being realized. What had commenced as the extra-legal manipulation of the constitutional organs of government soon involved the entire structure of Tudor society. Henry had found and fostered the support of the Protestant elements of the nation who had greeted the transfer of papal authority to the crown with loud applause. Indeed, the King did not have to be told the argument of Cranmer's chaplain, Richard Morice, who wrote Doctor Butts, the King's physician, that "if there be no better stay for the maintenance of these godly preachers, the King's authority concerning his supremacy shall lie post alone, hidden in the Act of Parliament, and not in the hearts of his subjects."[1] Gardiner, Tunstal, Lee, and Stokesley, although they complied with the Act of Supremacy, were not

---

[1] Foxe, VIII, "A letter of Master Morice sent to Sir William Butts" (1543), p. 33 (*L.P.*, XVIII, pt. ii [1543], Preface p. lii).

above suspicion. The loyalties and motives of each in turn were carefully scrutinized by a still unstable government, and it was not without reason that the astute King described the Bishop of Winchester's behavior during 1535 as one of "coloured doubleness."[2] As late as 1541 Bishop Longland was thrown into prison, his writings carefully perused and his friends called up for questioning, all because the Bishop's nephew, Richard Pate, had fled to the party of Cardinal Pole and the Pope.[3] The conservatives might be loyal but more than negative recognition of the supremacy was needed. It was not enough to have legislative sanction of Henry's new title, for the royal authority, as Morice warned, had to be instilled into "the hearts of his subjects." The advocates of the old faith might, as almost all of them were ordered to do, preach at Paul's Cross against the pernicious doctrines of Mistress Rose of Rome,[4] but it was infinitely safer and far easier to promote and favor a group of men who actually thought that the Pope was the "stinking whore of Babylon," and who could add religious conviction to political theory.

Unfortunately for the peace and stability of the country, the reformers, as we have already attempted to demonstrate, did not consider the abolition of the papal sovereignty to be the ultimate end of the English Reformation; they utilized the political breach with Rome and the protection which the government afforded them to encourage those who would have the Bible in English and who considered the Pope's doctrines as noxious and nefarious as the Supreme Pontiff himself. As early as the spring of 1534 the King was induced to set his royal pen to paper and write Archbishop Cranmer that he had been advised that "there swarmeth about a number of indiscreet persons which being neither furnished with wisdom, learning, nor judgment be nevertheless authorized to preach

[2] *L.P.*, VIII, pt. i [1535], No. 592.
[3] *L.P.*, XVI [1541], No. 449, p. 222.
[4] *L.P.*, X [1536], No. 282, p. 103.

and permitted to blow abroad their follies which among our subjects doth only engender contention." Henry then went on to warn the Primate to be more circumspect in his licensing of preachers "to the intent our people may be (better)? fed and enriched with wholesome food neither savouring the corruption of the bishop of Rome and his disciples nor by the setting forth of novelties and the continual inculcation of things not necessary brought in doubt."[5] Evidently Henry thought that he could promote his personal supremacy by protecting the episcopal reformers without sanctioning their doctrines. But the King was soon to learn the truth of More's words concerning Master Bayfield, when he said that any man "so blinded in the zeal of popery, so deadly set against the one side, and so partially affectionate unto the other, that in them whom he favoreth he can see nothing but all fair roses and sweet virtue; in the other which he hateth, there is never a thing can please his fantasy, but all is as black as pitch, vice, abomination, heresy, and folly, whatsoever they do, or intend to do."[6] The King, in his effort to consolidate this constitutional revolution, had placed the safety of his new regime in the hands of such men, individuals who were little interested in the legal niceties of the supremacy and whose motives were religious, not political. Under the circumstances, it is not surprising that the royal injunction against novelties in religion went unheeded. The extent of its failure was eloquently exemplified in the phraseology of a government proclamation issued the same year as Henry's letter to his Archbishop. The spread of "seditious" books throughout the realm had increased to alarming proportions and the government had become concerned by the rapid dissemination of Anabaptist and Sacramentarian ideas. The new proclamation took pains to point out that these seditious and unsettling books had encouraged the King's "simple loving subjects" "arrogantly and

[5] P.R.O., S.P. 6, vol. 2, No. 18, pp. 252-254, (*L.P.*, VII [1534], No. 750).
[6] Foxe, IV, p. 688.

superstitiously to argue and dispute in open places, taverns, and ale houses not only upon baptism, but also upon the holy and blessed sacrament of the altar. . . ."[7]

It was not until the mid-thirties that a clearly discernible party split began to appear within the episcopal organization. Cranmer had been elevated to the Primate's chair in 1533, and by 1537 eight more reformers were promoted under the patronage of Anne Boleyn and Thomas Cromwell.[8] With the appointment of Latimer, Hilsey, Barlow, Goodrich, and the other university divines and monks, the composition of the Episcopal Bench dissolved into two fundamentally opposed parties, and with this dissolution there developed all the personal acrimony consequent to party strife. Both Stephen Gardiner and John Stokesley were probably envious of the Archbishop's position, having themselves coveted the post,[9] and both men showed their distaste for the new Primate by appealing to the King against the legality of Cranmer's general visitation in 1534.[10] With men of both doctrines now strategically located in high ecclesiastical positions, there commenced a flood of vitriolic and contradictory criticism against the actions of individual bishops who engendered the hatred of one side or another. William Marshall wrote to Cromwell in 1536 lamenting that the poor people were being indicted for small matters of so-called heresy in the diocese of Lincoln while the Bishop, John Longland, was winking at the "proud and stubborn" persons who daily disregarded the word of God.[11] On the other hand, Thomas Bell, sheriff of Glouces-

[7] Wilkins, *Concilia*, III, p. 776.

[8] They were: Cranmer, Archbp. of Canterbury (1533); Barlow, Bp. of St. David's (1536); Goodrich, Bp. of Ely (1534); Hilsey, Bp. of Rochester (1535); Capon (Salcot), Bp. of Bangor (1534); Shaxton, Bp. of Salisbury (1535); Latimer, Bp. of Worcester (1535); Holgate, Bp. of Llandaff (1537); and Warton, Bp. of St. Asaph (1536).

[9] Pollard, *Thomas Cranmer*, p. 52; Muller, *Stephen Gardiner*, p. 48; Innes, *Cranmer and the Reformation in England*, p. 63.

[10] Cranmer, *Works*, No. CXLV, "Cranmer to Cromwell" (May 1535), p. 304 (*L.P.*, VIII [1535], No. 704); Strype, *Cranmer*, II, No. XV, p. 704.

[11] *L.P.*, XI [1536], No. 325.

ter, complained to John Stokesley that Hugh Latimer had been licensing lewd preachers and had admitted a black friar locally known as "Two-year old," who had previously been banished from the See of Worcester for abominable drunkenness and loose living. He ended by professing the hope that the Bishop and the Duke of Norfolk would exercise their influence to curb Bishop Latimer's indiscretions.[12] Minions on both sides carried on their masters' arguments with considerably more vehemence and less tact than the bishops themselves dared use. When Nicholas Shaxton, for example, came to Crutched Friars, inhibited a doctor and several others from hearing confession and placed in their stead the martyr, John Cardmaker, trouble was caused by one of the officials of the Bishop of London preaching to the people that Bishop Shaxton had no jurisdiction within his Lord's diocese and that his appointments were therefore invalid.[13]

On both sides the debate grew more violent and the cautious but usually accurate Anthony Waite reported to his mistress, Lady Lisle, "many preachers we have [at London], but they come not from one Master, for, as it is reported, their messages be divers. Latimer many blameth and as many doth allow. . . ."[14] It is little wonder that there were two schools of thought over the preaching of the new Bishop of Worcester, for in 1536, only a year after Waite's report to Lady Lisle, the Bishop stated at Paul's Cross that bishops, abbots and priors were "strong thieves" and that dukes and lords were little better. The King, he added, had made a "marvelous good Act of Parliament that certain men should sow, each of them two acres of hemp, but it were all too little, were it so much more, to hang the thieves that be in England."[15] It may be doubted that even Latimer preached this sermon as it was

[12] P.R.O., S.P. 1, vol. 104, f. 157 (L.P., x [1536], No. 1099).
[13] L.P., x [1536], No. 462.
[14] P.R.O., S.P. 3, vol. 14, No. 14 (L.P., IX [1535], No. 583).
[15] Wright, Suppression of Monasteries, Cam. Soc. XXVI (1843), No. XIII "Thomas Dorset to Mr. James Horsewell" (13 March, 1536), p. 38.

later reported in a letter of Mr. Thomas Dorset, but it did not augur well for the future stability of the realm if the words of divines could be construed in such an inflammatory manner. On all sides indiscreet if sincere preachers were voicing disturbing theories, and it must have given Thomas Cromwell quite a shock to read a letter addressed to him by one such extremist who suggested that the gospel should be set forth in all places, "even in brothels."[16]

The breach with Rome, and the commencement of reform within the church had set loose upon the land a host of amateur theologians who, as More warned, pictured their own side in terms of "roses and sweetness" and their opponents as "black as pitch." It was with a sense of foreboding that Bishop Longland wrote Cromwell relating the actions of Sir Swynnerton who "preached from day to day, and sometimes on the workdays, and twice upon a day for the most part," and whose "sermons are not fruitful but rather seditious." The Bishop claimed that the preacher, when called before him and questioned for speaking of "such doubtful matters as are not yet openly determined which was commanded in all dioceses not to be touched in sermons," the young man answered by saying that "he knoweth the King his mind." It was bad enough to have every amateur divine claim special knowledge of the King's mind, but Longland was even more worried that Sir Swynnerton was consorting with "light people," filling them with the words of the Bible and causing idleness and poverty within his bishopric. Moreover, the Bishop strongly suspected that there was a direct relationship between the growth of "such idle people" and the increase of robberies within the area of his jurisdiction, and he concluded his letter with characteristic academic snobbishness by saying that he felt sure that Sir Swynnerton had never seen the inside of a university despite his claims to the contrary.[17] The Bishop of Lincoln had

[16] *L.P.*, IX [1535], No. 611.
[17] P.R.O., S.P. I, vol. 103, f. 235 (*L.P.*, X [1536], No. 804).

cause to be alarmed, for dissension and confusion had grown apace with the increasing strength of the reformers, and, in reaction, the advocates of the old faith had become more vocal and violent. When one reformer could say it is time to cast off the works of darkness—"We must either [be] on God's party or else on the Devil's,"[18]—it was high time that the government took steps to reach a religious agreement before human reason and political prudence were engulfed by the brilliant faith of the elect of God's children and the darkness of the devil's creed.

Thus by 1536 there was a pressing need for some sort of codification of religious belief which the government and the Episcopal Bench could enforce. The King, by winking at ribald attacks against the clergy, by creating bishops whose doctrines were heretical if partially concealed, by secularizing the ecclesiastical wealth of the lesser monasteries, and by repudiating the spiritual and political supremacy of the Pope, had reduced the spiritual authority of the English church to the point where it was no longer possible either to discipline or to control its members. As early as 1535 Edward Lee had made a plea for unity and order, and had written Thomas Cromwell that the people of the northern counties were alarmed by the growth of heresy. He advised that a "book should be made to settle such matters of controversy and [that] the opinion of the holy ancient doctors of the Church, whose authority Melanchthon and others think necessary, [be] taken in doubtful passages."[19] Here was a plea for compromise based on authorities which both sides could accept as sacred. However, it was unity, not compromise, which was to be the order of the day, and on July 11, 1536, the government in the person of Edward Fox presented to Convocation a series of Ten Articles which were duly accepted. There is no record of a debate on the formation of these Articles, and it

[18] *Ibid.*, vol. 241, f. 3 (*L.P.*, Add. [1537], No. 1209).
[19] *L.P.*, IX [1535], No. 704.

seems unlikely that any extensive discussion took place. Fox arrived back from Germany on July 4 and seven days later the religious formulary was presented to Convocation. The Articles have been shown to have been based in part upon the Wittenberg Articles given to Fox by the German divines, as a foundation for a possible religious union between England and the German Princes,[20] and there was scarcely time during the week following Fox's return for a full scale debate.

The controversy over the nature of the Articles and the degree to which they constitute a breach with the old doctrines is long and detailed, and, in large measure, is founded on personal interpretation. The Abbé Constant has insisted on their basic orthodoxy while Professor Messenger has taken pains to prove their heresy.[21] Messenger's argument is based on the presence of what he claims to be Lutheran words in the Article dealing with the Mass. We need not go into the theological aspects of the discussion and it must suffice to say that the phraseology, as both authors admit, was ambiguous. There seems little doubt that the Articles, although completely orthodox as far as they go, were in certain instances open to a double interpretation which would appeal to both Catholics and Protestants. Certainly, however, the silence of the new formulary in regard to four of the seven sacraments was a serious blow to the believers in the old religion. The Articles themselves are divided, the first five dealing with things necessary to salvation, and the remainder with the outward aspects of the church, such as ceremonies. The Creed is given, and the three sacraments of baptism, penance, and the Mass are briefly recounted. Then follow the articles on images, saints, ceremonies, and purgatory.[22] The whole flavor of the work is one of breathless brevity, a concise survey of the essentials of Chris-

[20] Constant, I, pp. 400-404; L.P., XI [1536], Nos. 80, 123.

[21] Messenger, *The Reformation, the Mass and the Priesthood*, I, pp. 245-252.

[22] Two versions of the Ten Articles are printed in Lloyd, *Formularies*. See also Burnet, IV, Add. I, p. 166.

tian faith. It was orthodox in the strictest sense of the word, in that it did not state any heretical doctrines unacceptable to sincere Catholics, but its very conciseness constituted a marked victory for the advocates of reform. The sacraments of marriage, extreme unction, orders, and confirmation are not only omitted, but no hint is given that they ever existed. Moreover, the failure to expound a detailed and Catholic use of the various articles was tantamount to leaving the exposition to the individual preacher, who was ordered by royal injunction to explain their meaning at least three times a year. The element of compromise within the formulary has been assumed by some historians because of the fact that the names of most of the bishops are attached to the document,[23] but this would have been enforced regardless of whether the Articles represented agreement or not. The absence of any evidence that a debate was held, and the equivocal nature of the entire work, would appear to indicate that the formulary was dictated to the Convocation and represented an effort to achieve what its preamble avows—"unity and concord in opinion." In this the Ten Articles signally failed, for within three months of their publication occurred the rebellion of the north known as the Pilgrims of Grace.

This series of uprisings, which broke out in the late summer of 1536, started first in Lincolnshire and then spread northward to Yorkshire where the insurgents, calling themselves the Pilgrims of Grace, placed badges on their arms depicting the five wounds of Christ. For a time, at least, it looked rather as if the pilgrimage would reach London itself, but fortunately

---

[23] Messenger, *The Reformation, the Mass and the Priesthood*, I, p. 247. Eighteen of a possible twenty-one bishops signed the Ten Articles. Two were by proxy (Longland of Lincoln held proxies for Voysey and Roland Lee). Three bishops are not represented. Gardiner was out of the country; the See of Llandaff was vacant, Robert Holgate not being appointed to Llandaff until the following year; and John Kite appears to have been absent from Convocation. The Sees of Gloucester, Oxford, Peterborough, Westminster, Chester, and Bristol had not yet been created. See Burnet, IV, Add. I, p. 171.

for the government there was little internal unity within the ranks of the insurgents. The rebellion in the north failed to take advantage of the risings in Lincolnshire, thus affording the government's forces time to suppress the one before turning to the more serious revolt in the border counties. As most historians have claimed, the rebellion was essentially religious, and undoubtedly the publication of the Ten Articles played its part in the wave of religious reaction which swept northern England. In fact, one of the paramount claims of the rebels was the demand for the return of the four missing sacraments.[24] Certainly the government regarded the risings as having been caused by religious complaints, for Henry wrote an irate letter to his bishops accusing them of failing to read the Ten Articles to the people, and he peremptorily ordered his episcopate personally to read the articles on every holiday on pain of deprivation.[25] The administration's efforts to attain unity in religion was, however, only one of many causes which stimulated the passionate outbreak of the fall and winter of 1536. The revolt was the culmination of widespread discontent in all levels of society against almost every aspect of the Tudor regime. The badge of religion produced a unified appearance to a movement which otherwise was motivated by a host of social and economic causes. The old feudal nobility of the north were alarmed by the threat to their ancient independence produced by the increasing importance and power of the bureaucracy at London. They complained bitterly that their age-old prerogatives, especially their right to be represented on the King's Council, were being usurped by commoners and social upstarts, and their ire fell primarily upon the person of the blacksmith's son, Thomas Cromwell. The gentry demanded the repeal of the "quindezine" or tax on sheep enforced by a constantly penurious government,

---

[24] Gairdner, *Lollardy*, II, p. 318.
[25] Collier, *An Ecclesiastical History of Great Britain*, IX, No. XXXIX, "Henry VIII's letter to some of the bishops" (19 November, 1536), pp. 150-153 (*L.P.*, XI [1536], No. 1110).

while all classes in the north watched the destruction of the monasteries with ill-concealed distaste. These "Temples of God" were objects of local patriotism, and in the vast regions of wilderness in the north they played an important role as houses of hospitality where the wanderer could depend on food and board and the warmth of an open hearth. The testaments of many ancient families had been arbitrarily broken by the destruction of the religious foundations and not all the landed families had been so fortunate as to buy up the sites where the bones of their ancestors were interred. To the ranks of the Pilgrims was also added the great bulk of the peasants, who begrudged the strict collection of ecclesiastical taxes of tenths and first fruits and were threatened with pauperism by the steady growth of enclosure. A multitude of class interests were involved and most of them were conflicting and antagonistic, but for a moment, at least, religious emotionalism concealed divergent interests and maintained the illusion of outward harmony. Finally, internal cross-currents spelled the eventual collapse of the movement, but for a few weeks the whole future of Tudor despotism was at stake.[26] Henry was brutal in his suppression; his royal vanity outraged that "the rude commons of one shire" and "the most brute and beastly of the whole realm" should claim the right to dictate to their sovereign.[27] But the King was not blind to the dangers confronting his position, and almost the instant the rebellion of the north was crushed, he turned his attention to formulating the broad document of religious belief and social conduct known as *The Bishops' Book*—the first and only effort of the reign to achieve unity based on compromise.

In February of 1537 the King appointed a commission of

---

[26] *L.P.*, xi [1536], Nos. 585, 705, 828. For further details see M. H. and Ruth Dodds, *The Pilgrimage of Grace, 1536-37 and the Exeter Conspiracy, 1538*, 2 vols., Cambridge, 1915. For the relationship between the fall of the monasteries and the uprisings in the north see Baskerville, *English Monks and the Monasteries*, p. 156.

[27] *St. P.* i, No. xlviii, "King Henry VIII to the rebels in Lincolnshire," p. 463.

all the bishops and some twenty-five theologians and canonists, and ordered them in the interests of national concord to reach a permanent and lasting religious settlement. Compromise was to be the keynote of the sessions, and Cromwell at the first meeting addressed the members of this impromptu convocation, stating that they had been "called hither to determine certain controversies which at this time be moved concerning the Christian religion and faith. . . ." His Majesty, he said, "desireth now for Christ's sake that all malice, obstinacy, and carnal respect [be] set apart [to the entent that] ye will friendly and lovingly dispute among yourselves of the controversies moved in the Church, and that ye will conclude all things by the word of God without all brawling or scolding. . . ."[28] On the conclusion of the Vicar-general's speech, the bishops rose to return thanks to their gracious sovereign for his pious zeal, evidently choosing to ignore the ominous tone of Cromwell's oration, which seemed more suited to the schoolroom than to the sanctified atmosphere of the Episcopal Bench.

Compromise, however, was not to be attained without considerable brawling and scolding, and on the first day of the discussions the seriousness of the disagreement between the two parties became apparent. John Stokesley, as soon as the Vicar-general had returned to his seat, introduced the subject of the four missing sacraments, and a prolonged and irate debate ensued. The Bishop of London, along with Edward Lee, Longland, Clerk, Sampson, and William Rugge, contended that the meaning of a sacrament was not limited merely to the remission of sins but included the conferring of divine grace, while Thomas Cranmer, Latimer, Shaxton, Goodrich, and to a lesser extent Edward Fox, were equally violent in their opposition.[29] The temper of the argument was not im-

[28] Alane, *Of the Auctorite of the Word of God against the Bishop of London*, printed in Ellis, *Original Letters*, 3rd Ser., vol. III, pp. 196-197 (*L.P.*, XII, pt. i [1537], No. 790).
[29] *Ibid.*, p. 197.

proved by the presence of the Scottish theologian, Alexander Alane, whom Cromwell had imported into the session to lend support to the Protestant side. Alane and Bishop Stokesley became involved in an acrimonious debate in which the Scotsman accused the Bishop of basing his arguments upon "certain stinking glosses and old lousy writers"—remarks which Stokesley undoubtedly returned in kind. The diplomatic Edward Fox endeavored to pour balm upon the outraged vanities of the two men, tactfully warning the intruder that such bitter controversy was undermining the ultimate success of the meeting, and requesting him not to continue his argument with Stokesley about "the minds and sayings of the doctors and school writers, for ye know that they in many places do differ among themselves, and that they are contrary to themselves also almost in every article." Fox then turned to his brother bishops and attempted to impress upon them the seriousness of the situation, saying that they must either achieve agreement or lose the last vestiges of their waning authority and become the laughing-stock of the world.[30] Unfortunately, such worldly considerations had little effect upon the petulant Bishop and his stubborn adversary and the tension became so great that finally the Vicar-general was constrained to end the discussion at noon and adjourn the meeting to the next day. The presence of Alane had annoyed the national prejudices of both groups, and on the following day the Scot was politely but firmly requested not to reappear, while Thomas Cranmer wrote him that many of the bishops had been shocked by the interference of a foreigner in their midst.[31]

After Alane's dismissal the daily meetings, which lasted until July, disappear into the limbo of unrecorded history, but the sessions must have been heated and personal encounters vitriolic, for in late July one contemporary was still writing that even though the bishops had left Lambeth Palace,

[30] *Ibid.*, p. 200.
[31] *Ibid.*, pp. 201-202.

rumor had it that no solution had yet been reached.[32] That agreement was actually attained evidently came as something of a surprise to most Englishmen. At what cost to personal conviction it was achieved is still unknown, but certainly a bitter internal tug of war developed in which the uncertain, the undecided, and the fearful, were subjected to a barrage of arguments from both sides. When Richard Sampson, the newly installed Bishop of Chichester, showed signs of swinging over to the party of reform after his original stand in favor of the seven sacraments, John Stokesley and Cuthbert Tunstal took considerable pains to re-indoctrinate him with new propositions and proof. The three men used to share the same barge in their daily trips to Lambeth Palace from their London residences, and the unfortunate Bishop was induced to listen while his two friends expounded from weighty tomes in Greek and Latin.[33] Apparently their evidence was convincing, for Sampson remained a conservative and within three years had so antagonized his early patron, Thomas Cromwell, that he was attainted for treason and cast into the Tower for papal affection. One might wonder, however, whether compromise would ever have been reached had not chance in the form of the plague played into Henry's hands. Throughout the last month of the sessions, the Black Death descended upon the capital, and Henry, safe in his castle at Windsor, was adamant in his refusal to allow his divines to leave the contaminated "and smoky air" of London until some settlement had been concluded. Just what effect the lingering presence of the plague had upon personal convictions is difficult to judge, but the Archbishop, for one, wrote a terrified appeal to his

---

[32] *L.P.*, XII, pt. ii, No. 337, "John Hussee to Lord Lisle" (25 July, 1537). "The bishops," Hussee reported, "have left, not agreed, I think. Nothing is published as yet."

[33] Later Sampson when he had been imprisoned in the Tower described this episode in detail in a letter to Thomas Cromwell dated 7 June, 1540. See B.M., Cleo. E. v, f. 308 (300) (*L.P.*, XV 1540, No. 758). The letter is printed with fair accuracy in Strype, *Ecc. Mem.*, I, pt. i, No. XCIII, p. 381.

sovereign imploring him to give them all license to leave London, for, he said, the people were dying everywhere, in London, Westminster, and at Lambeth, and "they die at my gate, even at the next house to me."[34] There seems little doubt that the plague moved otherwise obstinate ecclesiastics to compromise, if only to escape such a sudden and frightful death.

The final solution was based on Melanchthon's theory of *adiaphora*. This was a philosophy which endeavored to draw a distinction between immutable divine law and mutable human legislation, or between what was necessary to salvation and what was merely indifferent and politically expedient.[35] Most of the ceremonies fell into this latter category since they were essentially of human origin and they could be abolished or retained depending on their use as rules conducive to religious order and tranquillity. The completed form of *The Bishops' Book*, or the *Institutions of a Christian Man* as the formulary was technically known, was clearly founded upon this distinction, and in the discussion of the jurisdiction of the clergy and the rules of the church the authors were explicit in pointing out that "the greatest part thereof consisteth only in outward ceremonies and such things as be of themselves but mean and indifferent things. That is to say, neither commanded especially in Scriptures nor necessarily contained or implied therein, nor yet expressly repugnant or contrary thereunto. Surely there is no other obedience required of us in this said third part [on ceremonies] but that men may lawfully omit or do otherwise than is prescribed unto us by the said laws and commandments of priests and bishops, so that they do it not in contempt or despite of the said power and jurisdiction, but have some good and reasonable cause so to do, and offend not nor slander not their neighbor in

---

[34] Cranmer, *Works*, No. cxc, "Cranmer to Cromwell" 21 July, 1537, p. 338; see also Latimer, *Sermons and Remains*, No. xx, p. 380.

[35] For further information and Thomas Starkey's use of Melanchthon's philosophy, see Zeeveld, *Foundations of Tudor Policy*, pp. 137-139.

their so doing."[36] Thus the ancient customs, holy days, the worship of saints and images, were reaffirmed as expedient and necessary, but they still lacked divine authority. Likewise the four missing sacraments were rediscovered and incorporated, not as equal to penance, baptism and justification, but because they were "of such antiquity, of such excellence, yea, and of such efficaciousness too, that many graces follow all those persons that reverently take" and use them.[37]

The philosophy of things indifferent was undoubtedly an attempt to discover a *via media* to which both sides could subscribe, but like most compromises under such circumstances it was soon evident that it satisfied no one. The Catholic doctrine had indeed been restated in its entirety, but it was no longer based on divine sanction but on human expediency, and the implication of the theory of things indifferent was perfectly clear: that there was no longer permanence or stability in religious belief, and what was now considered politically necessary might be discarded a few years hence as impracticable. Bishop Latimer expressed both the dissatisfaction of the reformers and the fears of the conservatives when he wrote that he would rather be the poorest parson than continue a bishop "not for anything that I have had to do therein, or can do, but yet forsooth it is a troublesome thing to agree upon a doctrine in things of such controversy, with judgments of such diversity, every man (I trust) meaning well, and yet not all meaning one way. But I doubt not but now in the end we shall

---

[36] P.R.O., S.P. 6, vol. 5, No. 8, pp. 245-246 (*L.P.*, XII, pt. ii [1537], No. 401, sec. 5). This passage is taken from one of the corrected drafts of *The Bishops' Book* and is in "Tunstal's hand and corrected and modified by him." It is interesting to note that almost all of the Bishop's modifications were later incorporated into the final and printed edition; cf. Lloyd, *Formularies*, pp. 107-123 and esp. 114-115.

[37] This description refers specifically to the sacrament of marriage and appears in a special letter of the "Archbishop and bishops of England to all and singular, the King's Highness' loving faithful and obedient subjects." P.R.O., S.P. 6, vol. 6, No. 2, pp. 55-59 (*L.P.*, XII, pt. ii [1537], App. 33). This letter is undated but probably was sent out in July 1537, a month or so before *The Bishops' Book* was published.

agree both one with another, and all with the truth, though some will then marvel." Latimer was giving notice that compromise had been forced for the last time, and he made his position quite clear when he added that he hoped the King would expurgate all that was uncertain and impure, or at least give notice to his subjects that he was aware of such impurities and merely tolerated them for the time being as a concession to "the fraility and gross capacity of his subjects."[38] To the Bishop of Worcester and many of his followers, *The Bishops' Book* was merely a temporary expedient drawn from them for the sake of unity and obedience to their sovereign.

It was the King himself, however, who delivered the final blow to the future success of this uncertain compromise by his refusal to bestow upon it his royal signature. The formulary had been the product of a multitude of minds anxious at all costs to gloss over issues of dangerous disagreement, and both sides had sought escape through vagueness and ambiguity. A host of Lutheran doctrines lay concealed beneath such undefined phrases as the "elect of God" or the use of such words as "exhibited" in describing the presence of the body and blood of Christ in the sacraments.[39] Throughout *The Bishops' Book* the doctrine was essentially Catholic as the Abbé Constant has avowed,[40] but in almost every controversial section the phraseology was sufficiently ambiguous to warrant a Protestant interpretation. Henry was well aware of the deliberateness of the wording of many crucial sections, and in his written correction of the work of his divines he made his disapproval quite clear. In the article on the sacrament of baptism the doctrine of justification by faith was worded as if to imply that the mitigation by penance and good works had little effect on eventual salvation for, said the article, "The penitent

---

[38] Latimer, *Sermons and Remains*, No. xx, "Latimer to Cromwell" (21 July, 1537), p. 380 (*L.P.*, XII, pt. ii [1537], No. 295).

[39] Messenger, *The Reformation, the Mass and the Priesthood*, I, pp. 260-262.

[40] Constant, I, p. 409.

must conceive certain hope and faith that God will forgive him his sins, and repute him justified, and of the number of his elect children, not for the worthiness of any merit or work done by the penitent, but for the only merits of the blood and passion of our Saviour Jesus Christ." The King suggested a significant change in this sentence, adding the two cardinal words "only" and "chiefly." Thus the revised sentence would have read: "The penitent must conceive certain hope and faith that God will forgive him his sins . . . not *only* for the worthiness of any merit or work done by the penitent but *chiefly* for the only merits of the blood and passion of our Saviour Jesus Christ."[41] Cranmer was quick to perceive the fundamental change which such an addition would have made to the sense of *The Bishops' Book* had the King insisted on its incorporation, and he wrote that the two words "may not be put in this place in any wise: for they signify that our election and justification cometh partly of our merits, though chiefly it cometh of the goodness of God. But certain it is, that our election cometh only and wholly of the benefit and grace of God. . . ."[42] Here was the core of the Catholic-Protestant dispute, and when the King suggested giving the new formulary a strongly Catholic interpretation in this key sentence, the reformers were equally uncompromising in their opposition. If the King was alarmed by the Protestant flavor of *The Bishops' Book*, we can well imagine that Bishop Stokesley and many of the other conservatives were even more critical. The astute monarch dexterously avoided taking the responsibility for a formula which obviously satisfied no one, informing his divines that business of state had prevented him from studying their worthy endeavor but that he would take their word for its godliness and would allow its publication

---

[41] Cranmer, *Works*, "Corrections of the *Institution of a Christian Man* by Henry VII with Archbishop Cranmer's annotations," p. 95; cf. Lloyd, *Formularies*, p. 97.
[42] Cranmer, *Works*, p. 95.

under their authority.[43] Thus the *Institutions of a Christian Man* was issued during August of 1537 under the auspices of the synod of bishops while the signature of the King was significantly missing. In fact, the debate continued even after the first volumes were in circulation, and in November George Day, Nicholas Heath, Thomas Thirlby, and John Skip were commissioned to revise the explanation of the Ten Commandments and the articles on purgatory and justification,[44] while the King spent the winter sending personally annotated copies to various members of the Episcopal Bench requesting that they should offer their further criticism, both on his own royal additions and deletions and on the phraseology of much that was open to doubt and confusion.[45]

In one field, however, the conservative element achieved a clear if limited victory. Theologically *The Bishops' Book* was an extension and modification of the Ten Articles, but as a testimony of Tudor social theory it was infinitely more. While the latter were essentially a brief statement of fundamental religious beliefs, the former was an endeavor to translate the Christian creed into social action. Throughout the thirties the disciples of law and order had begun to view with growing alarm the spread of Anabaptist doctrines, and had become convinced that the spreading religious anarchy was slowly undermining social morality and civil stability. When Bishop Longland suggested that there was a connection between the evangelical preaching of Sir Swynnerton and the prevalence of robberies in his bishopric, he was voicing a fear which was common to most of the conservative bishops. Again, one of the most disturbing criticisms of the Ten Articles had been their failure to include the sacrament of marriage as one of the divinely ordained orders of God, and many ecclesias-

---

[43] *Ibid.*, App. IX, p. 469 (*L.P.*, XII, pt. ii [1537], No. 618).

[44] *L.P.*, XII, pt. ii [1537], No. 1122, p. 393.

[45] B.M., Royal 7 C. XVI, No. 40, f. 199; and App. 78, f. 21 (*L.P.*, XIII, pt. i [1538], Nos. 141-142).

tics and civilians were worried that the bonds of matrimony had been permanently weakened as a consequence. Apparently, during the sessions on *The Bishops' Book* this argument had been strongly presented, for the explanation of the sacrament of marriage was issued as a proclamation by the archbishops and bishops to "all and singular, the King's Highness' loving, faithful, and obedient subjects," several months before the completed, printed edition of *The Bishops' Book* was offered for popular consumption. In the proclamation the synod of bishops admitted that they had now decided to add the missing four sacraments, "sorry that some men take occasion to think amiss by cause we left these out when the other articles were devised," and particularly they wished they had included the sacrament of marriage which, though not necessary to salvation, was nevertheless of great "effectiveness" and "excellence."[46] The government presumedly had taken the warning of Doctor Powell seriously, when he complained that evil men were wandering about the realm corrupting "the people with open sinning and ill ensample of living, as he that doth put away his first wife and take another without assent or dispensation of the church." The worthy Doctor had been even more explicit in stating the source of this evil, for, he added, it was especially demoralizing for innocent people when they beheld the King himself indulging in legalized adultery "which doth occasion others that heareth and seeth the same to follow and to do likewise. . . ."[47] There was no escape from the conclusion that the King's divorce had jeopardized the sanctity of the marriage bonds, and though it might be expedient to sanction such actions in a sovereign, the government could never allow similar behavior in the "common sort." In *The Bishops' Book* itself the authors stated their convictions even more categorically and they made it

[46] P.R.O., S.P. 6, vol. 6, No. 2, pp. 55-58 (*L.P.*, XII, pt. ii [1537], App. 33).
[47] *Ibid.*, vol. 3, No. 12, p. 113 (*L.P.*, VI [1533], No. 572, sec. 2).

perfectly clear that the marriage ceremony was instituted by God and "*whom God conjoineth man cannot separate.*"[48] Divorce might be granted by the proper authorities under certain circumstances but all else was condemned as bigamy.

Throughout the *Institutions of a Christian Man*, the Christian faith was carefully interpreted in terms of social conduct, and the Ten Commandments were correlated with the problems of daily life. For instance, the commandment, "Honor thy father and mother" was interpreted to include all levels of obedience, and the people were enjoined to obey "all the laws, proclamations, precepts, and commandments made by their princes and governors." Moreover, the commandment went on to encompass the obligation of reporting anything which might be "to the annoyance or damage of his prince's person or estate. . . . For of conspiracy and treason cometh never no goodness; but infinite hurt, damage, and peril to the common weal."[49] Also the duty due a master by his servant was emphasized, and it was stated as a divine commandment that fathers should remember "how much and how grievously they do offend God" when they bring their children up in "wantonness and idleness, and do not put them forth in time to some faculty, exercise, or labor, whereby they may after get their living, or occupy their life to the profit and commodity of the common weal. . . ."[50] Moreover, the enforcers of law and order were careful to incorporate under the heading of the Eighth Commandment, "Thou shalt not steal," most of the crimes known to a civilized society. Extortion, bribery and simony were condemned while such mercantile crimes as usury, false buying and selling, fraud and counterfeiting were included as being abhorrent to God's law.[51]

In view of the growing appeal of the Anabaptist doctrines of communal ownership, the bishops took pains to state the prevailing belief in the sanctity of private property under

[48] Lloyd, *Formularies*, p. 88.   [49] *Ibid.*, pp. 153-154.
[50] *Ibid.*, p. 156.   [51] *Ibid.*, pp. 163-164.

the guise of the Tenth Commandment. "For . . . this commandment," they wrote, "not only forbiddeth us to desire from our neighbor anything which is his, but by the same we be also commanded gladly to wish and will unto him that he may quietly possess and enjoy all that God hath sent him, be it never so great abundance."[52] Tudor statesmen were not slow to realize the force of the implied sanction of the existing inequality of wealth.

However doubtful the conservative victory in regard to the theological phraseology of *The Bishops' Book* may have been, the *Institutions of a Christian Man* was a clear expression of their social philosophy. Unfortunately, however, it was far from complete, as we shall see when we come to compare it with the second Tudor formulary, *The King's Book* of 1543. Henry himself was worried by the social implications of much of the book, and desired a more discriminating interpretation of many of the religious expressions which were open to serious social mistranslations. In the fourth petition, "give us this day our daily bread," the bishops had given legal sanction to charity saying "thou [good Lord] doth provide for thy poor people that have nothing, by them which have of thy gift sufficient to relieve themselves and others." Henry, however, was alarmed that this statement might be construed to mean that the wanton and idle might expect charity as a right, and he added the administrator's comment that "one thing herein is to be noted, that there be many folk which had rather live by the craft of begging slothfully, than either work or labor for their living; truely, these be none of them of whom we spoke before; for we think it right necessary that such should be compelled by one means or other to serve the world with their bodily labor, thinking it small charity to bestow otherwise alms on them."[53] It is an interesting commentary on con-

[52] *Ibid.*, p. 172.

[53] The copy of *The Bishops' Book* with Henry's annotations which is printed in Cranmer's *Works*, pp. 83-114, is from the Bodleian Library, Oxford. Since the editors had considerable trouble reading this particular an-

ditions in England during the Reformation that government officials felt obliged to reiterate the orthodox and conservative concept of society. And it is quite apparent that the conservative elements within the land had become aware that there was altogether too much truth in Bishop Gardiner's words when he warned the Archbishop that "the vehemence of novelty will flow further than your Grace would admit."[54] In an age when religion and society were intimately associated, novelty in faith could, and often did, breed revolution in society.

The reception of *The Bishops' Book* reflected its creation. It was avowedly a compromise in which neither side placed much faith, and its wording was so ambiguous that members of the same party could claim it as a victory for the old ways or condemn it as heretical. At Raynburn in Kent the advocates of the ancient faith were claiming that the Book "alloweth all the old fashion, and putteth all the knaves of the new learning to silence," and Archbishop Cranmer wrote a personal letter to Sir Thomas Cheyney, the local Justice of the Peace in Kent, accusing him of misleading the people into believing that the old faith had been restored. It is not true, wrote the Archbishop, that ceremonies, the worship of saints, and pilgrimages had been reintroduced into the church in their entirety, "but in very deed the people be restored by this book to their old good usages, although they be not restored to their late abused usages; for the old usage was in the primitive church, and nigh thereunto when the church was most purest. . . ."[55] In a second letter to the same man, Cranmer was even more critical and condemned the justice of "not discerning sincerely things commanded by God and by his word from things ordained by man and grounded upon mere devotion, without any foun-

---

notation (*Ibid.*, p. 108, n. 2), I have used a second copy of *The Bishops' Book* in which the royal comments, though varying in detail, are far more legible. See B.M., Royal 17 CXXX, f. 85.

[54] Gardiner, *Letters*, No. 124, "Gardiner to Cranmer" (1547), p. 308.
[55] Cranmer, *Works*, No. CCII, "Cranmer to a Justice" (1537), pp. 350-351 (*L.P.*, XII, pt. ii, No. 846, Letter 1).

dation and ground of the word of God. . . ."⁵⁶ The church might, with considerable rationalization, maintain the subtle philosophy of "things indifferent" but to the average man the distinction was of little significance. Years before, Martin Luther had written Erasmus warning him of the illusion of any theory of compromise and moderation, and "I may remark," he said, "that, unless I mistake, when you wrote that book you felt how easy it is to write about moderation and blame [my] excesses, but how hard or rather impossible it is to practice what you preach except by a special gift of the Spirit."⁵⁷ What was true when the German monk wrote the Dutch humanist in 1524 was even more apparent in 1538. The bishops had preached moderation only to discover that their flock were unwilling to practice what they preached. In fact, many of the ecclesiastics themselves showed little zeal in their task of making the *Institutions* a working formula. Sampson was quite frank in his disapproval, and though he wrote his friend, Mr. Welles, that "the King's Highness is yet content that the book lately put out . . . by the prelates, should be obeyed," the Bishop destroyed the effect by adding that the formulary should be taught only until "His Majesty shall otherwise order something with a more mature and deliberous council."⁵⁸ Obviously Sampson thought the Book both naive and a temporary compromise. Stephen Gardiner likewise was open in his criticism and did not hesitate to condemn *The Bishops' Book* as a makeshift and common storehouse of ill assorted ideas. The new work had been composed while the Bishop was on government service in France, but was issued under the signature of all the bishops of the realm, and the Bishop of Winchester was outraged that his name should have

---

⁵⁶ *Ibid.*, No. CCIV, "Cranmer to a Justice" (1537), p. 354 (*L.P.*, XII, pt. ii, No. 846, Letter III).

⁵⁷ Luther to Erasmus, 15 April, 1524; printed in Smith, *The Life and Letters of Martin Luther*, p. 205. The book referred to by Luther was Erasmus' as yet unpublished *Diatribe on Free Will*.

⁵⁸ B.M., Cleo. E. v, f. 305 (297) (*L.P.*, XIII, pt. ii [1538], No. 147).

appeared attached to a document which he found strongly objectionable. After perusing the new formulary he dismissed
this effort at moderation and compromise as "a common storehouse, where every man laid up in store such wares as he
liked, and could tell where to find [them] to serve his purpose."[59]

By March of 1539 the religious unity of the nation had so
far deteriorated that in London preachers were openly con-
tradicting the doctrine of *The Bishops' Book* and were treating
the Sacrament of the Altar as if even it were an indifferent
ceremony, necessary and expedient for the time being only.
The bread of the Mass, they said, was merely a symbol of
the body of Christ, and the Mass itself was called a rep-
resentation of Christ's passion and not a sacrifice. The legality
of clerical marriages was preached openly before the King and
his councillors, while images were being destroyed regardless
of whether they were abused or not.[60] In fact it was increasingly manifest to the meanest intelligence that the *Institutions
of a Christian Man* was a complete failure on almost every
level of society.

Both the dictated unity of the Ten Articles and the false
compromise of *The Bishops' Book* had been tried and had
proved themselves inadequate. There now remained only the
choice between the vigorous extension of the Protestant creed
or a return to Catholicism—minus, of course, the Pope. England was not yet ready for the pure light of the gospel, as
the risings in the north had indicated. The average man was
still attached to his patron saint, to the festive celebration of
holy days, and to the association of old and intimate images
and shrines which had for so long been an integral part of his
daily life. The English cared little for the theological niceties
of the relationship of God to man, and they tended to judge

---

[59] Gardiner, *Letters*, No. 125, "Gardiner to Cranmer" (1547), p. 351.
[60] *Original Letters*, II, No. CCLXXXVII, "John Butler and others to Con-
rad Pellican" (8 March, 1539), p. 624 (*L.P.*, XIV, pt. i, No. 466).

their religion by its outward expressions, by ceremonies and time-honored usages. They might accept reform, but the government rightly suspected that the average individual would never put up with the abolition of the faith of his fathers. The pendulum of reform had reached the revolutionary extreme and many men had begun to feel that a swing to the right was indicated.

At no time during Henry's reign did religious issues ever stand alone, and, as Friar Barnes in a moment of rare honesty confessed, Henry was far more interested in politics than in religion.[61] Social considerations, political expediency, the royal supremacy, and diplomatic prudence all united to sully the purity of religious policy. John Hooper, with what must be considered remarkable insight, wrote to his acquaintance, Henry Bullinger, in 1546, predicting that there would be a change in religion and a return to the Gospel of Christ if the Emperor were defeated in "this most destructive war: should the gospel sustain a loss, he [Henry] will then retain his impious mass. . . ."[62] Even such a reformer as Hooper realized that the success or defeat of Protestantism in England depended in large measure upon considerations of foreign policy, and what was true in 1546 can with reason be generalized into a criterion for the whole reign. England's theologically-minded sovereign with chameleon-like agility changed his religious complexion to suit his diplomatic and political designs, and in 1539-40 a host of religious, social and political motives joined together to persuade Henry to adopt a conservative policy in religious affairs.

It is tempting to explain Henry's reign in terms of his many matrimonial plunges and his extraordinary bad luck in his choice of queens. Catherine's dowdiness and barrenness and her blood relationship to the most powerful prince of Christen-

[61] *L.P.*, XVI [1540], No. 106.
[62] *Original Letters*, I, No. XXII, "Hooper to Henry Bullinger" (1546), p. 41.

dom, Emperor Charles V, caused untold misery for many Englishmen and cost More and Fisher their heads. Anne Boleyn's jealousy and ambition, and her questionable carrying-on with an organist who was introduced into her boudoir as a jar of marmalade, and Catherine Howard's illicit relations with her pianist, cost them both their heads and jeopardized the safety and political careers of a host of lesser lights. Catherine Parr's attraction to that even more dangerous lover, Protestantism, Jane Seymour's death shortly after childbirth, and Anne of Cleves' placid and Germanic features, affected, sometimes directly, sometimes superficially, the course of Tudor history. But the influence of these women is easy to exaggerate despite the glitter of their lives. Although Thomas Cromwell made a serious blunder when he argued his monarch into holy wedlock with the little Rhenish princess of Cleves, his basic mistake was diplomatic and only secondarily a miscalculation of Henry's taste in women. His fall and execution in the summer of 1540 were the result of a multitude of causes, and Anne of Cleves, whose looks won for her the uncomplimentary title of "the Mare of Flanders," was merely one of the eddies of the main current which rushed the Vicar-general to his destruction. It is at this point that we must turn to the details of these years, for the influences which resulted in Cromwell's death also paved the way for the victory of the conservative element within the Council and Episcopal Bench, and consequently to the final acceptance of their social and religious policy.

The first step in the swing to the right was taken in Parliament on May 5, 1539, when the Chancellor, Sir Thomas Audley, read the address from the throne. "His Majesty," he said, "desires above all things that diversity of religious opinions should be banished from his dominions; and since this is a thing too arduous to be determined in the midst of so many various judgments, it seems good to him to order a committee of the Upper House to examine opinions, and to report their decisions to the whole Parliament."[63] Here was tacit notice that the efforts at compromise had failed and that the King himself would take a hand in the formulation of a new religious policy. Cromwell, Edward Lee, Thomas Cranmer and six others were appointed to the commission in which the opposing parties were equally divided.[64] If, however, Henry thought that this was the way to attain a new religious settlement he was sadly mistaken, for ten days passed in futile discussion. Then on May 16 for the first time the secular authority stepped in to end the clerical deadlock. The Duke of Norfolk suggested to the Upper House that since a decision on the religious issue was unattainable through a committee of clerics, the questions under debate should be introduced on the floor of the House of Lords and the solution be enforced by penal statute.[65] The steady flow of injunctions, proclamations, and appeals to sobriety and order was to stop; henceforth conformity was to be fortified with the full weight of the civil authority.

Accordingly, the bishops voiced their convictions on the floor of the Upper House, and for three days the debate raged until the prattle of angry tongues was silenced by the person of the King himself. Cranmer, Goodrich, Hilsey, Shaxton, Latimer, and Barlow were induced to give way to Tunstal, Edward Lee, Gardiner, Stokesley, and a host of lesser conservatives, when Henry threw the weight of his authority on the side of conservativism.[66] One bishop at least refused to oblige his sovereign and an excuse was shortly found to bar Shaxton's presence from Parliament on the ground that sev-

---

[63] Smith, *Henry VIII and the Reformation*, p. 164; cf. *Lords' Journal*, I, p. 105.

[64] The following men were on the commission: Cromwell, Cranmer, Edward Lee, John Clerk, Tunstal, Thomas Aldridge, John Salcot, Thomas Goodrich, and Hugh Latimer. *Lords' Journal*, I, p. 105.

[65] *Lords' Journal*, I, p. 109; Smith, *Henry VIII and the Reformation*, p. 165.

[66] B.M., Cleo. E. v, f. 138 (129) (*L.P.*, XIV, pt. i [1539], Nos. 1004, p. 465; 1040).

eral members of his household had been taken with the plague, and the King, it was said, feared to expose his noble lords by permitting the Bishop to retain his seat in the House of Lords.[67] With Shaxton silenced and absent, and the rest of the reformers submitting with ill-concealed distaste, the Act for Abolishing Diversity of Opinion was passed with at least the outward appearance of unanimity during the concluding days of June. "The Whip with Six Strings," as the bill was popularly known, reavowed the doctrine of transubstantiation and communion in one kind, forbade the marriage of the clergy and classified the vow of chastity as one of the laws of God, sanctioned the celebration of private masses and ordered that henceforth auricular confession was to be considered necessary and expedient, if not of divine origin.[68] All six of the strings had been the source of constant argument, but proper belief in these debatable issues was now to be enforced by the double threat of burning at the stake without a chance of a last minute abjuration, and the confiscation of the property of the victims. It is little wonder that such an act sent a shock of terror through the party of reform, and its reception was met with bitter religious polemics. For the first time, the King himself was the subject of their attack. Myconius, one of the German delegates to London in 1538, voiced the disappointment of many Lutherans when he wrote that "Harry only wants to sit as Antichrist in the temple of God, and that Harry should be Pope. The rich treasures, the rich incomes of the Church, these are the Gospel According to Harry."[69] The reformers had suddenly discovered that more sordid considerations than the pure light of the gospel filled the breast of Bluff King Hal. They were well aware, as Luther said in 1540, that "what Juncker Heintz wills must be an article of faith [for Englishmen] for life and death,"[70] but for once they

[67] P.R.O., S.P. 1, vol. 152, p. 102 (*L.P.*, XIV, pt. i [1539], No. 1157).
[68] *Ibid.*, pp. 15-22 (*L.P.*, XIV, pt. i [1539], No. 1065).
[69] Rupp, *English Protestant Tradition*, p. 117 (no reference given).
[70] *L.P.*, XVI [1540], No. 106.

themselves were feeling the bite of that double-edged doctrinal sword.

Despite the violent criticism of the Protestants, the Act for Abolishing Diversity of Opinion, which William Turner referred to as "Gardiner's Gospel," was welcome to a nation still Catholic at heart, and the sight of their sovereign actually entering the arena of theological dispute to fulfill his pledge as Defender of the Faith appealed strongly to the average man. Most of England probably agreed with John Hussy when he wrote Lady Lisle in May that there was "good hope here that an Act will be passed, touching the Sacrament of the Altar, that people may be not so busy thereafter. . . . It will be the wholesomest Act ever passed."[71] However, the canny French ambassador, Marillac, was not convinced that Henry had committed himself to a Catholic stand solely for the sake of his simple, loving subjects. The Frenchman wrote his sovereign that it was true that "the people show great joy at the King's declaration touching the Sacrament, being much more inclined to the old religion than to the new opinions,"[72] but, he later added, the cardinal motive behind the new Act was to satisfy "the Christian powers who might take occasion to attack him," and to undermine the papal efforts at uniting France and Spain in an alliance against England on the pretext "that they [the English] were all heretics and infidels."[73] Diplomacy as well as religion was behind the "Bloody Act," for now Henry could with a reasonable show of truth claim that he was still orthodox in faith even though he denied the papal supremacy.

Though Latimer became a "bell without a clapper" as he called himself when he was induced to resign from the Episcopal Bench,[74] and Shaxton was peremptorily dismissed from his see, the immediate effect of the new bill, except for a

---

[71] *L.P.*, xiv, pt. i [1539], No. 1004.   [72] *Ibid.*, No. 1092.
[73] *Ibid.*, Nos. 1260, 1261.
[74] Becket, *The English Reformation*, p. 177.

momentary scare, went little further than to make it difficult for John Hilsey, Bishop of Rochester, to find godly preachers who were willing to risk a sermon at Paul's Cross.[75] Political reaction had not kept pace with religious conservatism, and both Cranmer and Cromwell maintained their influence at court. There is considerable truth in the assertion of Professor Pollard that both the Archbishop and the Vicar-general systematically undermined the effectiveness of the act,[76] and it was soon patent that there could be no permanent stability in religion if government officials were not willing to enforce what Parliament had enacted.[77] But, for the time being at least, it did not suit the royal pleasure to insist upon a strict application of the bill, and those who were convicted during the first rush of enthusiasm were acquitted in July by a general pardon.[78]

Cromwell's presence was still required in 1539, for the destruction of the great abbeys begun that year had not been completed, while on the diplomatic front the kaleidoscopic fluctuation of the international balance of power suddenly confronted Henry with a new threat of invasion. In February, before the passing of the Six Articles, Charles and Francis had begun to show every sign of reaching an agreement against England,[79] and it was during the following uncertain months that Henry had insisted on a restatement of English religious conservatism. At the same time, however, he allowed Cromwell to explore tentatively the possibilities of an alliance with the German princes through a marriage with Anne of Cleves. Fortunately for England, the two Catholic powers of Europe soon made it perfectly clear that they neither trusted one

[75] P.R.O., S.P. 1, vol. 152, p. 207 (*L.P.*, XIV, pt. i [1539], No. 1297).
[76] Pollard, *Thomas Cranmer*, pp. 132-133.
[77] Burckhardt, the Lutheran envoy, wrote Melanchthon in October of 1539 that the reformers were "in greater favour than ever, and the papistical faction . . . has nowise obtained its hoped-for tyranny, nor, God willing, ever will in England." *L.P.*, XIV, pt. ii [1539], No. 423.
[78] Smith, *Henry VIII and the Reformation*, p. 167.
[79] *L.P.*, XIV, pt. i [1539], No. 337.

another nor desired to bring on a crisis with England,[80] and though the policy of religious reaction was completed in May of 1539, the matrimonial angling with the Germans was abruptly called off. Then, in the late summer, rumors began to spread that His Catholic Majesty, Charles of Spain, had been invited by that Most Christian King, the sovereign of France, to pay a state visit to Paris and place the safety of his person in the hands of his traditional enemy. Serious as the offer was, it was infinitely more alarming when Charles showed every sign of taking such an unprecedented step and accepting the hand and friendship of his ancient rival.[81] To Henry this could mean little else than the beginning of an alliance between the two Catholic countries against the heretics in England, and as a result the negotiations with the Duchy of Cleves for the hand of the German princess was quickly renewed. Cromwell's Protestant policy seemed suddenly to have been vindicated and the actual marriage alliance was signed on October fourth of the same year. However, Anne did not arrive in England until late December, nor meet her future husband till the third day of January. In the meantime the reason for the alliance had vanished and though Charles did indeed visit his royal cousin at Paris, the spectre of a Catholic alliance seemed to go no further than lavish courtesy and artificial expressions of lasting friendship. Thus Henry found himself tied to an unstable and minority party in Europe and burdened with a queen who was not to his royal taste, while no diplomatic compensations were discernible.

The full responsibility for the diplomatic and marital blunder fell upon the Vicar-general, whose days were now numbered by the time it would take to arrange a speedy divorce with Henry's fourth queen. From January 1540 to Cromwell's fall in June, the political barometer showed alarming inclinations to violent and unpredictable oscillation. Stephen Gardi-

---

[80] *Ibid.*, Nos. 669, 804, 907, 908.
[81] *L.P.*, XIV, pt. ii [1539], No. 508.

ner had been recalled from France in September of 1538 where he had been exiled as a man so opposed to the Cromwellian policy that his presence in England was considered a threat to the Vicar-general's supremacy.[82] Since his return the Bishop had for the most part remained in his diocese and was not to be placed permanently on the Council until his rival's fall, but in April 1540 Winchester's prestige was sufficient to bring about the destruction of one of Cromwell's factotums, Robert Barnes. The Friar had made the grave error of attacking the Bishop by name in a sermon he preached in February. He had based his lesson upon the uncomplimentary allusion that Gardiner was an ungodly gardener of evil herbs in the garden of Scriptures, and not unnaturally Winchester took offense at such a comparison and brought it to the attention of the King. It is indicative of the political shift of the times that Henry should have interested himself in a question of personal slander. Barnes was ordered to recant and apologize; two things which he signally failed to do, and consequently he was imprisoned in the Tower on the third of April.[83] Political observers were quick to interpret the fall of Cromwell's minion as auguring a precarious future for the Vicar-general, and Marillac wrote home on April tenth that "there will be seen in this country a great change in many things: which this King begins to make in his ministers, recalling those he had rejected and degrading those he had raised. Cromwell is tottering. . . ." The ambassador also reported the rumor that Gardiner, Tunstal, and probably Clerk, all outspoken opponents of the Reformation party, were about to be returned to the Privy Council.[84] In the previous December

---

[82] *L.P.*, XII, pt. ii [1537], No. 960, "Report on the conversation of Edward Palades, yeoman," who was reported to have said that Bishop Gardiner "was kept abroad for a purpose, for if he were here many things would be brought to pass otherwise."

[83] For the details of this conflict see: Muller, *Stephen Gardiner*, ch. XIII "The End of the Vicar General and the Fate of Friar Barnes."

[84] *L.P.*, XV [1540], No. 486.

both Sampson and Gardiner had objected to the use of Barnes as an English representative abroad since, they said, he was a heretic, but during the Christmas month Charles was still at Paris and Cromwell still master of the political situation at home, and the two men had lost their seats on the council as a result of their opposition.[85] By April the pendulum had so far shifted that Tunstal was being considered for Cromwell's post,[86] and the Vicar-general was reduced to currying favor with his ancient rival, the Bishop of Winchester.

In June, however, the political complexion of the nation made one final convulsive swing to the left before settling down to a conservative victory. All political prognostications were upset by the imprisonment of Richard Sampson. During the last days of May 1540, the Bishop had been offered the newly created See of Westminster, a post which constituted a considerable promotion compared to his old diocese of Chichester. Exactly what occurred between the twenty-ninth of May and the first of June is still a mystery, but the political pendulum must have moved with whirlwind speed, for the French ambassador reported on June first that Sampson had been appointed Bishop of Westminster "with all solemnity" and "two hours later was led to the Tower as accused of treason, and before night was past his goods were confiscated, and he [was] left with life only, which he shall lose immediately according to the usual penalty decreed to high treason, as horrible to tell as frightful to see."[87] Sampson had given his assent to his elevation sometime before May,[88] and on the

---

[85] P.R.O., S.P. 1, vol. 155, ff. 190-192 (*L.P.*, XIV, pt. ii [1539], No. 750, sec. I and II); printed in Sturge, *Cuthbert Tunstal*, App. XVI, p. 369.

[86] *L.P.*, XV [1540], No. 486. On 10 April, 1540, Marillac wrote Montmorency that "it is said on good authority that Tunstal, Bishop of Durham, a person in great esteem with the learned, shall be vicar general of the spirituality, and that the Bishop of Belde [John Clerk, Bishop of Bath and Wells] shall be Keeper of the Privy Seal, which are Cromwell's two principal titles."

[87] *L.P.*, XV [1540], No. 737.

[88] P.R.O., Augmentation Office, Misc. Books, vol. 24, f. 34 (*L.P.*, XIV, pt. ii [1539], No. 429, p. 152). This book for a "scheme of Bishoprics"

twenty-ninth of that month his old benefice, the Deanery of Saint Paul's, was declared void "by the resignation and preferment" of Richard, Bishop of Chichester.[89] Presumedly then, the sudden change in policy must have occurred on or about the thirtieth of May. There was little doubt in the minds of contemporary observers that Cromwell's fine Italian hand was behind the Bishop's troubles, for Thomas Thirlby, the close friend of Cranmer and client of the Vicar-general, was almost immediately suggested as a candidate for the now vacant See of Westminster.[90] Marillac never doubted that Sampson's attainder for treason was primarily a strategic maneuver aimed at Stephen Gardiner, and he wrote his master that "things are brought to such a pass that either Cromwell's party or that of the Bishop of Winchester must succumb. Although both are in great authority and favor of the King their master, still the course of things seems to incline to Cromwell's side, as Winchester's chief friend, the said Dean of the Chapel [i.e. Sampson], is down, and the Bishop of Canterbury, his chief adversary, appointed in his place preacher and reader at St. Paul's where he has begun to put forward the contrary of what Winchester preached there in Lent last. Moreover, Dr. Barnes heretofore made prisoner is . . . to be soon released; and another doctor named Latimer, who last year forfeited his bishopric rather than subscribe what the others had concluded conformably to the ecclesiastical constitutions,

---

is undated. In the *L.P.* it is incorporated with documents for October 1539. Whatever the exact date may be, Sampson signified to "Mr. Chancellor of the King's Augmentation" that he was willing to take the See of Westminster in exchange for Chichester as the King desired.

[89] *L.P.*, xv [1540], No. 831, grant 13.

[90] *L.P.*, Add. [1540], No. 1457. This is a list of the new bishoprics with the names of possible candidates for election. The *L.P.* say that it was probably drawn up about April or May of 1540. However, until the last few days of May, Sampson, not Thirlby, was bishop-designate of Westminster. Since the list clearly gives Thirlby as the royal choice for the new see, it was probably composed in the middle of June when Thirlby's name first appears as "Bishop elect of Westminster." See *L.P.*, xv [1540], No. 826, sec. 19, 20.

is recalled, and will very shortly be anew made bishop." Not unnaturally, the Frenchman was baffled by the behavior of the English, and, with Gallic exasperation, concluded that the British were beyond analysis, "so great is the inconsistency of the English."[91]

But an even greater example of English inconsistency was in store for the puzzled ambassador, for on the tenth of June, less than two weeks after Sampson's imprisonment, Thomas Cromwell was marched off to the Tower accused of high treason and heresy. This time there was no last minute reprieve, and the man who had guided the course of the Reformation for some eight years, and who had only three months before been elevated to the position of Earl of Essex, was executed on the twenty-eighth of July, 1540. With the Vicar-general's death, and with the exponents of reform silenced and terrified, the way was prepared for the political as well as the religious return of conservatism. Men such as Heath, Thirlby, Bonner, Sampson, Day, and Skip, who had hesitated to oppose Cromwell during the decade of the thirties, but who had become convinced of the dangers of his policy, were now promoted to positions of governmental and administrative importance. Thirlby and Heath joined the Council in October 1540, while George Day was appointed Bishop of Chichester in 1543. Edmund Bonner made his peace with his old professional rival, Stephen Gardiner, while the Bishop's old friend, Thomas Wriothesley, returned to the conservative fold and was selected as Lord Chancellor on the death of Sir Thomas Audeley in May of 1544. Richard Sampson was promoted to the See of Coventry and Lichfield as compensation for his deprivation, and Cuthbert Tunstal, the oldest and probably the most respected leader of the conservative party, combined the duties of bishop and lawyer, being inaccurately described by Marillac as "first secretary."[92] Finally, Stephen Gardiner, the wiliest bishop of them all, became the King's

---

[91] *L.P.*, xv [1540], No. 737.   [92] *Ibid.*, No. 804, p. 378.

chief councillor, and, as rumor had it, was referred to by Henry as "his own bishop."[93] Though Henry did not always listen to the advice of his conservative majority, and though reform continued in certain instances, the political creed from 1540 until the King's death on the twenty-eighth of January, 1547, was essentially that of the conservative party—the doctrine of human prudence.

[93] *L.P.*, XIV, pt. i [1539], No. 662.

CHAPTER VIII

"THE NEW SOPHISTRY" (1540-1546)

To those men of the sixteenth century who placed political reality before religious idealism and who considered social
security more essential than doctrinal purity, the decade of the
thirties had afforded proof that the Reformation had given
birth to a monster, to a blind Samson whose undisciplined
strength was destroying both the pillars of the temple of God
and the citadel of the crown itself. If England was to escape
the example of the intestine wars of Germany and the humilia-
tion of Bohemia, hot-gospelers and wanton and unbridled social reformers would have to be curbed; Tudor society could
not afford the luxury of alehouse soliloquizing and Hyde Park
orating. "The Whip with Six Strings" had been enacted in
the spring of 1539 by a secular authority which was unwilling
that the extirpation of abuses should result in religious anarchy, and it was clear to all that the fall of the Vicar-general
just a year later was a delayed political expression of the
growing fear that the collapse of religious authority might be
a prologue to social revolution.

The Protestants were not slow to appreciate the motives
which underlay the political and religious changes of the turn
of the decade, and their wrath fell upon Bishops Stokesley and
Gardiner as the most outspoken exponents of the doctrine of
cautious expediency. "Do London and Winchester think they
are bringing a new philosophy down from Heaven?" asked
Melanchthon of Cranmer in March of 1539. "Hitherto we
have waged war with the old sophistry of the monks. Now
a new sophistry is brought forward, with powerful supporters
who measure and corrupt religions by human prudence,
which, if it gains strength, will produce a dreadful confusion

in religion and will engender a pestilent and pernicious custom and method."[1] The German divine was correct in suggesting that the party of reform had more to fear from worldly statesmen and trained civilian administrators than from the sophistry of the monks, but he grossly misjudged the character and strength of the opposition in assuming that the gospel according to Stephen Gardiner was either new or original. Men who saw in religion a divine sanction to social obligations and who considered that heresy and sedition were different sides of the same phenomenon were not peculiar to the latter years of Henry's reign. Long before, in 1521, the civilian-trained Archbishop of Canterbury, William Warham, had written to his equally astute rival, Cardinal Wolsey, that he had imprisoned a certain priest by the name of Sir Adam Bradshaw for removing "writings and seals as were set up at the Abbey of Boxley against the ill opinions of Martin Luther," but since then the Archbishop had been informed that the priest had also been spreading about London "seditious bills against the King's Grace most honorable council and other estates of this realm," and "because his offense in that behalf is of more weight than the pulling down and breaking of the said writings and seals," he had decided to send the culprit to the Cardinal "to be ordered further as ye shall think good."[2] Heresy was bad enough but treason was infinitely worse, and Warham had little doubt that the two were intimately related. Thus when Stephen Gardiner some seventeen years later warned his sovereign that "if he proceeds with the Reformation it will lead to commotion and the principal lords of England will be against him,"[3] he was voicing a fear common

---

[1] *Corpus Reformatorum*, III, No. 1790, "Melanchthon to Cranmer" (30 March, 1539), pp. 676-679. (*L.P.*, XIV, pt. i [1539], No. 631.) Melanchthon was an astute political observer, for this letter was written a month before the passage of the Six Articles and more than a year before Cromwell's fall from power.

[2] *Archaeologia Cantiana*, I (1858), "Warham to Wolsey" (16 June, 1521), p. 14 (*L.P.*, III, pt. i [1521], Mo. 1353).

[3] *Corpus Reformatorum*, III, No. 1852, "Bucer to Philip, Landgrave of

to all statesmen on whose shoulders rested the responsibility of government. As legalists and constitutionalists, as servants of the crown whose relations to the church were primarily those of a pensioner, the conservatives of the Episcopal Bench feared heresy, not because they were religious reactionaries, but because they were statesmen who perceived behind heresy the spectre of sedition and civil war.

It was during the years from the fall of Thomas Cromwell in 1540 to the death of the King early in 1547 that the disciples of political expediency and religious retrenchment were in control. The doctrine of conservatism was the spirit behind the legislation of these years, and it found its clearest exposition in Henry's final religious formula, *A Necessary Doctrine and Erudition for Any Christian Man*, published in 1543. But before turning to *The King's Book*, as the *Necessary Doctrine* was more popularly known, and to the history of the conservative supremacy, we must lay down the principles and premises on which the gospel of human prudence rested, principles which were conceived and developed by men whose training was in the Court of the Arches and the court of kings, and whose profession was diplomacy and administration.

When in 1522 John Clerk, Bishop of Bath and Wells, knelt before Pope Clement VII and presented King Henry's book against the pernicious doctrines of Martin Luther, he unwittingly voiced a philosophy of action which has since been echoed and reechoed by conservatives the world over. "Oh, most abominable and most execrable villainy of man!" he said, "What intolerable blasphemies, from an heap of calumnies and lies, without any *Law*, *Method*, or *Order*, does he [Luther] utter against God and his servants, in this book?"[4] To Gardiner, Tunstal, Sampson, and Clerk, the triple principles of

---

Hesse" (16 September, 1539), p. 775 (*L.P.*, XIV, pt. ii [1539], No. 186).

[4] John Clerk, "Oration" printed as a preface to Henry VIII, *Assertio Septem Sacramentorum*, 4th page. The italicized words are in block letters in the original.

law, method, and order were the abiding rules of human conduct, considerations which had been bred in them through years of legal training and a lifetime spent in the service of the state. These were precepts which colored their thinking, determined their actions, and made them determined opponents of reformers who, in an excess of zeal and idealism, were willing to sacrifice all order, all legality, and all method in order to attain their ends. Translated into terms of personalities, the full chasm which had opened up between the conservatives and the reformers was strikingly and ironically expressed by John Skip in a letter to Matthew Parker, the young Dean of Stokes and later the Elizabethan Archbishop of Canterbury. "I commend me heartily unto you," wrote the Bishop, "thanking you . . . for your last letters, wherein I perceive that the old and busy diligence in your new busy matters continueth still amongst you. We of the Convocation, by the reason of long absence from you, are decayed in quickness of wit, and so are become more dull and slow in our proceedings. Ye be hot and hasty: we be cold and tardy. We think that a great quantity of our qualities would do much amongst you, and a little portion of your qualities were enough for us. Ye are so prudent and expert in all things that ye need never to use deliberation though your matters were greater than they be, but we, for lack of your properties, are fain to respect and consult in all matters that we entreat of. Therefore, seeing this diversity between us and you, ye cannot blame us though we proceed diversely."[5] The cautious statesman is here criticizing the youthful zealot, and Skip showed remarkable insight when he concluded that differences in approach would produce diversity of action. The Bishop had recognized an essential fact, that the reformers with their terror-stricken consciences and preoccupation with salvation could never appreciate the earthly motives of the conservatives.

[5] Parker, *Correspondence*, No. IX, "John Skypp to Matthew Parker," p. 9 (*L.P.*, XV [1540], No. 663).

There could be no meeting of minds between the two parties when John Hooper warned "of this foolish and deceitful collusion, to think a man may serve God in spirit secretly to his conscience, although outwardly with his body and bodily presence he cleave, for civil order, to such rites and ceremonies as now be used contrary to God and his word. Be assured that whatsoever he be that giveth this counsel, shall be before God able to do you no more profit than the fig-leaves did unto Adam."[6]

Steeped in the law, the conservatives had a deep respect for tradition and the self-imposed rules of human society, and the reformers were not slow to realize the threat which such an attitude of mind presented toward any policy which advocated widespread change and the disruption of time-honored customs. Peter Martyr in writing to Henry Bullinger clearly recognized, even if he failed to appreciate, the conservative point of view, and he warned that his party was being opposed by a solid phalanx of lawyers who saw in the uprooting of ancient modes of thought and action a danger to all human authority, both ecclesiastical and secular. "There are certainly very many obstacles," he wrote, "especially the number of our adversaries, the lack of preachers, and the gross vices of those who profess the gospel; besides the worldly prudence of some parties who think it quite right that religion should be purified, but are willing only to make as few alterations as possible; for feeling as they do, and thinking as *civilians*, they consider that any great changes would be dangerous to the state."[7] Here, in fact, was the attitude of many traditionalists, men who were willing to countenance reform, but who stopped short when they perceived that reform was more dangerous to the fabric of society than the thing abused. Edmund Bonner expressed this same concern when he condemned the destruc-

---

[6] Hooper, *Later Writings*, No. XXXIII, "Another letter to certain godly persons" (14 June, 1554), p. 596.

[7] *Original Letters*, II, No. CCXXVIII, "Peter Martyr to Henry Bullinger" (1 June, 1550), p. 482. The italics are my own.

tion of the monasteries, not because it involved the desecration of sacred land but because the government had sanctioned the "unshameless breaking of the dead men's testaments, and their most godly intents and ordinances. . . ."[8] To a man who was primarily a lawyer and only secondarily a church official, the breach of legal contract pursuant to the fall of the great abbeys and chantries was infinitely more serious than sacrilege. The conservatives, as we have already seen, did not necessarily oppose the dissolution of the holy orders as a means of abolishing abuse, and in many cases they were outspoken advocates of limited reform, but it is quite evident from Bonner's comment that the Bishop of London, for one, considered their destruction a dangerous legal precedent. The Bishop's remark upon the abolition of the monasteries was not, however, the only occasion on which he voiced his opinion in regard to the legality of the Reformation, and in 1549, at his trial under Edward he became involved in an argument with Thomas Cranmer which epitomizes the depth of the gulf which existed between the two parties. From the standpoint of the government, Bonner's behavior during his deprivation was both arrogant and rebellious, for he prolonged and confused the question of his disobedience by raising a host of legal technicalities concerning the validity of the evidence brought against him. Thomas Cranmer, in the face of what must have seemed to him to be a series of pointless arguments, finally lost his temper and said to the Bishop: "If my matter and cause be good, what should I care who accuses me, yea although he were the devil in Hell?" Though Bonner was undoubtedly convinced of the justice of his cause, he not unnaturally insisted upon the legality of the conduct of his opponents and he claimed that the issue at stake was not purely a matter of godliness but of the "King's law used in the realm." "Well, my Lord," answered the Archbishop, "ye be too full of your law: I would wish you had less knowledge in

[8] Bonner, *Homilies*, f. 42.

that law, and more knowledge in God's law, and your duty."[9]
The legalist and the prophet had met and found no common
ground on which to agree, for the source of the knowledge of
one was earthly, of the other, divine.

Though many of the conservatives were canonists and civilians, they were also administrators of a complicated bureaucratic machine in which a wide variety of problems were daily
thrust upon them. The study of law gave them a deep regard
for constitutionality, but the exigencies of administration developed in them a flexibility which at times bordered upon
pragmatism. "Good is not good, when it is not well done, to
which well doing, time is a special circumstance."[10] These are
the words of the most prudent of all the disciples of human
prudence, Stephen Gardiner, and it is obvious that the Bishop
of Winchester considered that neither goodness nor justice
had meaning unless related to time and space, and that method
was just as important as the principle applied. The contemporary historian, John Hayward, once remarked of Nicholas
Heath that he was a man "who esteemed anything privately
unlawful, which was not publicly beneficial and good."[11] The
historian's judgment was not misplaced, for Bishop Heath
once went on record as saying that he considered that "necessity knows no law."[12] Again, Richard Sampson, though never
a lover of change, confessed a similar pliability when he wrote
to Thomas Cromwell that "Truth it is, my good Lord, that
surely I am not very friendly to novelties except that necessity, or a great expedient cause require it."[13] These conservative bishops may have been traditionalists, but they were rarely

[9] Foxe, v, "The second appearance of Bonner in the Chapel of Lambeth
before the Archbishop and other commissioners," p. 761.

[10] Gardiner, *Detection of the Devils Sophistrie* (1546), f. cxxxii.

[11] Hayward, *Annals of the First Years of the Reign of Elizabeth*, Cam.
Soc. VII (1840), p. 13.

[12] Burnet, IV, No. XXI, "The resolution of several bishops and divines of
some questions concerning the sacraments," question 13, p. 129.

[13] B.M., Cleo. E. v, f. 307 (299) (*L.P.*, XIII, pt. ii [1538], No. 278);
printed in Strype, *Ecc. Mem.*, I, pt. ii, No. XCII, p. 379.

absolutists, and if sufficient cause were shown almost all of them were willing to change both law and custom to meet the facts of government.

The gospel according to the conservatives was a predilection for the requirements of expediency, and if good was capable of coming from evil, they did not hesitate to sanction it. The church might be corrupt, worship superstitious, but better a little evil, a little laxity, than an irate and restless populace. Hugh Latimer, as we have already noted, was not fabricating the philosophy of the conservative bishops when he said that these apostles of earthly wisdom were whispering into the royal ear " 'It is but a little abuse, and it may be easily amended. But it should not be taken in hand at the first, for fear of trouble or further inconveniences.' "[14] John Skip in a sermon preached at the Chapel Royal in 1536 voiced this same sentiment in slightly different words, when he warned that "they that be a king's councillor have much more need to take heed that they go not about to make any renovations or alterations in civil matters that have been instituted for the common wealth by good men, for if any such thing should be taken away or altered, the community will murmur and grumble at it." Skip, however, did not stop merely at expressing a warning, but offered a startling and original scheme to prevent zealous reformers from meddling with the practical application of orderly government. He suggested that England adopt the system of one ancient nation which had been "much troubled and vexed with renovations and alterations in civil matters pertaining to their commonwealth." "They could never be quiet," he exclaimed, "but they were vexed by alteration upon alteration and statute upon statute until such time as they devised and made a very goodly and brief statute for the remedy and redress thereof. And that was this. They made a law or act that no man should bring into their parliament house any bill for the alteration of any civil matter

[14] Latimer, *Sermons*, p. 69.

concerning their commonwealth, but he should bring also a rope about his neck, and the people should lay their hands upon the rope to the intent, when the bill was read, they might pull the rope and strangle him if they proved that it was against their commonwealth. And so they were eased and delivered from alterations [for a] long time after, for there was no man that durst bring into their parliament house any such bill by the space of a hundred years. . . ."[15] Evidently John Skip as well as Nicholas Heath considered that no act was lawful unless it was publicly beneficial.

The Protestant stand, however, in regard to this issue was clear and uncompromising, and to men like Nicholas Ridley and Thomas Cranmer there was no doubt that the "license to sin was sin."[16] The wrath of the reformers towards those who judged law in terms of expediency was bitter and determined, and William Turner actually went so far as to accuse Bishop Gardiner of protecting houses of ill repute on the grounds of human prudence. "But Stephen master steward of the stewes, Priapus and keeper of the Pope's gardens," he ridiculed, "peradventure will defend his tenants, and say we uphold the stewes for the avoiding of a further inconvenience. If there were no stewes in London seeing there are so many wyveles and wanton courtiers there, there would great violence be offered unto men's wives and much more adultery should reign than reigneth now." Whether or not Master Gardiner actually advocated brothels for this reason is not recorded, but the argument is as old as man, and certainly the Bishop would not have hesitated to wink at a lesser evil in order to prevent a worse. But to the puritanical author such worldly considerations could not change the moral sinfulness of prostitution, and he concluded that "this politic answer will

[15] P.R.O., S.P. 6, vol. 1, No. 3, "The sense of the most special and principle part which Master Skyppe brought in his sermon," p. 20 (*P.L.*, x [1536], No. 615, sec. 4).
[16] Burnet, iv, "The Journal of King Edward's Reign," p. 214.

not serve, for Saint Paul saith . . . evil is not to be done that good may ensue there upon."[17] The controversy between the two parties was essentially one of relative values, and when the writer of this accusation made the suggestion that the English people were "spiritual Israelites"[18] the lordly Winchester must have given a skeptical chuckle, for Stephen Gardiner had little doubt that his fellow man was motivated by base and mortal instincts and that the countenance of a little more evil in the form of controlled prostitution could hardly injure him.

The advocates of what the reformers preferred to call "belly wisdom" had small regard for the intellectual capacity of the average man. Such men were trained in an authoritarian regime, and they expected the common man to do as he was told. When Stephen Gardiner addressed himself to his reader in his attack on Protestantism entitled *A Detection of the Devils Sophistrie* and said: "Believe not every spirit, and mistrust thine own judgment above the reach of thy capacity" he was reiterating a cardinal principle of Tudor government.[19] Authority came from above, not from within the individual, and the principle applied to religion as well as to the state. Bishop Bonner was equally scornful of imprudent preachers who migrated about the country teaching "the zely people" that individual judgment was more to be valued than the authority of the church.[20]

It was not for the "common sort" to question the source of jurisdiction or to decide the justice of a question in dispute. To men who were steeped in the problems of Tudor bureaucracy, order and authority were the basic principles of society, and they tended to judge all things, even religion, in terms of the secular problems of orderly government. The sardonic description of one reformer that the conservative

---

[17] Turner, *The Huntyng of the Romyshe Foxe* (1543), pp. 82-83.
[18] *Ibid.*, p. 84.
[19] Gardiner, *A Detection of the Devils Sophistrie* (1546), f. ii.
[20] Bonner, *Homilies*, f. 39.

bishops were "earthly men, and therefore they have an earthly god to serve at hand . . ."[21] was essentially true, for such men were creatures of a secular existence and their views on religion were accordingly obscured by the earthly considerations of mortal men. They saw in the church and its vast array of traditions and customs a bulwark to secular authority and social order. The church in its spiritual capacity might be of divine origins, but in its objective forms it was a social phenomenon as essential to the maintenance of civil stability as the crown itself. It is small wonder then that the conservatives were convinced that the growth of Protestantism in destroying ecclesiastical authority was endangering civil jurisdiction as well.

The association between ecclesiastical and secular jurisdiction in the mind of Bishop Gardiner was apparent when he consulted with the heretic, William Umpton, who had been imprisoned in 1532 for asking why St. Thomas à Becket was more a saint than Robin Hood. The case was undoubtedly a trifling one, but the Bishop took it seriously and asked Umpton why he did not also doubt and question "the King's right and title of lands and goods forfeit to his Highness by the offenders of his law. . . ?"[22] The right of the crown to seize the property of criminals was nothing more than a time-honored custom which had acquired the strength of law, and it was clear to the socially conscious Bishop that if men began to question the source of ecclesiastical authority they might well move on to doubt the basis of royal jurisdiction as well. To Stephen Gardiner each stone of the clerical structure had its human implication, and even the worship of images in-

---

[21] Gardiner, *De Vera Obedientia . . . with the Preface of Edmunde Boner*, Roane, 26 October, 1553. This is a relatively rare edition of Gardiner's work since it contains the so-called Preface of the "Translator" who was probably John Bale. This preface has been omitted from the more recent editions of the English translation because it is usually considered too outspoken for modern ears. The edition has no pagination and the quotation is taken from Bale's preface.

[22] P.R.O., S.P. 1, vol. 71, f. 2 (*L.P.*, v [1532], No. 1271).

volved an attitude of mind which was essential to the maintenance of law and order. "For the destruction of images,"
he wrote to Captain Vaughan in May of 1547, "containeth an
enterprise to subvert religion and the state of the world with
it; and especially the nobility, who, by images, set forth
and spread abroad, to be read of all people, their lineage
and parentage, with remembrance of their state and acts. And
the pursuivant carrieth not on his breast the King's name written in such letters as a few can spell, but such as all can read,
be they never so rude, being great known letters in images of
three lions and three fleur-de-lis, and other beasts holding
those arms. And he that cannot read the scripture written
about the King's great seal, either because he cannot read at
all, or because the wax doth not express it, yet he can read
St. George on horseback on the one side, and the King sitting
in his majesty on the other side; and readeth so much written
in those images as, if he be an honest man, he will put off
his cap."[23] The issue at stake was not merely religious symbolism, but the maintenance of social respect for the office of
royalty and the protection of class distinctions. Both were matters of mental discipline, and Gardiner was convinced that if
the practice of symbolic worship in the church were allowed
to disappear, it would have serious repercussions in other
spheres.

   Richard Sampson gave a similar warning when he wrote
to the clergy of his see that the people must give "respect to
such as are the ministers, not for their person but for their
office."[24] It was the office of state, both clerical and secular,
which had to be secured at all costs if deference for government and authority was to be maintained. The man who filled
the office might be corrupt, as might the noble who claimed
a distinguished coat of arms, but both the office and the rank
were expected to be objects of reverence for the common

[23] Gardiner, *Letters*, No. 119, p. 274.
[24] B.M., Cleo. E. v, f. 302 (294) (*L.P.*, XIII, pt. ii [1538], No. 278).

people. Veneration and discipline were the dual obligations
of religion and society, and many of the conservatives regarded the aura of religion which surrounded many secular
posts to be a valuable aid to social obedience and regimenta-
tion. In fact, the first criticism which the Bishop of Winchester made of the new ordinal on the consecration of priests
in 1550 was to point out that if the government denied the
sacrificial nature of the clerical power there would be no one
to anoint the king with divine authority. The new order of
consecration, he said, "touched the honor and dignity of the
King's person and succession, who, by this order, should never
after be anointed, having no Samuel left to execute it. . . ."[25]
To the reformers ecclesiastical laws stood or fell on their own
merits, but for the conservatives clerical authority could never
be divorced from the functions of government and the problems of temporal obedience.

The most fundamental complaint which the conservatives
had to make of the doctrine of the "New Learning" was its
emphasis upon predestination, for they soon perceived in such
a fatalistic creed the destruction of all moral responsibility
for human action. As humanists, they were unable to understand a God who denied to his creatures the exercise of free
will, for to such men the god of heaven and earth was humane
and merciful, and it was inconceivable that he should pre-
destine men to sin and then punish them for what he himself
had ordained. The crown of human action was the exercise
of choice, and its greatest jewel was the knowledge that human virtue would find its reward in heaven. To reduce man
to the status of a puppet subject to the caprice of destiny was
to destroy the basis of humanistic philosophy, the dignity of
man, for it was freedom of choice, as Gardiner said, which
set man above the rest of nature and made him different "from
other beasts unreasonable."[26] Sir Thomas More considered

[25] B.M., Harl. 249, "The trial of Stephen Gardiner," ff. 2-14, item
LXVI; Foxe, VI, p. 114.
[26] Gardiner, *A Declaration of true Articles* (1546), f. lxxviii.

the Protestant argument of foreordained election the most abominable of all their concepts, for it abolished the liberty of man's will, "ascribing all our deeds to destiny, with all reward or punishment pursuing upon all our doings; whereby they take away all diligence and good endeavour to virtue, all withstanding and striving against vice, all care of heaven, all fear of Hell. . . ."[27]

The conservative bishops, trained as they were in bureaucracy and administration, perceived in the doctrine of predestination the very antithesis of human law, for if the elect of God's children were secure in the knowledge of heaven, they might also regard themselves as immune from any earthly authority. Of what avail was social punishment if certain men were predestined to evil? What control could society enforce if individuals were assured of salvation in another world? Cuthbert Tunstal was convinced that such a certainty would eventually undermine all moral responsibility, and he predicted that the "common sort" would use such an argument to escape the pains of mortal retribution. He pictured the individual as claiming that "if God had predestined me to destruction, since his sentence is fixed . . . why should I defraud myself of pleasure? To what end should I vex myself uselessly with fast after fast, and torture myself with continual vigils, and pass sleepless nights . . . in unending prayer?" for "if I am indeed predestined by him to eternal life, however much I sin here on earth and however great the crimes I pile upon crimes I shall nevertheless be saved in the end. . . . Will it not be more sensible to devote myself to pleasure . . . than for a weak vessel such as I am to resist the potter, and for an earthen pot to clash with one of iron, and be broken?"[28] To the Bishop of Durham predestination was a justification for sin, corruption, and weakness—the very evils which law and

---

[27] Gairdner, *Lollardy*, I, App. to ch. v, "Abstract of More's *Dialogue*," p. 577.

[28] Tunstal, *Contra impios Blasphematores Dei Praedestinationis* (1555), pp. 5-6; English translation taken from Sturge, *Cuthbert Tunstal*, p. 337.

tradition attempted to limit and prevent. The Bishop of Winchester was even more fearful of the social consequences of a foreordained existence, and he claimed that the logical conclusion of the Protestant teaching was to believe that "all things come to pass by an absolute necessity, and so man's life, death, manners, behavior, state, condition, and everything is fixed and fastened in his place appointed, with nails riveted and clenched with mere necessity."[29] Gardiner saw in the doctrine of "mere necessity" a concept which "not only impugn[s] the whole process of Scripture, but also subverteth all stay of good direction and endeavour, either to godly exercise or politic behavior." "It is the extremity of all mischief," he concluded, "to say that man can not choose whether he will use God's gifts or no when they be offered him. . . ."[30]

The Bishop and his friends were wrong, of course, for predestination did not result in anarchy, licentiousness, and loose living. On the contrary, it produced a puritanical morality far more rigid and inflexible than that possessed by the advocates of free will, but this does not invalidate their argument. It merely constitutes another piece of evidence that history rarely follows the course of human prediction. Given the conditions of the sixteenth century their fears were real enough, and even the Protestants were not blind to the full force of the conservative argument that religious disobedience marched hand-in-hand with social anarchy. "Let not these worldly men," pleaded one unknown reformer to his sovereign, "make your Grace believe that they [the Protestants] will cause insurrection, envy and such mischiefs as they imagine of their own mad brains lest that he [God] be avenged upon you and your realm. . . . But peradventure they will lay this against me and say that experience doth show how such men as call themselves the followers of the gospel regard not your Grace's commandments . . . set forth by your parlia-

[29] Gardiner, *A Declaration of true Articles* (1546), f. xxxix.
[30] *Ibid.*, f. cxli.

ment, and that was proved by these persons which of late were punished in London for keeping of such books as your Grace hath prohibited by proclamation, and like as they regard not this, so they will not regard [any other of] your Grace's laws, statutes, and ordinances."[31] Human experience for this reformer was no basis on which to judge the actions of the "followers of the gospel," and he dismissed such a criterion as the "crafty persuasion" of earthy men. But unfortunately for the advocates of the Reformation, these "worldly men" had taken over the controls of government in 1540 and their decisions were, to a great extent, motivated by secular experience and human consideration.

The conservatives, however, did not have to rely solely on logic to prove their point: that Protestantism was socially dangerous. The argument of Gardiner that the destruction of religious images would weaken the social status of the nobility, or the reasoning of the Bishop of Durham that Predestination was dangerous because it tended to destroy the effectiveness of human law may have been important theoretical considerations, but these opponents of the Reformation had at their disposal actual historic proof in the lesson of Germany that religious reform, once sanctioned, could and did lead to serious social consequences. Even Martin Bucer had to admit in 1548 that this reminder of what Protestantism might mean to England was slowing up the process of the Reformation, and that many of his own party were "afraid that by reason of the unhappy events in Germany this kingdom would be yet more tardy, and employ new delays in fully taking up the cause of religion."[32] As we have already pointed out in a previous chapter, Gardiner, Sampson, and Heath all regarded the

---

[31] P.R.O., S.P. 6, vol. 7, No. 20, "A declaration againste the spiritualtys" (December 1530), pp. 195-196. Both Foxe (VII, p. 509) and the Parker Society (Latimer, *Sermons and Remains*, No. III, p. 297) attribute this document to Hugh Latimer. However, James Gairdner (*Lollardy*, II, pp. 261-263) has conclusively shown that this is impossible.

[32] *Original Letters*, II, No. CCXXV, "Peter Martyr to Martin Bucer" (December 1548), p. 469.

moral of Germany as a lesson in the result of tampering with the Catholic faith,[33] and Bonner likewise added his voice to the conservative alarm when he wrote to the people in his *Book of Homilies* to "look also upon Germany, and take example thereby; how they prospered among themselves, since they declined from the obedience of the See of Rome."[34] This warning was written in 1555 and by then the Bishop had begun to attribute all the evils of the Reformation to the schism with Rome. Long before the conservatives, however, had made up their minds to return to communion with the Papacy, the Peasants' Revolt in Germany had been held up to the people as glaring evidence of what Protestantism would mean to England. Germain Gardiner, the Bishop's nephew, had in 1534 written Edward Fox that "these heresies . . . , lately sprung up in Germany, . . . [are] spread abroad unto sundry parts of Christendom, tending to nothing else but to the division and rending asunder of Christ's mystical body, his Church, [and to] the pulling down of all power, and [the] utter subversion of all commonwealth."[35]

But it was Sir Thomas More who stated the conservative case most strongly, for the Lord Chancellor never doubted that the social ills of Germany were due to Martin Luther. The most pernicious of all the German monk's doctrines was, he said, "the liberty that he so highly commended unto the people, bringing them in belief that having faith, they needed nothing else," and as a consequence the people thought they were "so near cousins to Christ that they be in a full freedom and liberty discharged of all governors and all manner [of] laws spiritual or temporal except the gospel only."[36] His

---

[33] See ch. III, pp. 94-95.   [34] Bonner, *Homilies*, f. 52.
[35] *A letter of a yonge gentylman named Mayster Germen Gardynare wryten to a friend of his, wherein men may se the demeanour and heresy of Johnn Fryth late burned* (1534). There is an almost complete copy of this letter printed in Gairdner, *Lollardy*, I, pp. 405-412 from which this passage is taken. See esp. pp. 405-406.
[36] More, *English Works*, p. 257.

words are reminiscent of those of Cardinal Wolsey, when he spoke of the example which the religious and social revolutions of Bohemia presented to the governors of England. Like Wolsey, More was convinced that the Reformation in Germany could have been prevented had not the nobles been greedy and supported the Lutheran doctrines in the hope of absorbing the wealth and property of the church. The result, the Chancellor claimed, was self-evident: "For so was it shortly after that those uplandish Lutherans took so great boldness and so began to grow strong, that they set also upon the temporal lords. Which had they not set hand thereto the sooner while they looked for other men's lands, had been like shortly to lose their own." The Peasants' Revolt in Germany, More added, had been suppressed, but elsewhere, in Switzerland, the princes had not been so fortunate, and through negligence had allowed the people to grow so powerful in their Lutheran convictions that finally "the common people have compelled the rulers to follow them, who, if they had taken heed in time, they might have ruled and led."[37] The Marxian author Karl Kautsky has construed these words as evidence of More's awareness of "the class struggle which underlay the Reformation,"[38] but whatever else More had in mind, his words are primarily those of a statesman warning the members of his brotherhood of bureaucrats to take heed lest a similar negligence in England lead to the fate of Germany. When Sampson, Gardiner, and Cardinal Wolsey pointed to the history of Bohemia and Germany as an example of the consequences of allowing the people to think that "they might prevail," they all may have been unconsciously stating a class doctrine, but they were also quite consciously reiterating the guiding assumption of any Tudor administrator, that the common man was to be led, not followed.

The dividing line between religious revolution and social

[37] *Ibid.*, p. 258.
[38] Kautsky, *Thomas More and his Utopia*, p. 146.

[237]

war was never clear, and the two tended to unite in the minds of many reformers. In the case of Henry Brinklow, the two problems became one when he wrote of the wealthy burghers of London saying that "the great part of these inordinate rich, stiffnecked citizens will not have in their houses that lively word of our souls, nor suffer their servants to have it. . . ." In the eyes of this zealous reformer the religious idolatry of the "multitude of inordinate rich" was not their only or worst crime. "No, no! their heads are so given to seek their own particular wealth only, that they pass no honest provisions for the poor, which thing above all other infidelities shall be our damnation."[39] The readers of such words could take their choice as to whether the author was urging the people to rise up against the rich because they were ungodly or because they were rich. Bishop Gardiner was well aware of the confusion and Richard Hilles, in a letter to Henry Bullinger, reported that a man by the name of Collins had been imprisoned in Winchester diocese on the order of the Bishop for slanderous behavior towards images. Master Hilles, however, was not convinced that this was the sole explanation and he added that "many persons . . . say that this was not the cause of his imprisonment; but rather, because he was wont to exclaim against the nobility and great men of the kingdom, and rashly to bring forward against them many passages of holy scripture, especially the prophets, wherein there was any mention made of unrighteous judgments, or the cruel treatment of neighbors and dependents."[40] To most of the state officials the relationship between religious and social anarchy was clear, and Thomas Watson, later the Marian Bishop of Lincoln, never questioned that the ultimate end of Protestantism was "carnal and detestable living, conspiracy and treason."[41] Watson spoke

[39] Brinklow, *The Lamentacyon of a Christen agaynst the Cytye of London*, E.E.T.S., vol. 22, pp. 79-80.

[40] *Original Letters*, I, No. cv, "Richard Hilles to Henry Bullinger" (1541), pp. 200-201.

[41] Strype, *Ecc. Mem.*, III, pt. i, "A sermon by Thomas Watson before the Queen" (1553), p. 119.

these words in a sermon preached in 1553, but Sir Thomas More expressed the same thought many years earlier when he wrote that with the final victory of the "New Learning," "then shall all laws be laughed to scorn, then shall servants set naught by their masters, and unruly people rebel against their rulers. Then will rise up rifling and robbery, murder and mischief and plain insurrection, whereof [what] would be the end, or when you should see it, only God knoweth."[42] Such was the "belly wisdom" of the conservatives, a wisdom founded on human knowledge and experience and which in the end made them fear all reform however worthy it might appear. The conservatives were fast acquiring an attitude towards reform akin to that of the ruling classes in England for liberalism during the French Revolution. As the picture of the excesses in France in the last decade of the eighteenth century and the fear of revolt at home blinded the average landowner to the benefits of any form of liberalism, so in the sixteenth century the example of the Peasants' Revolt in Germany and the social implications of Protestantism at home prevented the conservative members of the Episcopal Bench from sanctioning any religious reform, and in the end drove them back to allegiance to the See of Rome.

During this period of conservative supremacy the vast uprising of 1549 had not yet occurred, nor had England been subject to the studied mismanagement of self-interested and unscrupulous courtiers of Edward's reign. Henry VIII was still on the throne, and the disciples of human prudence found in their sovereign a man who was fully cognizant of the lesson of Germany and the threat to law and order which Protestantism implied. The King in his attack on Lutheranism in 1522 had written that Luther "robs princes and prelates of all power and authority; for what shall a king or prelate do, if he cannot appoint any law, or execute the law which is appointed, but even like a ship without a rudder suffer his people

---

[42] Harpsfield, *Life of Sir Thomas More*, p. 71.

to float from the land."[43] Henry had not hesitated to use and even support the advocates of Lutheranism in order to maintain his Royal Supremacy and to confiscate the wealth of the monasteries, but he had no intention of putting harness upon his back and bowing to the will of the people. With Gardiner as the King's "own bishop," with Tunstal as one of his chief advisers, and with Sampson as Lord President of the Council of Wales, there was little fear that the government would ignore the warning of two Lord Chancellors and allow negligence to breed revolution. During the last six years of the reign, the administration maintained a cautious watch upon the actions of the reformers, and though it is impossible to narrate the course of reaction in full, we can at least indicate the direction of government policy throughout these years, and scrutinize the last of the Henrician formularies of faith, *The King's Book*, which was *par excellence* the work of the conservatives.

It is indicative of the trend which had set in during the early months of 1540 that the government insisted on the complete and detailed recantation of William Jerome, one of the most advanced and vocal of the reformers. Who was responsible for his abjuration sermon is unrecorded, but it has all the earmarks of having been drawn up by one of the conservatives. On the date determined for his public disavowal of heretical beliefs, the government sent a number of observers to witness the fact that Jerome preached as he had been ordered, and it is on the basis of the notes of one of these witnesses, a Henry Dowes, that the topics of Jerome's sermon have been preserved. The first of the three articles which the radical divine had been commanded to recant was the old question of justification by faith alone, but it is the last two articles which so clearly show the government's alarm concerning the anarchistic implications of the Protestant doctrines. "The second article was this," reported Dowes to Gregory Cromwell, "whereas he had in the

[43] Henry VIII, *Assertio Septem Sacramentorum*, p. 60.

said sermon preached that the magistrate as concerning things left indifferent by God's word could not make any laws that should bind men's conscience, he now revoked the same as erroneous, false and contrary to the Scriptures, forasmuch as the rulers whom we are bound to obey should thereby run in contempt and the people be brought into disobedience which should be the subversion of the public weal and breaketh of all honest order." After treating the problem of the royal authority, Dowes reported that Jerome continued with his third article as follows: "whereas in a sermon made in the summer, he was now convinced by witnesses according unto the law, to have used opprobrious words against the burgesses of the Parliament as calling them butterflies, dissemblers, and knaves, he now protested the same to be ill and slanderously spoken, since thereby such things as they shall determine and conclude upon, might be had in the less regard and estimation."[44] The government could not afford to allow preachers the liberty of exclaiming to the people that the King's powers were in any way limited, nor could it pass unnoticed remarks which so clearly attempted to undermine the respect and dignity of Parliament. By adding secular authority to religious doctrine through the passage of the Six Articles in 1539, the government may have strengthened religious orthodoxy, but at the same time it had brought Parliament itself under attack as the source of an ungodly religious creed. Such attacks the administration could never sanction, and it exemplifies the growing conservative alarm that only one article of Jerome's recantation dealt with strictly religious heresy while the rest was a direct disavowal of what the government must have regarded as sedition.

The authorization and placement of the Bible in all the churches of the realm during 1537-38 had been viewed for several years by such men as Edmund Bonner and Cuthbert

[44] P.R.O., S.P. 1, vol. 158, "Henry Dowes to Gregory Cromwell on Jerome's sermon of recantation," ff. 124-125 (L.P., XV [1540], No. 414).

Tunstal with increasing consternation, for the availability of the Scriptures had not resulted in the moral uplifting predicted by Cranmer. Instead, amateur theologians had taken to reading and expounding the gospel, causing heated discussions and interrupting religious services. By 1542 the commotion and uncertainty which the Bible in English was causing induced Bishop Bonner to issue a lengthy admonition to his diocese in regard to the proper respect expected of those who delved into the mysteries of the gospel, and he warned his flock that "the abuse, default and evil behavior of a few, who for lack of discretion and good advisement [in reading the Bible], . . . [have rather hindered] than set forward the thing that is good of itself. . . ."[45] The Bishop was still willing to admit the benefits of the Bible in English but he was no longer convinced of the truth of More's advice that a "commodity ought not be kept back for the harm that may come of it," and he coldly ordered that no unlicensed person should expound the Scriptures or read the Bible during time of services. In 1543, however, the central government finally took a hand in quieting the commotion which the English Bible was causing, and ordered that "no manner of person or persons . . . shall take upon him or them to read, preach or teach openly to others in any church or open assembly . . . the Bible or any part of Scriptures in English . . . unless he be so appointed thereunto by the King's Majesty. . . ." But the act involved far more than the silencing of indiscreet theologians, for it reflected the growing conviction of many Englishmen that the knowledge of the Bible among the common people was a demoralizing influence. The government now ordered that only noblemen and gentlemen householders might read the Bible and keep a copy in their homes to be read by their families. Merchants, if they were householders, were likewise

[45] Burnet, IV, No. xxv, "An admonition and advertisement given by the Bishop of London to all readers of this Bible in the English tongue," p. 139.

given permission to read the Scriptures privately, but since the liberty had been abused by the "lower sort," all women, artificers, prentices, and others under the rank of yeoman, were to be prohibited from reading the Bible either privately or publicly.[46] Henry's administration had given official voice to its fears that the Bible in the hands of the people was a threat to law and order, and the Protestant reaction to this stand was almost instantaneous. William Turner said in a last minute addition to his book, *The Hunting and Fynding Out of the Romishe Fox*, published in September of 1543, that he had just heard that "the bishops had made an act that none but gentle men and gentle women might read the Scripture and certain rich men." Then he went immediately to the heart of the issue when he wrote that "some politic man perchance will say the rich men and the nobles are wiser than the poor people and can order it well and so cannot the ignorant poor people well." Undoubtedly this is exactly what the conservatives and their sovereign did think, and Turner's conclusion "that there are more gentle fools than yeoman fools number compared to number,"[47] must have convinced them of the justice of their argument that the Bible in the hands of "the lesser sort" constituted a serious threat to the security of the realm. Without doubt the factor which prevented the growth of Protestantism during these final years of conservative supremacy was the failure of many reformers to discern whether the rich man and the noble were evil because they were ungodly or because they were wealthy. Though the episcopal leaders of the Reformation preached that evilness lay in ungodliness, the masses of the underprivileged, as Miss White has pointed out, saw in religious change "the hope of social betterment."[48] For the "lesser sort" at least, the evilness of the "senior or alderman with the multitude of the inordinate rich" lay in their coffers, not in their souls.

[46] *Statutes of the Realm*, III, 34 and 35 H. VIII, c. 1, pp. 895-896.
[47] Turner, *The Huntyng of the Romyshe Foxe* (1543), pp. 85-86.
[48] White, *Social Criticism*, p. 82.

In May of 1543 the last of the religious formularies of Henry's reign was read in the Council before the nobility of the realm. *The King's Book,* or to use more official language, *A Necessary Doctrine and Erudition for Any Christian Man,* was the final expression of conservative thought, an official statement of the view that religion was a social as well as a metaphysical problem. It does not seem to have been the work of one man, though Gardiner, Thirlby, and Heath seem to have been the guiding spirits behind its creation. All three men were busy during the sessions of Convocation in the spring of 1543 reading and presenting sections of the work to the Lower House,[49] and in August of the same year Henry wrote to Ralph Sadler in Scotland that he was to dispel the rumor that any one man had been responsible for this most recent religious settlement. Sadler was instructed to inform the Scottish government that the work had been the result of the common consent of "learned men of divers judgments," and had been penned by the bishops of Westminster, Rochester, and Chichester (Thirlby, Heath, and Day) and by Doctors Cox, Redman, and Robyson.[50] The name of Stephen Gardiner is significantly missing from this list, and what part he played in the making of the formulary is not clear, but his contemporaries were quite certain that *The King's Book* was essentially his, and George Joye described the work as "a book belike penned by you, for it savoureth everywhere of your damnable doctrine."[51] There is little doubt that the underlying philosophy behind the new formulary did savor of Gardiner's "damnable doctrine" for only two years before, in 1541, Gardiner in a long letter to Bucer laid down the cardinal principles which should control the writing of such a book. "It is the duty of preachers and of those who declare Christ," he said, "not to cite to the people such texts from Scripture,

[49] *L.P.,* XVIII, pt. i [1543], No. 365.
[50] *Ibid.,* pt. ii, No. 68.
[51] Joye, *The Refutation of the Byshop of Winchester's derke Declaration* (1546), f. cxxxi.

as not being brought forward in their proper place, or not being unfolded sufficiently, beguile the people into the refusal of obedience. Of which sort are the following words: subjects are only entrusted to the prince's fostering care and protection, and are not subject to princes in any other way than for the sake of God. Then again: all outward things have been founded and instituted in a heavenly way for the sake of man. Which assertions are not altogether false: but yet they are spoken in such a way as to seem in favor of the people, and to tend to anarchy; which latter is not without cause suspected of many, to be the aim of this your sect, which, under colour of godliness, endeavours meanwhile to confound all things human. If it be said that God's law contains in itself, without exception, the prescription of all things good, and the prohibition of all things evil, is it not tacitly hinted that all human laws are to no purpose? which laws are now and again branded with the infamous name of traditions: sometimes indeed the following words are added: In vain ye worship me with the commandments of men."[52] The Bishop may not have been the particular legalist behind *The King's Book*, but the new formula of faith certainly did attempt to present the Christian creed in such a way so as not "to seem in favour of the people and to tend to anarchy."

Genetically the *Necessary Doctrine* stemmed from its earlier counterpart, *The Bishops' Book* of 1537, and the conclusion of Canon Smith is essentially exact when he wrote that "Much of *The Bishops' Book* was incorporated in the new one, but there is an improvement in the arrangement of the matter; it shows a better sense of proportion, and the style is less redundant—it contains more in less space. What, however, is of far more importance is the fact that the doctrine is

---

[52] *Gardiner's answer to Bucer; The contempt of human law, made by rightful authority, is to be punished more heavily and more seriously than any transgression of the divine law* (probably written during the latter part of Henry's reign). Translated and printed in Janelle, *Obedience in Church and State*, p. 205.

far more Catholic, and stated with greater precision."[53] All
the controversial elements of the Catholic creed were reiterated in an explicitly orthodox manner; such debatable phrases
as "the elect of God's children" were deleted; the sacrament
of the altar which had warranted only a page of description
in the previous book was extended and narrated in a detailed
Catholic form; the doctrines of Free Will and Good Works
were lengthened and given separate treatment; and finally the
via media of the older formulary, the theory of things indifferent, was abandoned. The theology of *The King's Book*
need not detain us except to say that Cardinal Pole was willing to use the formulary under Queen Mary,[54] and the Spanish ambassador, Chapuys, wrote his sovereign that the recent
book "for the extirpation of the heresies and errors which
have heretofore reigned" restores "ceremonies and other
things of the Christian religion to their first state, except what
concerns the authority of the Apostolic See."[55]

It is in the sphere of the conservatives' view of religion as
a prop and support to social stability and order that the new
codification is pertinent to this discussion, for it presents a much
more complete and careful picture of their attitude than did
The Bishops' Book of the previous decade. Doctrinal phrases
and sentences which might be construed as an excuse for disobedience and insurrection were carefully omitted, or their
interpretation limited. For instance, to the fifth petition in
The Bishops' Book, "and forgive us our trespasses, as we forgive them that trespass against us," *The King's Book* adds
the significant qualification that the people "shall understand
that forgiveness, afore spoken of, is not so meant in Scripture,
that by it justice or laws of princes should be broken, condemned or not executed."[56] To the eighth commandment,

[53] Smith, *Henry VIII and the Reformation*, p. 375.
[54] Constant, I, p. 429.
[55] *L.P.*, XVIII, pt. i [1543], No. 684.
[56] Lloyd, *Formularies, The Bishops' Book*, p. 197; cf. *ibid.*, *The King's Book*, p. 349.

"thou shalt not steal," the new formulary, after listing almost every crime known to a civilized society, adds a final offense in the form of vagabondage, which the originators of the first Book had not bothered to consider. Thus *The King's Book* says: "Also all idle vagabonds and sturdy beggars, which, being able to get their living by labor, take such alms wherewith the poor and impotent folk should be relieved and sustained, do offend against this commandment."[57] With the fall of the monasteries and the increase of enclosure the problem of charity and vagabondage had become a serious concern of the secular government, and evidently the custodians of the state felt that divine intervention was needed to help remedy this difficulty.

By 1543 the doctrine of the equality of man in the eyes of God as stated in the Bible and taught by the early Church Fathers had acquired alarming social implications, and in the first petition of the Lord's Prayer the disciples of human prudence expurgated all mention of this equality. The authors of *The Bishops' Book* had written that "in these words, *Our Father*, is signified, that we ought to believe, not only that Almighty God is the common Father of all Christian people, and equally and indifferently regardeth the rich and the poor, the free and the bond, the lord and the subject, but also that all Christian people be Christ's own brethren, and the very coinheritors and compartioners with him in the kingdom of heaven. . . ." Thirlby, Heath, and Day, however, penned the same petition in a much more subdued and politic manner. "Moreover," *The King's Book* says, "by these words *Our Father*, is signified, that we ought to believe that Almighty God is the common Father of all true Christian people, and fatherly regardeth all, through and by means of our Saviour Jesus Christ, unto whom all faithful and obedient Christian men be brethren by grace and adoption, and called to inherit

[57] *Ibid., The King's Book*, p. 327; cf. *ibid., The Bishops' Book*, pp. 163-164.

with him the kingdom of heaven. And they be also brethren each one to [the] other, having all one Father, which is God Almighty."[58] The "damnable doctrine" of Stephen Gardiner and his advocates apparently did not consider it prudent to impress too strongly the equality of the rich and the poor, the free and the bond, the lord and the subject, for there was always the possibility that some one might take it literally.

In the final paragraphs of *The King's Book* occurs a summation of the conservative view concerning the relationship of man to his religion. To the advocates of earthly wisdom, religion for the average man was a code of social and moral behavior relative to this world. The full force of this concept appears in the "Article of Good Works" when the authors wrote that "Saint Paul saith: The grace of God hath appeared to bring salvation unto all men, teaching us, that we, renouncing all ungodliness and worldly desires, should live in this present world soberly, justly, and devoutly, looking for the blessed hope and appearance of the glory of the great God, and our Saviour Jesus Christ. . . . In which godly sentence of St. Paul, besides other great plenty of fruitful learning and edifying, he toucheth in three words all the good works of a true Christian man, where he saith, *soberly, justly,* and *devoutly.* For in this word *soberly* he comprehendeth all abstinence and temperence, and our duty touching our body: and in saying *justly,* he containeth all works of charity towards our neighbor, with due obedience to our princes, heads, and governors: and in this word *devoutly,* he concludeth all our works spiritual, which be done immediately unto God, as prayers, thinking of God, desiring of his glory, etc."[59] The community here pictured is not the theocratic state of Calvin's Geneva, but a society in which the individual would quietly accept the mores and customs of his civilization and obey the

---

[58] *Ibid., The Bishops' Book,* p. 182; cf. *ibid., The King's Book,* p. 336.
[59] *Ibid., The King's Book,* pp. 374-375.

orders of his masters and betters. It is the administrator's ideal, not the theologian's.

The Necessary Doctrine and Erudition for Any Christian Man, for all its prudent words and cautious phraseology, remained the religious creed of Englishmen for only three years, for in January 1547, the most persistent believer in the Book died. With Henry's death Stephen Gardiner, who had been feared by his opponents as "the best learned [man] in his faculty," lost his influence and power, and Cuthbert Tunstal for all his "stillness, soberness, and sublety" was relegated to a minor position in the new Edwardian government.[60] With the commencement of the new reign, the reformers returned to control, and many of them were men who thought as Martin Luther had once thought, that "the Word of God can never be advanced without whirlwind, tumult, and danger. The Word is of infinite majesty, it is wonderful in the heights and in the depths; as the prophet says: 'It slew the fattest of them and smote down the chosen men of Israel.' One must either despair of peace and tranquility or else deny the Word."[61]

During the last months of Henry's reign the political barometer had evinced a tendency toward erratic oscillation in anticipation of the King's death. During one of the swings to the left after the disgrace and imprisonment of Gardiner's old friend, the Duke of Norfolk, in December of 1546, John Burcher wrote to his acquaintances in Germany that nothing is "wanting but Winchester alone, and unless he also be caught the evangelical truth cannot be restored."[62] Within a month

---

[60] *Archaeologia*, XXIII (1831), "Memorial from George Constantyne to Thomas Lord Cromwell," pp. 62-63.

[61] "Martin Luther to George Spalatin" (February 1520), printed in Smith, *The Life and Letters of Martin Luther*, p. 72.

[62] Original Letters, II, No. CCXCV, "John Burcher to Henry Bullinger" (31 December, 1548), p. 639. There is considerable evidence to believe that even before Henry's death the tide was running against the conservative party. It was rumored that Henry had broached the subject of a possible reformation to the French ambassador in September of 1546, and had

that want was to be rectified, for on January 28 the old King died, and within two years Wily Winchester was safely imprisoned, as much a bell without a clapper as Latimer had been after his deprivation in 1539.

---

suggested plans for the abolition of popery and a change in the Catholic Mass in both countries. Moreover, Bishop Gardiner himself was in disfavor during the final months of the reign, and was absent from the Council. Likewise, his name was excluded at the last moment from the Council of Regency named in Henry's will. Whether all this signifies, as A. F. Pollard suggests, that the Reformation would have been revived whether Henry had died when he did or not, is far from certain. However, it is quite apparent that even during the years of conservatives supremacy (1540-1546) there were powerful reforming elements at court. Cranmer, though a subject of constant conservative attack, was always protected by the King; Catherine Parr, Henry's last Queen, was probably sympathetic toward the Reformation ideals; and finally, the influence of the Seymour-Dudley faction continued to grow until, by the closing months of the reign, it was able to exclude Gardiner from the Council. See Pollard, *Henry VIII*, p. 421, n. 2; *ibid.*, *Thomas Cranmer*, pp. 180-183; Smith, *Henry VIII and the Reformation*, pp. 220-225.

CHAPTER IX

THE CONSERVATIVES' DILEMMA
(1547-1550)

O N the 16th of February, 1547, Stephen Gardiner administered the last rites in honor of his dead sovereign, and preached the final sermon before the royal body was lowered to rest beside the grave of Jane Seymour, the mother of Henry's only legitimate son, Edward VI. The text of the Bishop's sermon was "Blessed are dead who die in the Lord," and his words were those of a man who had suffered a personal loss. What a "pitiful and dolorous loss," he lamented, have all men "sustained by the death of so gracious a King."[1] Catholics and radical reformers may have doubted whether Henry actually did die "in the Lord," but for the two old rivals, Bishop Gardiner and Archbishop Cranmer, Henry had indeed been a "gracious" sovereign. Whatever his crimes may have been before the throne of heaven, on earth the King had won the devotion of both the divine and the lawyer. For all his greed and cruelty, for all his egotism and lust, the King's personal charm and magnetism had produced an allegiance and loyalty which transcended the prick of religious conscience. When the Bishop of Winchester said: "No man could do me hurt during his life," he may have been overestimating his monarch's good faith,[2] and Cranmer's grief may have been misplaced when as a token of his emotions, he grew a fine flowing beard, but both men were sincere in their sense of a personal loss.

Neither that "godly and virtuous imp," Edward, nor his

---

[1] Strype, *Ecc. Mem.* II, pt. ii, Repository A, "The ceremonies and funeral solemnities paid to the corpse of Henry VIII," p. 309.

[2] Gardiner, *Letters*, No. 121, "Gardiner to Somerset" (6 June, 1547), p. 287.

neurotic half-sister, Mary, were able to stimulate the individual devotion which had been their father's greatest asset, for what had been considered in Henry parental severity, became under his two successors ungodly tyranny. The second Tudor had been able to maintain a sanguinary middle course, forcing the individual to acquiesce in a policy which at times he regarded as unjust and unchristian, but the judicious tempering of extremism with reaction had won the support of both parties in the belated hope that the future would bring a change for the better. Whatever history may feel towards Henry's policy, his own personality was an important ingredient in the English Reformation, and the anomaly of Catholicism without the Pope was a *via media* which was buried with the person of the King. With Henry alive and in control of England, Master Gardiner had little fear for the present; it was the future which was foreboding, and he confessed to William Paget in 1545 that he feared "not these fond malicious follies" of the Protestants during the King's life, but "when those that now be young shall, with the frailty of youth, win a contempt of religion and conceive another opinion of God than is indeed true," then, he predicted, was the time to worry about "what is like to ensue thereof."[3] What did ensue is the story of this chapter.

The new government, by the terms of the dead king's will, was placed in the hands of a commission, headed by the young sovereign's uncle, Edward Seymour, better known as the Duke of Somerset, who shortly assumed full control with the title of Lord Protector. The regime was supported by a strange union of religious fanaticism and economic avarice, of reformers who sincerely desired the problematical example of the primitive Christian church as the standard of both religious and social life, and of courtiers and sycophants who perceived in the Protestant doctrines of religious simplicity a heaven-sent excuse to profit from the further acquisition of clerical

---

[3] *Ibid.*, No. 79, p. 161 (*L.P.*, xx, pt. ii [1545], No. 732).

wealth. The relationship between economic self-interest and religious purity was recognized by the Spanish ambassador in one of his rare prophetic moments when he observed in September of 1547 that the new royal commissioners had been appointed to visit the bishoprics in order "to examine the clergymen and enquire into their knowledge, manner of life and income." "It may well turn out," he sagely concluded, "that the question of incomes is the principal one."[4] The truth of this prophecy became apparent when Nicholas Ridley, on being promoted to the See of London after the deprivation of Edmund Bonner, accepted the vastly curtailed income of 1,000 pounds yearly. Likewise, Stephen Gardiner, whose bishopric, said one Venetian observer, "was perhaps his greatest sin, as it yielded him a rental of 12,000 crowns," was deprived under Warwick in 1551 and his see bestowed on John Poynet, who renounced the old income in return for a yearly salary of 2,000 marks paid him by the government.[5] The character of the Lord Protector, the titular head of this unfortunate marriage of antithetic interests, remains even yet an unraveled enigma, and though we may accept the sincerity of his words when he wrote Stephen Gardiner "that he would suffer no innovations in religion during the king's majesty's young age,"[6] the basis of his power made such a policy impossible. Without the severities of Henry's reign and without the prestige of the dead monarch's personality, it proved impossible to curb the tongues of reformers who once again began to mutilate images and strive for the return of Biblical purity in religious life.

The preparatory steps were taken in the spring of 1547 when all episcopal authority was suspended in anticipation of the royal visitation of the dioceses in September. Then in July injunctions were issued, ordering the destruction of all

---

[4] *Cal. St. P. Sp.*, IX, p. 148.
[5] *Cal. St. P. Ven.*, V, No. 703, p. 349; cf. *Cal. St. P. Sp.*, X, pp. 261-262.
[6] Foxe, VI, p. 106, item VI.

superstitious images and the setting up of Erasmus' *Para-phrases* and Cranmer's short *Book of Homilies* in all the churches of the realm. Both Bonner and Gardiner protested against the *Book of Homilies* as a deliberate and illegal effort on the part of the reformers to disseminate the Protestant doctrine of justification by faith alone, and the Bishop of Winchester condemned the *Paraphrases* as a dangerous mistranslation of sections of the New Testament which even Erasmus had lived to regret.[7] It had been difficult enough under the preceding reign to discriminate between abused and worthy images, but under Edward, with the government giving tacit support to the radicals, the intestine conflict over what constituted abuse reached such a peak that the government, in February of 1548, was induced to settle the controversy by siding with the Protestant elements and ordering the abolition of all images. Moreover, the royal visitation during the early winter of 1547 stirred up a multitude of religious controversies which had remained latent during Henry's life. Avowedly enforcing the injunctions of the previous spring and selling the *Paraphrases* and *Book of Homilies*, the visitors, by their presence and as prophets of approaching religious change, excited contention over the sacrificial nature of the Mass and the question of transubstantiation. The alehouse had become the local arena for religious debate, and a host of ardent reformers indulged in the dubious humor of calling the Mass the "Jack-in-the-box," and in conceiving the singularly bad pun of referring to the time-honored words of the consecration—*Hoc est corpus*, as hocus-pocus.

It was becoming painfully apparent throughout these months that Henry's death had set loose upon the land a bitterness of religious dissension which at times bordered on anarchy, and if doctrinal peace was ever to be reestablished

---

[7] Burnet, IV, "The Protestation of the Bishop of London made to the Visitors," p. 261; Gardiner, *Letters*, No. 126, pp. 361-368, and No. 130, pp. 380-400.

it was evident that some new basis of religious concord would have to be found. The government in December 1548, issued injunctions forbidding either party from preaching about the sacrament of the altar until the King and his Council had had a chance to redefine the religious faith of Englishmen. However, it proved easier to legislate internal tranquillity than to enforce it, and amateur theorizing continued unabated. Even licensed preachers showed little discretion, and in September of 1549 the Council took steps to inhibit the privileged few from any discussion of doubtful matters. This last inhibition, however, was in preparation for *The Book of Common Prayer* of 1549, the first of the two Edwardian efforts at doctrinal definition. It was high time that governmental action was taken, for the uncertainty surrounding the question of the Mass had resulted in actual rioting between the two parties in St. Paul's Cathedral. Finally in September a group of theologians and canonists met under circumstances which are still obscure to draw up the new formulary, and some three months later the draft of the *Prayer Book* was introduced into the House of Lords. In a week-long colloquy the Book was subject to the bitter attack of the conservative bishops and the equally determined defense of the reformers, and finally on January 21, 1549, the first *Book of Common Prayer* received statutory sanction in the form of the first Act of Uniformity.[8]

This brief history of the religious events of the first years of the new reign, cursory as it is, need not be extended, for it was on the issue of the *Prayer Book* of 1549 and the events

[8] For the political details of these years see A. F. Pollard, *England under Protector Somerset*. There is no satisfactory biography on Edward VI. However, J. G. Nichols, *Literary Remains of King Edward VI*, gives in his introduction a short but accurate account of the known facts of the young king's life. Religious affairs are adequately covered by G. Constant, *The Reformation in England*, vol. 2, while G. H. Smyth, *Cranmer and the Reformation under Edward VI*, presents a controversial treatment of many of the theological problems of the reign. The best work on the Book of Common Prayer is Gasquet and Bishop, *Edward VI and the Book of Common Prayer*.

immediately following it that the conservatives took their last stand and were forced to make their final decision between the obedience they owed their King as loyal subjects and state officials, and the conviction they felt for their faith and religious doctrines. By the time the second Edwardian *Prayer Book* was issued in 1552, Bonner and Gardiner, Heath and Day, had been deprived of their episcopal garb and safely imprisoned, while John Voysey had been forced to resign his see and William Rugge was dead.[9]

The new *Book of Common Prayer* united under a single cover a Breviary, a Missal and a Ritual, but neither the first nor the last sections of the book need detain us. The Missal, however, or what Cranmer preferred to call "The Book of Communion," must be given considerable attention, for it was here that the reformers had a chance to introduce the Lutheran concept of the Mass and for the first time to rewrite the ancient mode of the Missal so as to destroy the sacrificial nature of the ceremony and transform it into a simple communion service. The tone of the new work was established by the renaming of the old ritual, which now became "The Supper of the Lord and the Holy Communion, commonly called the Mass." The Catholic Mass has always been both a thanksgiving celebration or memorial and a sacrifice or oblation, and generally speaking the new *Prayer Book* endeavored to emphasize the former and as far as possible to destroy the latter. The central feature of any mass or communion is the ritual of consecration, and in the ancient ceremony this portion of

---

[9] Edmund Bonner was deprived on 1 October, 1549; Gardiner on 14 February, 1551; Heath and Day in October of 1551. Voysey resigned his see on 14 August, 1551, while William Rugge gave up his Bishopric of Norwich on 26 December, 1549 and died in September of the following year. Of the conservative leaders only Tunstal retained his see until after the publication of the Second Prayer Book. Although he was deprived on 14 October, 1552, he had been in "lenient custody" since September of 1550, and was actually imprisoned in October 1551. He was tried and found guilty of felony on 1 December, 1551. For the still controversial story of Tunstal's fall, see Sturge, *Cuthbert Tunstal*, ch. XXIV "Tunstal and John Dudley."

the Mass had been accompanied by a series of prayers which were particularly odious to the Protestants, since they clearly announced the sacrificial element of the ritual. Luther regarded the Canon, as this section of the Mass is called, as "a heap of filth," and the English reformers did their best to change the meaning of these prayers while at the same time still retaining their actual form.[10] Thus, for example, the prayer, *Te igitur*, in which God is asked to accept and bless "these gifts, these offerings, these holy [and] undefiled sacrifices," was rewritten so as to omit the essential words "gifts," "offerings," and "sacrifices," and merely requested God "to receive these our prayers, which we offer unto Thy Divine Majesty. . . ."[11] The efforts to impress upon the communicant that the Mass was a memorial service and not a sacrifice likewise involved the revision of the ancient prayer, *Unde et memores*, in which the priest states that "[We] offer unto Thy excellent Majesty . . . the holy bread of eternal life, and the cup of everlasting salvation." The revised prayer, however, completely omits the concept of a sacrifice and concentrates on the idea of a memorial, and simply says: "Wherefore Oh Lord and heavenly Father . . . we Thy humble servants, do celebrate and make here before Thy Divine Majesty, with these Thy holy gifts, the memorial which Thy Son hath willed us to make. . . ."[12] The implication to the reader was quite clear, the Mass was to be regarded as a thanksgiving and not an oblation. The inspiration for the new ritual, as the Abbé Constant has said, was clearly Lutheran and recognized as such by contemporaries.[13] "We have an uniform celebration of the Eucharist," wrote Richard Hilles to a German friend in

[10] Constant, II, pp. 73, 78.

[11] Gasquet and Bishop, p. 200, have printed the prayers of the Canon as published in the First Prayer Book side by side with the ancient Sarum Ritual; cf. Constant, II, p. 74. See also *The First and Second Prayer Books of Edward VI* (Everyman edition), p. 221.

[12] Gasquet and Bishop, pp. 207-208; cf. Constant, II, p. 75. See also *The First and Second Prayer Books of Edward VI* (Everyman edition), p. 223.

[13] Constant, II, pp. 76-77.

June of 1549, "throughout the whole kingdom, but after the manner of the Nuremberg churches and some of those in Saxony."[14] The author of this letter, however, is not altogether accurate in implying that the Missal was by any means an exact copy of the Lutheran ceremony, for the reformers, while transforming the meaning of the prayers of the Canon, had not dared to abolish them completely, and as a result the *Prayer Book* was still capable, though with some difficulty, of an orthodox interpretation.

As the Ten Articles of 1536 had been drawn up by a pseudo-Catholic government, in an effort to mollify the reformers by giving to the work a mildly Protestant flavor, so now, in 1549, the first *Prayer Book* was conceived by an essentially Protestant regime which wished to carry with it as many of the moderate conservatives as possible. James Gairdner has remarked that "there was really little in it [the *Prayer Book*] to which even good Catholics could object, except things omitted. . . ."[15] This is probably a far too positive statement of the situation, but for men who were looking for some means of satisfying both their duty to their government and their faith in the old religion, the new book did allow a solution. The prayers of the Canon had been changed but not removed, and Stephen Gardiner was quick to point them out as still implying, even in their modified form, a Catholic interpretation. Ceremonies had been removed, he said, but the Catholic doctrine had not been touched, and he concluded that although he himself would never have written the *Prayer Book*, "he could with his conscience keep it and cause others in his diocese to keep it."[16] This was evidently the stand taken by most of Gardiner's followers, for although Tunstal, Bonner and Day all voted against the new service when it was being discussed

[14] *Original Letters*, I, No. cxxi, "Richard Hilles to Henry Bullinger" (4 June, 1549), p. 266.

[15] Gairdner, *The English Church in the Sixteenth Century*, p. 267.

[16] Foxe, VI, "A long matter proposed by the Bishop of Winchester," p. 114.

in the Lords,[17] none of these men were deprived and imprisoned for refusing to accept or enforce the Book once it had been given legal sanction. That they disliked the new doctrine concerning the Mass, however, is perfectly clear, for during the colloquy on the *Prayer Book* in December of 1548, the sections dealing with the Breviary and Ritual were passed over, and the conservatives concentrated their attack on the Missal, which they considered at best an objectionable and dangerous innovation and at worst actually heretical.[18]

Mere dislike for religious innovation and the fear of the consequences of meddling with ecclesiastical problems was not, however, enough to drive the conservatives into open opposition, for the government could call upon two influences to which the conservatives were peculiarly susceptible. Religious, political, and social unity were the abiding principles on which the Tudor governmental machine relied, and as bureaucrats and administrators, the conservative bishops were acutely aware of the importance of maintaining that unity even at the cost of individual conscience. Moreover, Gardiner, Tunstal, Thirlby, and Edmund Bonner, and a host of lesser bishops had attained episcopal rank as a reward for service to their state and sovereign, and they were deeply influenced by the personal loyalty which they owed their sovereign both as subjects and as servants. I am "but a cipher" John Stokesley had remarked to Geoffrey Pole during the previous reign when he was explaining his inability to prevent heretics from preaching at Paul's Cross. Thomas Cromwell, he said, in his capacity of Vicar-general, and not he, made the appointments, and as long as the King cared to support the advocates of reformation it was not for a Bishop of London to question either the reason or the right.[19] Edward Lee of York had been even more abject

---

[17] *Lords' Journal*, I, p. 331.

[18] B.M., Royal 17 B. xxxix, "The debate on the Sacrament," printed in Gasquet and Bishop, App. v.

[19] P.R.O., S.P. 1, vol. 138, "The examination of Sir Geoffrey Pole," f. 17 (*L.P.*, xiii, pt. ii [1538], No. 695, sec. 2).

in his humility and openly confessed that he owed "all things save his soul" to the King, a statement which was not far from the truth.[20]

The tradition of obedience to the king and state, however, was a principle universal to Tudor England and affected conservative and reformer alike. What was unique to the conservative bishops was the appeal to national unity and solidarity. It must be remembered that the duties of these ecclesiastics were dual, for they not only were the spiritual leaders of the nation and overseers of the souls of their bishoprics, but they were also state officials to whom order was dearer than life and to whom obedience was the very heart of administrative power. Both unity and law stood above the individual, and for a time at least these men considered that their consciences were discharged by the legal sanction of a majority vote in Parliament. Educated in the law, trained in statism and owing their worldly success to their sovereign, they were confronted with the pronged dilemma of loyalty to their own convictions and obedience to the state. Like most men, they clung to the familiar patterns of thought, to legality, order, and obedience, the products of a lifetime of training. It was only when they discerned in the Protestant reformation the antithesis of these three principles that they turned to faith and individual conscience as the rock on which to take their stand. The breakdown of old loyalties and cultivated patterns of thought, the refusal to heed the appeal to national solidarity was a slow one, and under Henry and during the first years of the new reign these men undoubtedly preferred unity and compromise to the social and personal consequences of treason.

During the previous reign, Henry had been quick to perceive the strength of the appeal to unity and utilize it in his efforts to bend the nation to his royal will. In 1531 he placed Cuthbert Tunstal in an embarrassing and equivocal position when he wrote the Bishop in regard to his opposition to the

[20] *L.P.*, VIII [1537], No. 870, p. 343.

government's policy asking "Why do not you, in this case, with yourself, as ye willed us in our great matter, conform your conscience to the conscience and opinion of the great number?"[21] One may question the validity of the assumption that the majority did rule in Tudor England, but once a law had been passed by Parliament it was assumed that the nation had given its consent. The conservatives, for the most part lawyers, had a deep respect for this type of argument, and Bishop Gardiner confessed that although he might be absent from Parliament or even be opposed to a particular bill during the course of a debate, he "must and will, after they be passed without my knowledge or against my mind, honour and reverence them nevertheless as laws of the realm. . . ."[22]

It was Edward Fox, however, who best exemplified this conservative preoccupation with the political and social aspects of the religious issues of the Reformation, and stated most clearly the consequences of disunity. During the debate on the formation of the so-called *Bishops' Book* in 1537 he warned his fellow bishops that "ye must consider earnestly what ye will determine of these controversies, that ye make not yourselves to be mocked and laughed to scorn of all the world, and that ye bring them not to have this opinion of you to think ever more hereafter that ye have neither one spark of learning nor yet of godliness in you. And thus shall ye lose all your estimation and authority with them which before took you for learned men and profitable members unto the commonwealth of Christendom."[23] Very much the same warning was expressed by another conservative bishop a dozen years later during the debate on the first Edwardian *Prayer Book* of 1548-49. At that time Thomas Thirlby confessed that though he would never compromise the fundamentals of his faith, there

[21] B.M., Cleo. E. VI, f. 216 (*L.P.*, V [1531], App. 9).

[22] Gardiner, *Letters*, No. 125, "Gardiner to Cranmer" (1547), p. 350.

[23] Ellis, *Original Letters*, 3rd Ser., vol. III, pp. 196-202 (*L.P.*, XII [1537], No. 790).

were "other things, in consideration of the unity at home, [which] might be altered."[24]

If government officials could not agree, how could the Episcopal Bench or any other state administrative body expect to govern the realm? The leaders of society had to have at least the outward appearance of unity before the nation would follow. It was this knowledge, plus loyalty to their monarch, which induced many of the conservatives to seek for a compromise with their reforming opponents, and to enforce laws of which as individuals they disapproved. To reiterate the already belabored remark of Bishop Bonner: "In matters of state, individuals were not to be so much regarded as the whole body of the citizens."[25] The principle was a universal dictum and applied to their own actions as well as to the behavior of the "lesser sort."

Thus the conservatives of the Episcopal Bench were confronted with the problem of divergent allegiances, of antithetic loyalties. They were presented with a dilemma to which no solution was found. As churchmen and guardians of souls they owed a moral obligation both to themselves and to their flock to regard religious problems as of paramount importance; but as administrators and diplomats and as creatures of the crown, their primary duty was to the state and nation. Under Henry this dual nature of their office had rarely conflicted, but under the youthful Edward the two positions were often antagonistic. In fact, many of the seemingly contradictory actions of these bishops are attributable to this inability to solve the enigma created by their dual office and their conflicting loyalties. Edmund Bonner, for instance, when the royal visitors presented him with the injunctions of July 1547, and ordered him to set up the *Book of Homilies* in the churches of his bishopric, received the injunctions with the

---

[24] Gasquet and Bishop, App. v, "The debate on the Sacrament," p. 405.
[25] Sanders, "Report to Cardinal Moroni on the change of religion in 1558-59," *Catholic Record Society*, 1 (1904-1905), p. 39.

"protestation, that I will observe them, if they be not contrary and repugnant to God's law and the statutes and ordinances of the Church."[26] The Bishop was shortly called before the Council to explain this statement, and at that time he confessed to the Lords of the Council that "upon better consideration of my duty of obedience, and of the ill example that may ensue to others thereof," he had decided to renounce his original protestation since it seemed "neither reasonable, nor such as might well stand with the duty of an humble subject."[27] Bonner was undoubtedly sincere in his change of opinion and there is no reason to believe that his renunciation was induced through fear, for the Bishop within two years was to prove himself quite ready to accept the consequences of open disobedience to the state.

The Protectorate was quick to appreciate the influence which such an appeal to national unity would have over the minds of the conservative opposition. When, during the discussion of the *Prayer Book* in the chamber of the Lords, Thirlby rose to point out that the bishops had not agreed to the doctrine of the Mass as a memorial when the book was first drafted in the previous September and that he, for one, would never accept it, the Earl of Warwick mildly chastised him, saying that "it was a perilous word spoken in that audience; and [he] thought him worthy of displeasure, [who] in such a time when concord is sought for, would cast such occasions of discord among men."[28] On the following day, Thirlby, though admitting the need for unity, made his opposition to the new service quite clear. In fact, the Bishop's "obstinate opinions" were considered so dangerous that the Duke of Somerset was forced to add to the warning of the Earl and cautioned Thirlby that "these vehement sayings showeth rather a wilfulness and an obstinacy to say he will die in it."[29]

---

[26] Burnet, IV, No. XII, p. 261.   [27] *Ibid.*
[28] Gasquet and Bishop, App. V, "The Debate on the Sacrament," p. 403.
[29] *Ibid.*, p. 406.

If the appeal to unity and internal concord did not suffice, the government was perfectly willing to insinuate the unpleasant consequences of "obstinacy."

The unfortunate conservatives endeavored to solve their difficulty by the questionable expedient of distinguishing between their two offices. As spiritual lords and churchmen they refused to sanction the principles on which the new religious legislation relied, but as administrators and state officials they acknowledged their duty to accept and enforce what Parliament and the Council had enacted. Evidently the prick of conscience was alleviated by their parliamentary opposition to the *Prayer Book*, for, as we have already noted, not one of the conservatives failed to administer it once the Act of Uniformity had been passed. Years before, under Henry, both John Fisher, Bishop of Rochester, and Sir Thomas More had sought refuge in the same type of rationalization, when they were forced to reconcile their obedience to the See of Rome with their duty to their sovereign.[30] More had always stated his willingness to conform to the facts of Henry's supremacy if not to the principle, and when Thomas Cromwell interviewed him in the Tower, More remarked that since "his Highness" was "in possession of his marriage and his noble woman really anointed Queen, [he would] neither murmur at it nor dispute upon it. . . ."[31] The political and matrimonial results of the breach with Rome he was willing to accept, but not the ideals on which it was presumed to rest, and More stood adamant in his refusal to swear to the preamble of the Act of Supremacy which named Henry as the head of the English church and denied the papal authority.[32]

---

[30] Cranmer, *Works*, No. cv, "Cranmer to Cromwell" (17 April, 1534), pp. 285-286.

[31] B.M., Cleo. E. vi, f. 155; printed in More, *Correspondence*, No. 199, p. 497.

[32] Chambers, *Thomas More*, p. 300. One of the fundamental difficulties for the more scrupulous of Henry's subjects was that the Oath of Succession not only required them to swear to support the Act itself, but also "all other

The Bishop of Winchester endeavored to utilize the same distinction, when, in July of 1550, he was presented with a series of articles which the Council ordered him to sign. Gardiner showed little reluctance in obliging his superiors, for the articles for the most part were restatements of events which he had either approved or to which he had signified his acquiescence. Ever since Henry's assumption of the supremacy, he had acknowledged the King to be Supreme Head of the church, while he had never denied that the government could legislate on such "indifferent" rituals as Lent, fasts, holy days, and images. One of the articles required that he acknowledge that the *Prayer Book* of 1549 was "a godly and Christian book and order, and to be allowed, accepted, and observed of all the King's most true subjects,"[33] and while the Bishop might have doubted the godliness of the work, he had already given his opinion that it should be accepted by "all the King's subjects."[34] But to these six articles there was added a preface of a far more compromising nature. In it the Bishop was expected to acknowledge that he "had been suspected as one too much favoring the Bishop of Rome's authority, decrees, and ordinances, and as one that did not approve or allow the King's Majesty's proceedings in alteration of certain rites in religion, and was convented before the King's Highness's Council and admonished thereof." He was ordered to confess that he was "right sorry therefor and knowledge" himself "condignly to have been punished. . . ."[35] Such a confession of guilt was tantamount to admitting that the principles and ideals on which his life had been based were wrong and ungodly, and this the Bishop refused to do. "I should sooner," he said, ". . . by commandment, I think, if ye would bid me, tumble myself desperately into the Thames"[36] rather than sign such a con-

---

acts and statutes made since the beginning of this present Parliament." (*Lords' Journal*, I, p. 82).

[33] These articles are printed in Dasent, *A.P.C.*, III, pp. 68-69.

[34] Foxe, VI, p. 113.   [35] Dasent, *A.P.C.*, III, pp. 67-68.

[36] Foxe, VI, p. 73.

fession, for what "pleasure," he asked, "were it to me to have my body at liberty by your procurement, and to have my conscience in perpetual prison by mine own act?"[37] Gardiner's sense of duty as a subject and as a crown official obliged him to accept what was authorized, but this in no way implied his approval, as an individual and as a cleric, of what the government had ordered.

At almost the same time as the Bishop of Winchester was salving his conscience by means of dubious rationalization in regard to the dual nature of his position, both Nicholas Heath and George Day encountered similar difficulties. In February 1550, Heath was placed on a commission of twelve ecclesiastics to rearrange and revise the ceremonial forms of ordaining and consecrating the clergy. The new Ordinal was presented to the Council the same month, and was signed by eleven of the commissioners, but Nicholas Heath's signature was strangely missing. The Bishop had categorically refused to give his approval to a ceremony which he considered basically heretical, and he was ordered before the Council on the last day of February to explain his position. Heath's refusal to conform to the will of the majority evidently baffled even his contemporaries and the minutes of the Council register the government's perplexity. "It is thought convenient by the Lords," an unknown clerk of the Council wrote, "that, seeing the rest appointed to devise the form for consecrating of priests have agreed upon the book and set their hands to the same, that the Bishop of Worcester shall also do the like, especially for that he cannot deny but all that is contained in the book is good and godly."[38] The Bishop later added to the confusion by indicating his willingness to obey the new Ordinal even though he still declined to sign it, an argument which the Council found difficult to appreciate.[39] However, Heath's position is not altogether perplexing if we realize that he was

---

[37] *Ibid.*, p. 74.   [38] Dasent, *A.P.C.*, II, p. 403.
[39] Dasent, *A.P.C.*, III, p. 361.

applying the same form of reasoning that More had used before him and which Stephen Gardiner would employ later the same year.

The Reformation historian, Gilbert Burnet, has confessed his perplexity concerning the Bishop's seemingly contradictory statements, and has acknowledged his inability to understand why Heath accepted imprisonment rather than give his consent to a form of consecration which Burnet considered of trifling importance.[40] Actually, however, the new ritual for ordaining priests was just as serious a blow to the Catholic faith as the *Prayer Book* of 1549, and the Bishop's reactions to both were identical. The issue behind the two works was the same, for as the *Prayer Book* had attempted to depreciate the sacrificial and emphasize the memorial nature of the Mass, so now the Ordinal of 1550 endeavored to picture the clergy merely as church ministers and not as sacrificing priests. Churchmen, by the terms of the new ritual, were to be regarded solely as teachers and preachers and superintendents of public worship, while any mention of their sacrificial powers was almost entirely omitted.[41] The new Ordinal, in fact, gave legal recognition to the concept of the nature of clerical ordinations which Cranmer had expounded many years before in 1540, that "there is no more promise of God, that grace is given in the committing of the ecclesiastical office, than it is in the committing of the civil office."[42] The *Prayer Book* had at least allowed a Catholic interpretation of the Mass, but now the Ordinal made such a construction even more difficult by depriving the priest of any miraculous authority. It is obvious that Heath, as a conservative ecclesiastic and a Catholic in all but his recognition of the papal power, could not sanction such a concept of the clergy, and in the same way as he had voted against the *Book of Common Prayer* in Parliament but enforced it once

---

[40] Burnet, III, pp. 294, 296.   [41] Constant, II, pp. 215-216.

[42] Cranmer, *Works*, "Questions and answers concerning the Sacraments and the appointment and power of bishops and priests" (1540), p. 116, No. 9.

the doctrine had received legal backing, so now in the case of the new Ordinal, he felt obliged to register his dissent even while signifying his willingness to administer what the law had stated to be "good and godly." His refusal to sign what the majority had approved was predicated upon his position as a clergyman and upon his individual conscience; his readiness to enforce what the government had decreed was based upon the obedience he owed his state both as an official of the crown and as a loyal subject.[43]

The case of George Day, Bishop of Chichester, involves yet another aspect of the essential question of the Mass as a sacrificial celebration. In the early winter of 1550, Day was ordered to appear before the Council for failing to enforce the government's order to replace all the altars of the realm with tables, and for refusing to preach a sermon justifying this procedure. The Bishop acknowledged his guilt but requested exemption from the order to preach in favor of the removal of the altars. This, however, the Council refused to allow and he was imprisoned in the Fleet, in the hope that his conscience might be modified by the discomforts of the body.[44] Finally he was deprived for his obstinacy and disobedience, along with Nicholas Heath, in October of 1551. Later, however, he was apparently offered his freedom if he would conform his conscience to the will of the Council, for Secretary Cecil wrote him in January of 1552 in the hope that a year in prison had weakened his resistance. Day's answer was as obstinate as ever, and he merely reiterated his old position. "I cannot tell," he said, "what I should write therein, otherwise than I answered unto my

---

[43] Messenger, *The Reformation, the Mass and the Priesthood*, pp. 498-500, takes another view of Heath's prevarications, and says: "Heath's statement that he would not disobey may quite well have meant that *he would not hold ordinations according to the Pontifical rite*. It does not imply that he himself would have held ordinations according to the new English rite." Had Heath confined himself to a negative statement and insisted merely that he would "not disobey" the new Ordinal, Messenger's theory might be acceptable. Unfortunately, however, the Bishop quite clearly stated his willingness to "obey" the new ritual. See Dasent, *A.P.C.*, III, p. 361.

[44] Dasent, *A.P.C.*, III, pp. 168-170, 172-173, 176, 178.

Lords of the Council (before I was committed to prison) and afterwards to the Commissioners at the time of my deprivation: viz. that I stick not at the alteration either of the usual form of the altar, either of the situation thereof, either of the matter (as stone or wood) whereof the altar was made, but I then took as I now take these things to be indifferent, and to be ordered by them that have authority. But the commandment, which was given to me to take down all altars within my diocese and in the lieu of them to set up a table, implying in itself (as I take it) a plain abolishment of the altar (both the name and the thing) from the use and ministration of the Holy Communion, I could not with my conscience then execute. . . . If I may by your help and Sir John Cheke in consideration of the loss of my living, and two years imprisonment, freely now obtain the liberty of a subject (which if I should hereafter abuse I would not desire to live) I will daily pray to God for the King's most excellent Majesty and most honorable Council. . . ."[45]

From a Protestant view, the Bishop's argument is not altogether logical. He was willing to change both the shape and the material of the altar and presumably to set up tables in their place, but he would not call a table a table, and insisted that even in its transformed shape it should still be referred to as an altar. Obviously Day was willing to fulfill the act of the Council's commandment but not its spirit. He would comply with the fact but not the principle of the Reformation legislation, and no amount of persuasion or imprisonment would induce him to compromise his conscience as an individual to fit the will of the Council. However, as a state official he was ready to administer the physical work of replacing altars with tables, and as a loyal subject not to complain or preach against the injunction. Burnet has again described the Bishop's posi-

---

[45] B.M., Lans. ii, No. 53, f. 121, "Bishop Day to William Cecil" (1552); printed in Ellis, *Original Letters*, 3rd Ser., vol. iii, No. ccclxviii, p. 303, and incorrectly dated 1550.

tion as "unaccountable,"[46] but George Day must have been fully aware of the motives behind the order, for in November 1551, Cranmer in a letter from the Council to Bishop Ridley wrote that "The form of a table shall more move the simple from the superstitious opinions of the popish mass, unto the right use of the Lord's Supper. For the use of an altar is to make sacrifice upon it; the use of a table is to serve for men to eat upon. Now, when we come unto the Lord's board, what do we come for? to sacrifice Christ again, and to crucify him again, or to feed upon him that was once only crucified and offered up for us? If we come to feed upon him, spiritually to eat his body, and spiritually to drink his blood (which is the true use of the Lord's Supper), then no man can deny but the form of a table is more meet for the Lord's board, than the form of an altar."[47] It made small difference to George Day whether the sacrifice was accomplished upon a table or an altar, but he obstinately refused to sanction the spirit of the new order by acquiescing in calling the new structure a table simply because, as Cranmer said, it denied the concept of a sacrifice.

Unfortunately for the conservative bishops this philosophical hair-splitting proved of little avail in an age when religious fanaticism had exceeded the limits of human reason and prudence. The Duke of Somerset gave expression to this collapse of human standards when he answered Cardinal Pole's letter suggesting that the religious issues dividing England and Rome be settled by a meeting of indifferent men. "And yet," he wrote, "your device were not the best or likeliest, whereof the sum is that there should be indifferent men chosen betwixt the realm and the church of Rome." Before any meeting of judicious and liberal men could be organized, the Duke said, "indifferent men should set an order first for the indif-

[46] Burnet, III, p. 295.
[47] Ridley, *Works*, "Injunctions given in the visitation of . . . Nicholas Bishop of London" (1550), p. 322.

ferences," and this, he implied, was now patently impossible, for no such basis of discussion existed. "If the controversy," he continued, "be of taking away abuses, superstition, idolatry, . . . we may peradventure in the way of reasoning grant them to be indifferent towards men, but surely to Godwards, which is the true trial and judge, they be ungodly, devilish, and wicked."[48] Whether the Protector was stating his own sentiments is open to question, but he was certainly echoing the attitude of many of the reformers who judged the doctrines and institutions of the church by the absolute standards of what God considered as "ungodly, devilish, and wicked." Considerations of human knowledge and expediency could never enter into the actions of men such as Hooper and Ridley who regarded the keeping or the abolition of abuse and superstition as equivalent to the difference between salvation and damnation. The form of the altar might in itself be indifferent to both Catholics and Protestants, but the issues dividing the two parties had transcended ceremonial forms, and now included the fundamental principle of Catholicism—the concept of the sacrificial Mass. The forms of ritual reflect the faith of the participant, and as the Bishop of Worcester pointed out in the debate over the *Prayer Book* of 1549, "Reason will not serve in matters of faith."[49] In the same debate, Edmund Bonner stated the question which was uppermost in the minds of many Englishmen when he asked: "As we seek and hear, what shall we do then when we have searched [for the truth]?" The only answer the Bishop could give, and possibly the only answer possible, was to say: "Believe then we must."[50] In matters of belief there could be no indifference, for the divine knowledge ultimately claimed by both sides could admit of no earthly compromise.

Under such conditions the negative acquiescence of many

---

[48] Pocock, *Troubles Connected with the Prayer Book of 1549*, Cam. Soc. XXXVII (1884), "Somerset to Pole" (4 June, 1549), p. xi.

[49] Gasquet and Bishop, App. v, "The debate on the Sacrament," p. 399.

[50] *Ibid.*, p. 439.

of the conservatives in the acts of the Reformation government was not sufficient, and the Council demanded the full
measure of obedience, the positive approval of the principles
and ideals upon which the innovations were founded. This
Gardiner, Bonner, Heath, and Day refused, and, like More
before them, preferred imprisonment and possible death rather
than to admit the injustice and wickedness of their cause. A
generation of mediation and compromise, years of endeavoring
to hold the middle line between Papism and Protestantism had
finally led to open disobedience. The truth of the warning
of the first of the Catholic martyrs, John Fisher, had been
realized when he told Convocation, many years before, the
parable of the ax which lacked a handle. "An ax, which wanted
a handle," he said, "came upon a time unto the wood, making
his moan to the great trees, that he wanted a handle to work
withal, and for that cause he was constrained to sit idle; therefore he made it his request to them, that they would be pleased
to grant him one of their small saplings within the wood to
make him a handle; who mistrusting no guile, granted him
one of their smaller trees to make him a handle. But now,
becoming a complete ax, he fell so to work, within the same
wood, that, in process of time, there was neither great nor
small tree to be found in the place where the wood stood."[51]
Bishop Fisher could never have foreseen the outcome of these
prophetic words, for he spoke them in 1524, when Wolsey
was attempting to persuade Convocation to grant him permission to dissolve several of the smaller monasteries in order to
finance his college at Oxford, and the Bishop considered the
request a dangerous precedent. Consciously or unconsciously,

---

[51] Bailey, *The Life and Death of the Renowned John Fisher*, p. 108.
This passage has been incorrectly dated 1536. Fisher was already dead by
the time of the dissolution of the smaller monasteries of that year. The
parable must then have been given in 1524 when Wolsey met with
considerable opposition in his efforts to get Convocation to sanction the
dissolution of several small houses, the profits from which the Cardinal
intended to use in the building and endowing of his new college at Oxford.

the conservatives had learned the lesson of Fisher's parable, for on Elizabeth's accession to the throne in 1558 only one of the Marian Episcopal Bench, Anthony Kitchen, was willing to give again a handle to the ax and recognize a new breach with Rome and a new Act of Supremacy.

In another sphere also the wisdom of the older Henrician state servants was fully vindicated, and the warning of Wolsey and More that the nobility would live to regret their greed in countenancing the destruction of the property of the church and clergy was realized in the social and religious upheavals which convulsed the country during 1549. The consequences of the union of reformers who in their zeal to establish the early simplicity of the primitive church were willing to strip the clergy of their wealth, and of politicians and courtiers whose questionable belief in the Protestant doctrines was largely motivated by the far from pious desire to absorb as much of the church's property as was legally possible, were not slow in appearing. The reformers certainly did not desire and probably did not foresee the results of their religious policy, but in their eagerness to evangelize society they disturbed a host of time-honored customs and stirred up a multitude of social problems. Like reformers before and after them, they were convinced that the mere application of godly legislation and the preaching of God's word would make of Englishmen "spiritual Israelites," and they never realized the truth of the ancient maxim that "Alas, the greatest evil sent by the gods to man is this: that we should know the good and do it not."[52] Bishop Hooper was convinced that sedition was the direct result of ignorance of divine law, and in a sermon preached during Lent in 1550 he said: "It is a fond opinion, most Gracious King . . . that in case the doctrine of Christ and his holy sacraments should not be decked and set forth with these plausible and well liking ceremonies (that is, to

[52] *Tragicorum Graecorum Fragmenta*, ed. A. Nauck, 2nd edition (Leipzig, 1926), No. 841, p. 635.

speak plainly, with papistical superstition), it were to be feared of sedition and tumult. Doubtless, if the Pope's members would not deceive the people but teach them God's words, the people would soon see the truth, and willingly leave as much as God and their King should command them. . . ."[53] The Bishop had little sympathy for those who thought "peace and quietness shall come to the realm a better way than to have the true religion of God restored."[54]

In the previous reign, Sir Robert Wisdom had encountered the wrath of old Bishop Stokesley for preaching very much the same doctrine. The preacher had made the suggestion that his parishioners should take their Bibles with them on Sundays and holidays when they met together at the local alehouse and "talk and converse and reason of it." When Stokesley was informed of this suggestion, his immediate reaction was to say: "Yea, but when they are drunken they shall unreverently handle the Scripture and much mischief may come by it." Sir Robert was unable to appreciate the warning of the Bishop, and he answered that he had "exhorted them to have the Scripture in their hands that remembering the fear of God they might abstain from excess and drunkenship. . . ." The worldly Bishop of London must have listened to this pious hope with considerable amusement, but the determined minister was quite sincere in his faith in the salubrious effects of the Scriptures, for he continued his argument by asking "What is the cause of so many drunkards? So much pride that men set so much by themselves and so little by God, that they are so covetous, so puffed up, such shameful hypocrites, such horrible swearers, so cursed tongued, so disobedient to their parents, so unthankful, so ungodly and unnatural, such breakers of promise and covenants, such railers, so intemperant, so cruel, so neglecting of all goodness, such traitors and so false-hearted to their princes . . . ?" Stokesley might have answered

[53] Hooper, *Early Writings*, p. 440.
[54] *Ibid.*, p. 439.

that men did all these evils simply because they were human, but Sir Robert Wisdom was quite sure that this long list of crimes was due to "nothing else but that they have thrown from them the word of God and there is no wisdom in them."[55] Despite the pun, he undoubtedly believed exactly that.

Following the path of earthly wisdom, Bishop Stokesley promptly clapped Sir Robert into prison on the excuse that such idealized sentiments were too dangerous to society to be left unpunished. The conservatives with considerable justice felt that the determined faith of such fanatics would lead to rioting and sedition, and Bishop Bonner, for one, never doubted that it was this same type of idealism which had caused the series of rebellions which broke out in the spring of 1549. Whether justly or not, he attributed the revolts directly to the religious innovations of the Edwardian government and the indiscreet actions of the leading reformers. During his trial in June of that year, his ire fell particularly upon his two denouncers, William Latimer[56] and John Hooper, who, he informed his judges, would have them believe "that they have made their said pretensed denunciation, not moved of any malice or evil will, but for the good tranquillity and governance of this realm, which, as they pretend in their gay and glorious proem, they would seem to have a great care and solicitude of, whereas in very deed they and such as they are, by sundry ways, and especially by their corrupt doctrine, and heretical naughty preaching, and infecting of the King's Majesty's people, have disturbed and greatly inquieted the good tranquillity and governance of this realm, as evidently and notoriously it is well known. . . ."[57] To Bonner the fruits

---

[55] B.M., Harl. 425, ff. 4-7, "Robert Wisdome's letter, written in the Lollard's Tower, to the brethren, giving an account of the reason of his imprisonment" (*L.P.*, xviii, pt. i [1543], No. 539).

[56] William Latimer was Parson of St. Lawrence Pountney, and should not be confused with his more distinguished contemporary, Hugh Latimer, ex-bishop of Worcester.

[57] Foxe, v, pp. 755-756.

of the new Protestant learning were clearly to be found in the rebellion of 1549.

Actually, of course, the revolts of that year, known as the risings of the East and West, were only in part caused by religious discontent on the part of the believers of the old faith, or the desire of religious radicals to spiritualize or communize the daily life of the nation. As in the revolt of the Pilgrims of Grace thirteen years before, a multitude of conflicting interests were involved. England was floating rudderless through a sea of economic troubles, and these, just as much as the religious innovations of the reign, underlay the demands of the rebels. The government of the Protectorate had inherited a bankrupt and dangerously inflated economy; the wealth of the New World had resulted in a sharp increase of prices while the wages of a still predominantly agrarian society had not kept pace with the rising cost of living. The expenses of the new bureaucratic machine created by the first two Tudors were prodigious, and far exceeded the royal income. Frugality had filled the coffers of the first Tudor, and the wealth of the monasteries had helped finance the government and foreign policy of the second, but even by the closing years of Henry VIII's reign, the government was running into debt and had sought the temporary expedience of debasing the currency. Under Edward the process of inflation continued, resulting in a serious dislocation of trade and the further increase of prices. To add to the trials of the yeoman and peasant classes, the process of enclosure, whereby the landlord encroached upon the communal rights of the peasants to use the common land of the manor and converted arable land into pasture, continued at a rapid rate as the profits from the wool trade increased. We need not narrate in further detail the host of social evils which burdened sixteenth-century England, except to add that the weight of the economic dislocation fell primarily upon the laboring sections of society.[58]

[58] The standard account of the revolt in Norfolk is still F. W. Russell,

As Gardiner predicted to Cranmer, if "the wall of author-ity" was once broken, "and new water let in at a little gap, the vehemence of novelty will flow further" than even the reformers were willing to accept. Authority had been under-mined in religious matters, and it was only a matter of time before secular jurisdiction likewise collapsed. Dangerous so-cial concepts had been disseminated throughout the land under the guise of the Bible in English, while it had proved impos-sible to prevent the Anabaptist belief in communal ownership from attracting peasants and laborers, who were burdened with rising prices and taxes and were confronted with the disagree-able picture of widespread inequality of wealth. "It is not agreeable with the gospel," stated one champion of the under-privileged classes in 1550, "that a few persons shall live in so great abundance of wealth and suffer so many their Chris-tian brothers to live in extreme poverty."[59] Nor did the words of some of the leaders of the Reformation help to instill in the people a proper Christian forbearance in the face of this world's evils. When Hugh Latimer cried out against the greedy gentry, saying "You landlords, you rent-raisers, I may say you step-lords, you unnatural lords, you have for your possessions yearly too much,"[60] he was merely giving divine sanction to the demands of peasants who bitterly resented the efforts of wealthy farmers to raise their rents and enclose their lands.

Thus religious innovation and social grievance played their part in the uprising during the summer of 1549. In the west, in Cornwall and Devonshire, the rebellion was primarily re-ligious, and the insurgents demanded the return of the Cath-olic Mass and the reenactment of the Act of Six Articles, in a word, the demand of the western rebels was a complete and

---

Kett's Rebellion in Norfolk. See also Frances Rose-Troup, *The Western Rebellion of 1549.* Constant, *The Reformation in England,* II, pp. 102-122, has an admirable but brief description of the risings of 1549.

[59] *Pyers Plowmans Exhortation,* quoted in White, *Social Criticism,* p. 29.
[60] Latimer, *Sermons,* p. 84.

purposeful rejection of the *Prayer Book* and the religion on which it stood.[61] In the east, around Norfolk, however, the rising was far more serious, for the rebels led by Robert Kett were in some ways more advanced in their Protestantism than either Cranmer or Ridley. Their grievances were social and their demands at times bordered upon communism.[62] For a time, the situation was so serious that London was placed under martial law and troops had to be recalled from Scotland and France, but by August the rebellions both in the east and west were crushed. Whatever the true causes behind the insurrections of 1549, they were sufficiently religious in their outward appearance to convince the conservatives of the truth of their fears—that Protestantism would lead to social revolution. The picture of those summer months in 1549 when Englishmen were killing Englishmen was before the eyes of the Marian Lord Chancellor, Stephen Gardiner, when he preached at St. Paul's in December 1554, and joyfully announced the "awaking" and final reconciliation with Rome after the long sleep which had been the schism of the past twenty years. The nightmare was over, he said, and England had awakened from the terrible dream "of killing, of maiming, of burning, and of such beastliness as I dare not name. . . ."[63] To Edmund Bonner, as well as to Gardiner, the lesson of "the dolorous experience of the inconstant government" of Edward's reign was confirmation that internal tranquillity and quiet could never be maintained, except by the restoration of the papal authority and the Catholic church. Consequently, Bonner took pains to mark the moral of a generation of schism which, he claimed, was to be found in the destruction of "all good order, as well in the church, as in the commonwealth. . . ." The appeal to internal security and order was the strong-

[61] The articles of the Devonshire and Cornwall rebels are printed in Pocock, *Troubles connected with the Prayer Book of 1549*, Cam. Soc. XXXVII (1884), pp. 145-188.

[62] Constant, II, p. 116.

[63] Foxe, VI, "Notes of a sermon of the Bishop of Winchester," p. 577.

est argument which the conservatives of Mary's reign possessed, and the Bishop of London did not hesitate to emphasize the bloody history of the preceding years. "Now here Christian people," he pleaded in his *Book of Homilies*, published in 1555, "though you do not consider the play of sundry sins, that hath in this late schism, possessed many men's souls, yet do not dissemble, nor forget the misery, that we all have suffered outwardly, since we were separate from the Church of Christ: Alas, what Christian blood within this Realm, even by our own countrymen, hath been shed? Oh Lord, how many poor widows without comfort have been left? How many fatherless children without succour?"[64]

The claim that heresy breeds civil strife was undoubtedly true, at least in the sixteenth century, but some of the reformers suspected, not without cause, that the conservative insistence on religious orthodoxy for reasons of human prudence was merely clever dissembling. "Mark also another subtlety of the fox," wrote William Turner of Stephen Gardiner "where as in my former hunting I made such arguments against the Pope's ceremonies and traditions as he could not solute, now because he seeing that he cannot defend the Pope under the name of ceremonies and traditions now calleth him good politic laws where with the king's subjects are enclosed . . . and after this marvelous transformation he maketh the Pope's ceremonies the King's politic laws."[65] The appeal, as Turner suggests, to the gospel of human prudence, to the arguments of a legally trained mind and the fears of a statesman and administrator, may indeed have been a form of worldly rationalization of problems which were fundamentally matters of faith. It is difficult to conceive of Gardiner, Bonner, Heath, and Day preferring years of imprisonment to accepting the Reformation legislation, merely because they considered such laws socially dangerous and politically unde-

[64] Bonner, *Homilies*, f. 42.
[65] Turner, *The Rescuynge of the Romishe Fox* (1545), Sig. B. II.

[279]

sirable. These men did not face physical jeopardy because they were administrators and lawyers any more than Cranmer and Hooper withstood the torments of the stake because they were theologians and university dons. Their strength lay in their religious faith—the one Catholic, the other, Protestant. But it must be remembered that conservative and reformer alike stemmed from the same educational, social, and religious background, and it was only after their lives had diverged that they began to manifest different approaches to religious questions. The conservatives, after leaving Oxford and Cambridge, had little time or occasion to question the basic precepts of their Catholic beliefs, while their education in law and experience in diplomacy and administration merely confirmed the truth of what they had heretofore accepted on faith. Had Gardiner entered Jesus College and not Trinity Hall, had he spent his life in probing the deepest mysteries of religion, and had he never been subjected to a multitude of practical considerations relative to a long career in the service of the state, he might not, it is true, have ended a Protestant martyr as did Cranmer, but he certainly would have been a very different person from the man who eventually became Lord Chancellor under Queen Mary.

The law, the study of humanism and the demands of a diplomatic career made these conservative bishops what they were—statesmen who sought truth in the book of human knowledge and theory in the ageless lesson of daily experience. As administrators they saw in religion society's greatest bulwark, a divine authority which lent moral sanction to social order. Paradoxically, the conservatives were far closer in their thinking and social philosophy to the attitude of the new nobility and the "middle class" gentry than were the reformers, and as Professor Tawney has so sagely perceived: "The most scathing attack on social disorders came, not from the partisans of the old religion, but from divines on the left wing of the Protestant party, who saw in economic individualism but another expression of the laxity and license which had degraded the purity of religion, and who understood by reformation a return to the moral austerity of the primitive church, no less than to its government and doctrine."[66] This is not to say that the conservative bishops necessarily approved of enclosure and rent-raising, but unlike the reformers, they had little desire to achieve the theocratic utopia of creating a heaven on earth. The foundation of their thinking was secular, not religious, and though faith may have been the ultimate basis of their Catholicism, reason and the practical considerations of this world confirmed and strengthened them in their opposition to ideas and doctrines which involved the destruction of cultivated and inherited patterns of religious thought.

[66] Tawney, *Religion and the Rise of Capitalism* (Pelican edition), p. 121.

CHAPTER X

EPILOG: THE STERILE REIGN (1553-1558)

O~N~ the 6th of July, 1553, that "godly and virtuous imp," Edward VI, died of consumption, and despite the desperate calculations of the Duke of Northumberland England rallied to the support of its legitimate sovereign, Catholic Mary. As a consequence, the prison gates of the Fleet and the Tower of London were cast open and the imprisoned conservatives of the Henrician episcopate were set at liberty while their places were taken by Latimer, Hooper, Ridley, and Cranmer. An accident of history, a palace revolution, had reversed the tables, and as Bishop Bonner acidly observed, the reformers were soon to discover that "their sweet shall not be without sour sauce."[1] But the future of the conservatives was not without its "sour sauce" also. The individual bishops might be liberated and returned to their episcopal dignities but the age of the legally trained ecclesiastical administrator was over and their species proved itself to be as barren as the new Queen herself. Moreover, they shortly realized that the "bellie wisdom" of their gospel was as much out of place under a Catholic queen guided by the small but persistent voice of her conscience as it had been in the Protestant atmosphere of the previous reign.

The ecclesiastical diplomats, jurists, and administrators were, as F. W. Maitland has pointed out, an expiring race, a fact which the new reign made painfully apparent.[2] The decline of the episcopal statesman was a reflection of the times, and the encroachment of the laymen upon preserves previously limited to clerics was a process which had begun under

[1] Burnet, IV, No. VII, "Bonner to Thomas Shirley *et al.*" (6 September, 1553), pp. 330-331.
[2] Maitland, *English Law and the Renaissance*, p. 51, n. 18.

Henry VIII. Although Gardiner and Heath became Lord Chancellors under Queen Mary and Thomas Thirlby was temporarily appointed custodian of the Great Seal,[3] the Chancellorship, except briefly under James I, was never again to be held by a clergyman.[4] Heath, after his release from prison, was made Lord President of the Marches of Wales, but when he released that post to become Lord Chancellor in 1555 the office was returned to the Earl of Pembroke and thereafter remained in the hands of a layman. Though Henry VIII had maintained two high ecclesiastics, Tunstal and Holgate, as Presidents of the Council of the North, the Edwardian government bestowed that position on the Earl of Shrewsbury, who significantly retained his post under Mary.[5] But the shift to a lay government is best exemplified by Mary's council.[6] Out of a total of almost fifty councillors only five held episcopal rank[7] while in the sphere of diplomacy only two bishops, the veteran Thirlby and the new Bishop of St. Asaph, Thomas Goldwell, were ever used on foreign missions.

At the accession of Mary the old Henrician episcopal civil servants were, for the most part, elderly men in an age which accounted three score and ten the maximum life span. Aldridge, Chambers and Sampson were all in their 60's; Tunstal, Kitchen and King were elder ecclesiastics in their 70's; Salcot and Voysey were relics of a still more distant past, both being over 80, while some of the younger bishops such as

[3] *Cal. St. P. Ven.*, VI, pt. i (1555-1556), No. 246, p. 213.

[4] Powicke, *Handbook of British Chronology*, p. 70. John Williams, Archbishop of York (1641-1650), was Lord Chancellor from 16 July, 1621 to 1 November, 1625.

[5] Reid, *The King's Council in the North*, App. II, pp. 487-488. The office remained in the hands of a layman except for a period of seven years when Thomas Young, Archbishop of York, held the post from May 1564 to June 1568 and Matthew Hutton, Archbishop of York, from February 1596 to August 1599.

[6] Harbison, *Rival Ambassadors at the Court of Queen Mary*, pp. 61-62; Pollard, *History of England*, pp. 94-96.

[7] They were Reginald Pole, Stephen Gardiner, Cuthbert Tunstal, Nicholas Heath, and Thomas Thirlby.

Gardiner and Day, men still in their 50's, had grown old under the strain of ceaseless labor and imprisonment. Mary's reign is branded by the merciless extermination of the leading reforming prelates, but although the new Queen may have been partial in her selection of martyrs, death itself was far less prejudiced. Of the 14 conservatives who were alive to greet the Queen only five survived her reign.[8] This high death rate among the Henricians might not have been serious had it been possible to replace them. But unlike the Protestants, where the blood of the martyrs was the seed of the church, there were no replacements for the ecclesiastical civil servants who died of overwork or old age. The falling off of the proportion of doctors of civil and canon law among the new Marian episcopal appointments is startling—of the 19 new bishops only three were Doctors of Law,[9] while with the exception of Cardinal Pole, Archbishop of Canterbury, none were members of the Council. More and more the control of government was being monopolized by laymen while the church and especially the Episcopal Bench were being restricted to men of God. Mary may have stood for the restoration of the old regime, but even had she so desired she could not restore the conditions of the pre-Reformation society out of which the ecclesiastical statesman had sprung. In fact, the new Queen accelerated the process of decay by continuing the policy of her brother. The Protestant leaders of the previous reign had reserved the bishoprics and deaneries for divines "and thus what had been the prizes of his profession were placed beyond the jurist's reach."[10] As the proportion of jurists to theologians among the Marian episcopal appoint-

---

[8] Richard Sampson died 25 September, 1554; John Voysey on 23 October, 1554; Stephen Gardiner on 12 November, 1555; John Chambers on 7 February, 1556; Robert Aldridge on 5 March, 1556; George Day on 11 August, 1556; Robert Parfew on 22 September, 1557; John Salcot on 6 October, 1557; Robert King on 4 December, 1557. Those of the old guard remaining were Heath, Kitchen, Thirlby, Bonner, and Tunstal.

[9] See App. v.

[10] Maitland, *English Law and the Renaissance*, p. 51, n. 18.

ments indicates, this policy continued unabated during the Catholic reaction.

It was not, however, merely the older conservatives who died under Mary; the mortality rate of the entire episcopate is extraordinarily impressive and one might almost conclude that elevation to episcopal rank was to risk divine retribution. Besides the nine Henricians, three of the Queen's appointments died before her own death, while five more survived their sovereign by a single month.[11] By January of 1559 the death toll had become such that John Jewel wrote Peter Martyr that "if the bishops go on as they have begun, bishoprics will shortly become very cheap . . . there are at this time no less than fourteen sees vacant."[12] The venerable divine's figures are inaccurate, but his pleasure in the fall of "those oily, shaven, portly hypocrites,"[13] as he preferred to describe the Catholic prelates, was none the less obvious.

Thus in the closing months of 1558, when the third new reign and fourth religious upheaval in one generation commenced, only sixteen bishops were able to attend Elizabeth's first Parliament or to send their proxies. Five of the Henrician and eleven of the Marian episcopate remained, while death had made the new Queen's position easier by conveniently removing the remaining ten.[14] For a second time the opponents of Protestantism were forced to search their con-

[11] George Coates, Bp. of Chester, died in 1555; William Glynn on 21 May, 1558 and James Brooks in September of the same year. Reginald Pole and Maurice Griffin, Bp. of Rochester, both died in November of 1558 while John Christopherson, Bp. of Chichester, John Holyman, Bp. of Bristol, and John Hopton, Bp. of Norwich, died in December.

[12] *Zurich Letters*, No. VIII (26 January, 1559), pp. 6-7.

[13] *Ibid.*, No. XXXII, "Jewel to J. Similer" (November 1559), p. 64.

[14] Bayne, Bonner, Kitchen, Oglethorpe, Pate, Scott, White, and Turberville were all present at the first session of Parliament which met on 25 January, 1559. Bourne, Morgan, Pole, Thirlby, and Tunstal were represented by proxies while Goldwell was not summoned and Watson was absent through sickness after the 4th of March (*Lords' Journal*, I, pp. 541 and 565; Birt, *Elizabethan Religious Settlement*, pp. 44-45). The Sees of Canterbury, Norwich, Rochester, Oxford, Chichester, Hereford, Salisbury, Gloucester, and Bangor were vacant (Dasent, *A.P.C.*, VII, p. 28).

sciences and decide between their divergent loyalties—between their allegiance to their sovereign and to their faith. For the most part however, the decision reached in 1559, the refusal to support in Parliament the new Act of Supremacy and the consequent failure to accept the oath of supremacy,[15] was merely a reiteration of a stand taken almost a decade before. Two-thirds of the Marian prelates had already reached the real crisis of their lives; what happened in the early months of Elizabeth's first Parliament was little more than a tragic anticlimax.

Bonner, Heath, Thirlby, and Tunstal had all taken up their position in 1549 when they voted against the first of the Edwardian Acts of Uniformity and all but Thirlby had accepted deprivation and imprisonment as the price of their recalcitrance.[16] Thomas Watson of Lincoln and John White of Winchester had both been imprisoned during Edward's reign for being too closely associated with the party of Bonner and Gardiner.[17] Richard Pate, Bishop of Worcester, had sacrificed a promising diplomatic career under Henry VIII when in 1541 he fled to the party of Cardinal Pole at Rome.[18] Likewise Thomas Goldwell, Bishop of St. Asaph, had preferred exile rather than conform to the Henrician religious settlement.[19] Gilbert Bourne's record is not so clear, for the Marian bishop of Bath and Wells had been a relatively obscure man during Edward's reign and as Rector of High Ongar in Essex seems to have escaped the wrath of the Protestant government. However, under Henry VIII, he had been chaplain to Bishop Bonner and had risked his ecclesiastical career by being one of the Bishop's most devout supporters during his trial in 1549.[20] Finally, Owen Oglethorpe, Bishop of Carlisle, also seems to have merely repeated in 1559 his decision reached when he

[15] *Lords' Journal*, I, pp. 565, 568. [16] See ch. IX *passim*.
[17] *DNB*, Arts. "Thomas Watson" and "John White."
[18] *L.P.*, XVI [1541], Nos. 446, 448, 449; *DNB*, Art. "Richard Pate."
[19] Gillow, *Literary and Biographical History*, II, pp. 513-514.
[20] *DNB*, Art. "Gilbert Bourne"; Fox, V, pp. 784-786.

was President of Magdalen College under the Protestant regime. Like many of his contemporaries he reluctantly accepted the religious changes instituted at his college but in 1552 he was finally deprived of his office even though he escaped being imprisoned.[21] With the exception of Anthony Kitchen, Bishop of Llandaff, the remaining five prelates seem to have avoided the difficult question of reconciling their consciences and their duty to the crown, or at least were not publicly forced into making a decision.

For the old Henricians as well as for a number of the newer Marian appointments consistency may have been in large measure the determining argument in their resolution to resist the Elizabethan religious settlement. There is considerable truth in John Jewel's remark to his reforming colleague, Peter Martyr, when he wrote that "The bishops, rather than abandon the Pope whom they have so often abjured before, are willing to submit to everything. Not, however, that they do so for the sake of religion of which they have none, but for the sake of *consistency* which the miserable knaves now choose to call their *conscience*."[22] The worthy divine wrote in derision but except for his failure to appreciate the religious basis of his opponents' actions, he came surprisingly close to the truth. A lifetime had convinced many of these men of the value of authority and although Tunstal and Thirlby may have insisted on the maintenance of authority for social considerations, while the Theatine monk, Bishop Goldwell, did so because of religious scruples, the result was very much the same. With the exception of one man, the entire Marian episcopate persisted in supporting the authority of the Pope.[23] Time and time again under Mary both the old Henricians and the newer ecclesiastics had reiterated the importance of an ultimate source of authority. A generation of controversy had been released by

[21] *DNB*, Art. "Owen Oglethorpe."

[22] *Zurich Letters*, No. XXVII (1 August, 1559), p. 54.

[23] Anthony Kitchen twice voted against the Act of Supremacy (*Lords' Journal*, I, pp. 565, 568), but later accepted the oath and retained his see.

the Protestant Reformation and the bishops were convinced that this controversy would lead to spiritual and social anarchy as well as to damnation. "If you will not have the church to be certain, I pray you by whom will you be judged in matters of controversy," George Day once asked John Philpot in answer to one of that reformer's more oracular theological assertions. The young man answered that in "all manner of controversies the word ought to be judge" and the Bishop not unnaturally asked him "what if I take it one way, and you another; how then?"[24] There seemed to be no answer to this question for unless there was one authoritative interpretation, the word of God could be taken in a variety of ways.

This same problem of ultimate authority also worried James Brooks, the Marian Bishop of Gloucester, and he once informed Nicholas Ridley that if the deprived bishop refused "the determination of the Catholic church, you must needs be singular and wise in your own conceit, for you bring Scripture for the probation of your assertions, and we also bring Scripture; you understand them in one sense and we in another. How will you know," he asked, "the truth herein?" Bishop Brooks was quite sure that "except we do constitute the church our foundation, stay and judge, we can have no end of controversies, no end of disputations."[25] Possibly however, it was the French ambassador, Charles de Marillac, who put his finger on the underlying dilemma when in 1540 he reported to his government in words reminiscent of more modern times that some middle-of-the-road settlement was being sought for in England but that he predicted that any attempt at religious compromise would "result like the diets in Germany, of which one engenders several others . . . and doubts, instead of ending, will increase."[26] For the doctors of divinity as well as those in law there seemed to be in 1559 only one way to remove the constant doubt, to end the incessant controversies,

---

[24] Fox, VII, p. 673. [25] *Ibid.*, p. 538.
[26] Kaulek, *Correspondance Politique de Marillac*, p. 188; *L.P.*, XV [1540], No. 737.

and that was to maintain at all costs the supremacy of the Pope.

Though the ecclesiastical lawyers and diplomats were being deprived of the rewards of their profession, though their breed was gradually disappearing, the real tragedy of their lives lies in the history of their age. The Henricians had been born to one set of values and had died under another. Bred to the enthusiastic humanism of the Renaissance, they perished in an atmosphere of emotional bigotry epitomized by the meaning which the expression "the new learning" eventually acquired. Originally it had embodied a variety of meanings relative to the quickened tempo of intellectual life and especially to the revived study of Greek and Latin authors, but by the time Henry died in 1547 it had lost this academic flavor and had been swept into the religious polemics of the age. "The new learning" was now used to signify solely the study of the Reformation doctrines. As the phrase remained the same throughout the generation of Henry's reign but its meaning changed, so the protagonists of those militant years remained constant but the values of their society altered; from enthusiastic supporters of the "new learning" they developed into its most obstinate opponents.

Moreover, the Catholic church had not remained untouched. Catholicism both at home and abroad had been transformed by the Protestant Reformation. The church which accepted the prodigal daughter back into the fold was now the Papacy of Cardinal Caraffa, a man who regarded his elevation to Peter's chair in May of 1555 as proof of the personal interference of God in the affairs of men. The new Pope was an acrimonious old man with extravagant concepts of his papal prerogative, willing to sacrifice both Papacy and church to his violent antipathies and religious zeal. Significantly, he was a member of the new Theatine monastic foundation, an organization which along with the Jesuits was the symbol of a rejuvenated but authoritarian Catholicism. The old Henrician conservatives may have been sincere penitents in their return to Rome but they were of the humanistic Catholic tradition and could not entirely escape the taint of heresy for having sanctioned so many of the early religious reforms in England. Even Cardinal Pole, who had spent a lifetime in exile working for the reunion of England and the Papacy, was not free from the stain of liberal Catholicism which in the eyes of Caraffa constituted heresy, and at the time of his death he was on the verge of excommunication by the very institution to which he had consecrated his life.[27]

If the comfortable but corrupt Papacy of Clement VII had been purged in the fire of the Reformation, so also had much of the liberal spirit within the Catholic church in England. The change is nowhere more apparent than in the composition of the Marian episcopate. The new incumbents of the dioceses of England were different both in temperament and training from the older Henrician prelates. Almost half of Henry's Episcopal Bench had been Doctors of Law, while under Mary only three of the new appointments were trained in the civil or canon law and 15 had degrees in divinity.[28] Moreover, the basis of selection had altered since the days of the second Tudor. Bonner, Gardiner, Thirlby, and Tunstal had owed their promotion to long years dedicated to the service of the state; the Marian bishops, on the other hand, were men who for the most part had earned their sees through their devotion to their religious faith. Five of the new Catholic prelates had given clear indication of their episcopal qualifications through many years of exile under Henry or his son.[29] Like their Protestant counterparts the Marian bishops tended to be men of God and although they were imbued with the spirit of the Catholic Counter Reformation, in many ways they had more in com-

---

[27] Schenk, *Reginald Pole*, pp. 118, 164-165; Haile, *Life of Reginald Pole*, pp. 512-519.

[28] See App. v.

[29] They were Reginald Pole, Richard Bayne, Thomas Goldwell, Richard Pate, and John Christopherson.

mon with their evangelical opponents than with the cautious and worldly ecclesiastical statesmen of Henry's reign. Like Ridley, Cranmer, Latimer, and Hooper they were theologians and university professors. Richard Bayne was a distinguished Hebrew scholar, while John Christopherson, John White, James Brooks, George Coates, Owen Oglethorpe, and Cuthbert Scott had all been masters, wardens, or presidents of various collegiate institutions.[30] As for John Hopton, he was Mary's personal confessor throughout Edward's reign and risked imprisonment when he persisted in maintaining the Catholic rites in his patron's household.

Again like the reforming prelates, little is known about the early careers of most of the Marian appointments except that they were conscientious men who viewed the religious conflict of their age in its simplest form—the inevitable war between the powers of light and darkness. They tended, as did the reformers, to place matters of God above those of expediency and questions of state, and their attitude at times came surprisingly close to that of such men as Latimer and Hooper. At the Queen's funeral in December of 1558 Bishop White of Winchester, in a sermon which would have shocked his worldly predecessor, said: "Better is one lively preacher in the church that dareth to bark against sin, blasphemy, heresy; better is one lively officer or magistrate in the commonweal that dareth to speak against injuries, extortions, seditions, rebellions, and other discords, than the dead lion; that is to say, men, perhaps, of great dignity and vocation, who dare not open their mouths and bark, but suffereth while all goeth to ruin, to the decay of Christian religion, and the subversion of the public wealth."[31] Significantly, it was the Archbishop of York, Nicholas Heath, who was still a member of the Privy Council, who peremptorily ordered the Bishop before the Council for having preached such a sermon at a moment of

[30] See App. v.
[31] Strype, *Ecc. Mem.*, III, pt. ii, No. LXXXI, p. 544.

[291]

national crisis, and as a consequence the indiscreet prelate found himself confined to his house.[32] We need only compare Bishop White's outburst with some of the more fiery dictums of such men as Hugh Latimer to realize that militant Catholicism and Protestantism were rapidly joining hands in a common denunciation of the practical creed of Mammon which placed the security and stability of this life before the theological purity of the next.

Although not typical of the caliber of men on the Episcopal Bench, Thomas Goldwell, Bishop of St. Asaph, indicates the growing spiritual and religious preoccupation of its members and supplies the link between the militant, anti-nationalistic faith of the Elizabethan Jesuits and the milder but equally determined convictions of the Marian Catholics. Goldwell was the son of a prosperous county family in Kent and was educated at All Souls, Oxford, where he received his degree of Bachelor of Divinity in 1534. Probably as early as 1532 he had become a member of Pole's household at Padua,[33] but he does not seem to have remained in Italy for he must have returned home in 1534 to receive his divinity degree. However, shortly thereafter he renounced a promising ecclesiastical career and permanently joined Pole in voluntary exile, and along with his patron was attainted for high treason in 1538. Goldwell joined the Theatine house of St. Paul at Naples in 1547 and eventually became a full member three years later. When the Cardinal returned from exile during the Marian reaction, the Theatine monk accompanied him to England and was shortly made Bishop of St. Asaph. On the succession of Elizabeth he managed to escape imprisonment and retired into permanent exile. Refusing both a cardinal's hat and the offer of an Italian bishopric, he reentered his monastery becoming the Superior of his order in 1561. The exiled Bishop seems to have had two missions in life to which he gave himself un-

[32] *Zurich Letters*, No. VIII, p. 16.
[33] *L.P.*, V [1531-1532], No. 1155.

sparingly—his faith, and his hopes for the return of England to the Catholic church. Undoubtedly a deeply sincere man, he was regarded by that astute judge of character, Elizabeth, as a "very simple and fond man."[34] He was probably both of these, and as a consequence took a completely unrealistic view of events in England. In 1580 he obtained with considerable difficulty from a skeptical Pope permission to join Edmund Campion in that Jesuit's tragic, if well-intentioned, efforts to wrest England from the bewitching charms of her Protestant Queen. Dying in 1585, Thomas Goldwell was the last surviving Marian prelate. He was a man who harkened to the call of the spirit before that of his nation, a man who in many ways was similar to the more radical Protestants in that he placed spiritual salvation before political security.[35]

Although "Bloody Mary's" death on November 17th, 1558, meant the end of papalty in England, it made but little difference to the older conservatives such as Heath, Tunstal, Thirlby, and Bonner. Whether Mary had lived or borne an heir, the future would not have been theirs; instead, it lay with the militant authoritarian Catholicism of the Jesuits and the Counter Reformation and with the Protestant, nationalistic spirit of the "beardless boys" of Elizabeth's reign. Almost everything for which the Henrician prelates stood had vanished, and though Bonner, Heath and Thirlby lived many years into the new reign, their age was in fact over. What one reformer said on hearing of the death of Cardinal Pole can almost be generalized into a proper epitaph for all of the Henrician conservatives. "We have nothing . . . to fear . . . ," he said, "for dead men do not bite."[36] Not all, of course, of the older generation were dead, but they certainly had lost their "bite."

Although "all the churches in London did ring" and men

[34] *Cal. St. P. Foreign* (1561-1562), No. 948, p. 563.
[35] Gillow, *Literary and Biographical History*, II, pp. 513-522.
[36] *Zurich Letters*, No. III, "Edwin Sandys to Henry Bullinger" (December 1558), p. 4.

"did make bonfires" and "drink and make merry" to celebrate the succession of Good Queen Bess,[37] a mere change of
sovereigns could not destroy the policy of human prudence
which had been the guiding light of the Henrician prelates.
Gardiner, Heath, Tunstal, and Day and the other disciples
of "bellie wisdom" may have been enthralled by a cherished
if vain illusion—the belief that the sanely ordered reality of
this world must be protected against the figments of the ideal-
ist's imagination. Their apprehension may have been unwar-
ranted, but like men before and after them they sought a firm
foothold against the tide of human fancy. The appeal of the
gospel of human prudence and the reaction against it was to
continue unabated; the same slogans, the same arguments both
for and against were to be bandied back and forth in only
slightly modified form indefinitely. Elizabeth and her "beardless boys" were to impose a new religious *via media* but they
were as much addicted to cautious expediency as ever Henry's
ecclesiastical statesmen had been, and Protestant divines who
in their younger days had been convinced of the blessings of
the kingdom of God on earth grew more conservative with
each passing year. Thus the new Archbishop of Canterbury,
Matthew Parker, prayed that God and Queen would keep
England "from such [a] visitation as Knox has attempted in
Scotland; the people to be orderers of things."[38] The pendulum had shifted a little farther to the left, but the relation-
ships had remained constant, and as Gardiner had feared the
social consequences of Parker's mild Protestantism, so the new
Archbishop in his turn was concerned over the revolutionary
implications of Knox's Presbyterianism. Likewise, the demands
of the extreme left under Elizabeth are reminiscent of the
Henrician evangelists, and when Rodolp Gualter appealed
to Elizabeth in 1559 against the proponents of a cautious religious compromise he was merely reiterating many of the

[37] Machyn, *Diary*, p. 178.
[38] Parker, *Correspondence*, No. LXXII, p. 105.

[294]

ideas of men like Latimer and Hooper. He pointed out to the new Queen the "saying of Christ who declares that the *new pieces* of evangelical doctrine will not suit the *old garments* of superstitions. And he also solemnly warns us not to put the fermenting and wholesome *new wine* of his gospel into *old leathern bottles*, unless we would have not only these to perish, but that to be spilled at the same time."[39]

The gospel of human prudence as preached and practiced by the Henrician episcopal statesmen is merely one instance of human conservatism. Like many practical men of affairs who recognize the need for reform but who are fearful of its social implications, their apprehension in the face of revolution became so great that they ended by renouncing all change however mild. For the Henrician conservatives, the drift from practical if limited reform to something bordering on reaction was completed in one generation. When Stephen Gardiner officiated at the coronation of Anne Boleyn to Bluff King Hal in 1533 he and Tunstal and John Clerk had written to Sir Thomas More asking him to join them in celebrating a ceremony which, more than any act of Parliament, symbolized the breach with Rome. The retired Chancellor refused and wrote his friends a letter the full import of which took them twenty years to realize. "Though your lordships," he said, "have in the matter of the matrimony hitherto kept yourselves pure virgins, yet take good heed, my Lords, that you keep your virginity still; for some be there that by procuring your lordships first at the coronation to be present, and next to preach for the setting forth of it, and finally to write books unto all the world in defense thereof, are desirous to deflower you, and when they have deflowered you, then will they not fail to devour you."[40] Twenty-six years later the lesson of More's prophecy had been belatedly but thoroughly learned,

[39] *Zurich Letters*, No. v (January 1559), pp. 8-9. The italics are Gualter's.

[40] Harpsfield, *Life of Sir Thomas More*, pp. 148-149.

and Nicholas Heath gave expression to a generation of bitter experience when he spoke the epitaph of humanism and liberal Catholicism by categorically stating "whatever is contrary to the Catholic faith is heresy; whatever is contrary to unity is schism." "It is the same thing, so far as schism is concerned, to do a little or to do all."[41]

[41] Sanders, "Report to Cardinal Moroni on the change of religion in 1558-59," *Catholic Record Society*, 1 (1904-1905), p. 38.

APPENDICES

ABBREVIATIONS USED IN NOTES
AND APPENDICES

MANUSCRIPTS are cited and their location given under their usual abbreviations, which are as follows:

Bodleian Lib.	Bodleian Library, Oxford.
Ash.	Ashmolean Mss.
B.M.	British Museum, London.
Cleo.	Cotton Mss., Cleopatra.
Galba	Cotton Mss., Galba.
Tib.	Cotton Mss., Tiberius.
Vit.	Cotton Mss., Vitellius.
Add.	Additional Mss.
Harl.	Harleian Mss.
Lans.	Lansdowne Mss.
Royal	Royal Mss.
P.R.O.	Public Record Office, London.
S.P. 1	State Papers, Henry VIII.
S.P. 3	Lord Lisle Papers.
S.P. 6	Theological Tracts, Henry VIII.
S.P. 10	State Papers, Domestic, Edward VI.

In the citation of printed books, the following abbreviations have been used:

Cal. St. P. Span.	*Calendar of Letters . . . Relating to the Negotiations between England and Spain.*
Cal. St. P. Ven.	*Calendar of State Papers . . . Preserved in the Archives of Venice.*
Cam. Soc.	Camden Society Publications.
Dasent, *A.P.C.*	Dasent, *Acts of the Privy Council.*
DNB	*Dictionary of National Biography.*
E.E.T.S.	Early English Text Society.
EHR	*English Historical Review*
H.S.	Harleian Society Publications.
Leland, *Collectanea* ..	Leland, *Antiquarii de Rebus Britannicis Collectanea.*

[297]

L.P. .... *Letters and Papers, Foreign and Domestic, of the Reign of Henry VIII.*
Lords' Journal .... *Journals of the House of Lords.*
N. and Q. .... *Notes and Queries.*
St. P. .... *State Papers during the Reign of Henry VIII.*
Strype, Ecc. Mem. .... *Strype, Ecclesiastical Memorials.*

Fuller titles, names of editors, and dates of editions may be found in the bibliography of printed books. Several well-known histories and collections of documents such as Burnet, Foxe, Constant, and Gasquet and Bishop, are cited under the names of author or editor only. Titles and editions used may be found in the bibliography of printed books.

It should be noted that the spelling and punctuation of manuscript quotations have been modernized in order to facilitate reading.

APPENDIX I

BISHOP BONNER'S PARENTAGE

THE question of Edmund Bonner's parentage rests, in large measure, upon what books one cares to read. Protestant historians have usually accepted the story of his illegitimacy without question (see Burnet, *History of Reformation*, II, pp. 430-431), but Catholic writers such as G. E. Phillips have vigorously denied or completely ignored the stigma of the bar sinister (*The Truth about Bishop Bonner*, p. 1). The problem has more or less become a matter of religious preference, for Edmund Bonner was an outstanding opponent of the Protestant party, and such authors as Bale and Poynet in their zeal for their faith have not hesitated to portray "Bloody" Bonner as a veritable monster—a legend ably preserved by John Strype who describes the Bishop as a "bastard all over. He a bastard, his father a bastard, his grandfather a notorious whoremaster" (*Ecc. Mem.* III, pt. ii, p. 172).

It was in reaction to this kind of polemical writing that S. R. Maitland was induced to investigate the problem of Bonner's illegitimacy which he dismisses as malicious Protestant slander, fabricated in order to "furnish a ground for denying the validity of his orders, and, therefore, of all acts performed by him in his episcopal character" (*Essays on the Reformation*, p. 58). Maitland is not the only historian, however, to query the legend of the Bishop's illegitimacy, and strangely enough, Strype himself felt obliged to cast doubt on it. After assuring his reader that Bonner was "a bastard all over," he later recounts the story of his conversation with one Nicholas Lechmere who assured Strype that his grand-father had known the Bishop and that the Lechmere family papers held proof of Bonner's lawful birth (*Annals*, I, pt. ii, p. 300).

Unfortunately, the evidence of Bonner's legitimacy rests primarily on Maitland's able but unsubstantiated conjecture, Lechmere's undocumented conversation, and the argument that any proof of illegitimacy is merely Protestant forgery. The story of the Bishop's unsavory lineage stems from an existing pedigree showing that Bonner was one of seven baseborn children of George Savage, parson of Daneham. There are at least three versions of this pedigree which differ from one another in detail only (see B.M., Tib. E. VIII, f. 213; Petyt 538, vol. 47, f. 4; and Harl. 1424, f. 134, printed in the *Visitation of Cheshire*, H.S., XVIII, p. 205). The dates of these documents are unknown. Presumably they were compiled before 1597 since Sir John Savage, who is described in the Tiberius and Petyt versions as "now living," died in that year. In all probability the original was composed during the first years of Elizabeth's reign and before the Bishop's death in 1569.

It seems improbable that anyone would have dared to associate the Savage family of Cheshire with such an unpopular man as Bishop Bonner unless there were considerable truth in the assertion that the Bishop was an illegitimate offshoot of that family. This is especially so inasmuch as the Savages were related to the Earls of Derby, the Earls of Worcester, to Lord Barkeley, and to the Bulkeleys of Anglesey. Moreover, whoever wrote the pedigree had intimate and accurate knowledge of the Savage family tree (cf. *Visitation of Cheshire*, H.S., XVIII, pp. 203-204 and p. 205). Finally, it is highly unlikely that this unknown genealogist fabricated the details of Bonner's life, for they can be checked against verified facts. Thus the Harleian version says that Bonner was the "son of George Savage, priest, parson of Daneham [Danham] in Cheshire, who was slain before Boulogne when Henry VII laid siege to it, which priest begot Edmund of one Elizabeth Frodsham who was sent with child out of Cheshire to one that was called Savage of Elmley in Worcester. And when she was delivered of Edmund, one Boner, a sawyer with Mr. Armingsham, married her and begot other children and lived at Potters Hanley in Worcester . . . ." and ". . . one

[299]

Serle, living in Bushly . . . was a cousin of Boner." We know that a branch of the Savages of Cheshire did live at Elmley in Worcestershire (see their pedigree: *Visitation of Worcestershire*, H.S., XXVII, p. 125); that Bonner did have relatives living in that county; and that he was a close friend of a Mr. Serle (B.M., Vit. B. XXI, f. 148). Moreover, it is known that Bonner as a young man held a benefice from the Savage family, for Sir Richard Bulkeley wrote Thomas Cromwell in 1533 requesting him to give to his brother, John Bulkeley, the "benefice of Danam in Cheshire which is in the gift of Mr. Savage, now the King's ward, especially as it is said by those coming from London [that] Dr. Bonar is to be Bishop of Chester" (P.R.O., S.P. 1, vol. 74, f. 200). It is very probable that this is a variant spelling of the same benefice held by Bonner's natural father, George Savage, parson of Daneham.

Illegitimacy in the sixteenth century had not acquired the social stigma that it was later to assume during the Victorian period, and it is not unnatural that Bonner should have been baseborn. Many of the landed and clerical families of the Tudor reign had illegitimate offspring, and even Cuthbert Tunstal, Bishop of Durham, was born out of wedlock (Sturge, *Cuthbert Tunstal*, pp. 3-7), while Cardinal Wolsey had several natural children. The only other piece of evidence relating to the Bishop's lineage is the provocative but unverified statement of S. R. Burke in his *Historical Portraits* (III, p. 285) that Bonner "was indebted for his promotion to his kinsman, Lord Cromwell." Certainly the Bishop was indebted to the Vicar-general, but I can find no evidence of a blood relationship.

APPENDIX II

THE BULKELEYS OF ANGLESEY

AND CHESHIRE

THE case of Arthur Bulkeley is an example of the difficulties which confront the genealogist when he endeavors to place a man in his exact family position. This is especially true when he is dealing with a second son of a cadet line. The Bulkeley family of Cheshire was a remarkably prolific branch, and though it is obvious that Arthur was related, it is impossible to give his exact relationship. He was certainly connected with Sir Richard Bulkeley of Beaumaris, the Vice-Chamberlain of Wales, whose family originally stemmed from Cheshire, for Sir Richard refers to the Bishop as his "cousin" (*L.P.*, xii, pt. ii [1537], No. 998) and Arthur mentions him in his will (Willis, *Survey of the Cathedral Church of Bangor*, No. xxviii, p. 256). The future Bishop was probably one of two Arthur Bulkeleys who appear in the various pedigrees of the family. He may have been the third son of Charles Bulkeley of Burgate whose father was Sir William Bulkeley, Kt., of Eaton and Deputy Justice of Chester (*Visitations of Hampshire*, H.S., lxiv, p. 4). However he may also have been another Arthur who appears in the same pedigree as the brother of Charles Bulkeley of Burgate and as the second son of Sir William of Eaton—a possibility increased by the fact that Bishop Arthur Bulkeley's coat of arms is the same as that of the Bulkeleys of Eaton (cf. *Visitation of Cheshire*, H.S., xviii, p. 54, and Bedford, *The Blazon of Episcopacy*, p. 17). However, George Ormerod, *History of the County Palatine and City of Chester*, iii, pt. i, p. 269, gives this Arthur Bulkeley a son Thomas. Bishop Kennett, moreover, has a completely different version of the Bishop's antecedents, and states that he was "the son of Richard Bulkeley, son of another Richard, the son of John, son of another John Bulkeley, but whether he was of the Anglesey or Cheshire branch I find not" (*Bp. Kennett's Notes*, B.M., Lans. 980, f. 117). Unfortunately Bishop Kennett fails to mention where he found such an array of ancestors, and for lack of evidence to the contrary we must assume that Arthur Bulkeley was one of the Eaton Bulkeleys.

APPENDIX III

GENEALOGICAL INFORMATION

SECTION A

The following are those bishops whose pedigrees have been recorded in the College of Heralds or can be found in manuscript form at the British Museum.

Thomas Cranmer, *Visitations of the County of Nottingham*, H.S., iv, pp. 70-71.

William Barlow, Meyrick, *Visitations of Wales*, i, pp. 117-118.

George Day, *Visitation of Shropshire*, H.S., xxviii, p. 162.

Thomas Goodrich, *Lincolnshire Pedigrees*, H.S., LI, pp. 415-417.

John Voysey (alias Harman), *Visitation of Warick*, H.S., XII, p. 105; *Bp. Kennett's Notes*, B.M., Lans. 980, f. 142; Oliver, *Lives of the Bishops of Exeter*, p. 120.

John Wakeman (alias Wicke), B.M., Harl. 6185, f. 75 (74).

John Skip, Robinson, *A History of the Mansions and Manors of Herefordshire*, p. 170; Bodleian Lib., Ash. No. 831.

Richard Sampson, There is some confusion concerning Bishop Sampson's pedigree, cf. B.M., Add. 5524, f. 157 (163), and *Visitations of Berkshire*, H.S., LVII, p. 207. In the former, the Bishop is included and given his proper title of Bishop of Coventry and Lichfield; in the latter, this Richard Sampson is deprived of his episcopal rank and given several children. However, despite the *Berkshire Visitation* pedigree, it seems that this Richard, who was a brother of Robert of Bynfeld, Berkshire, clerk of the Council to Henry VII and VIII, was actually the Bishop of Coventry and Lichfield since his coat of arms, except for a difference in color, is the same as that of the Sampsons of Berkshire (cf. *Visitations of Berkshire*, p. 207 and Bedford, *Blazon of Episcopacy*, p. 66). Unfortunately, however, there is still much to be explained. For instance, Richard, Bishop of Coventry and Lichfield, had a brother named Nicholas Sampson (*L.P.*, XI [1536], No. 543) who does not appear in either of the above pedigrees. See also *N. and Q.*, ser. 10, XI (1909) pp. 16, 117, 396.

Henry Holbeach (alias Randes), *Lincolnshire Pedigrees*, H.S., LII, p. 810.

Edmund Bonner, B.M., Harl. 1424, f. 134, printed in *The Visitation of Cheshire*, H.S., XVIII, p. 205; Inner Temple Library, Petyt Ms. vol. 47, No. 538. f. 4; and B.M., Tib. E. VIII, f. 213 (177, 179); see also App. I.

William Rugge (Rugg, Reppes), *Visitations of Norfolk*, H.S., XXXII, p. 229.

Nicholas Ridley, *Visitation of Yorkshire*, H.S., XVI, p. 263; Foster, *Pedigrees Recorded at Heralds' Visitations of Northumberland*, p. 102.

Thomas Thirlby, *Visitations of Essex*, H.S., XIV, p. 556.

Robert Holgate (Holdegate), Hunter, *Familae Minorum Gentium*, H.S., XL, p. 1282.

Cuthbert Tunstal, Sturge, *Cuthbert Tunstal*, App. I.

Arthur Bulkeley, *Visitations of Hampshire*, H.S., LXIV, p. 4; Ormerod, *History of the County Palatine and City of Chester*, III, pt. i, p. 269; see also App. II.

Robert King, B.M., Add. 24488, p. 1. For further details and the Bishop's relationship to Thomas Cromwell, see *DNB*, Arts. "Robert King" and "Thomas Cromwell."

SECTION B

Stephen Gardiner, Nicholas Heath, and Robert Ferrar have no pedigrees, but their relationship to families of moderate wealth is quite clear. Gardiner was a younger son of John Gardiner, a cloth-maker of Bury St. Edmunds of "comfortable circumstance" (Muller, *Stephen Gardiner*, pp. 1-2). Heath was the son (probably the second) of William Heath, "citizen and culter of London" and his wife, Agnes (see Agnes Heath's will recorded at Somerset House, Dyngeley—28, and William's will, Dyngeley—3). The *DNB*, Art. "Nicholas Heath," says that Nicholas was born in London and was descended from the Heaths of Apsley, Tamworth. However, it is probable that William and his son Nicholas were related to the Heaths of Twickenham in Middlesex, since the Bishop's arms are very similar to those of John Heath, gent. of Twickenham who married Agnes, dr. of Lee (cf. *Visitation of London*, H.S., I, p. 37, and Bedford, *Blazon of Episcopacy*, p. 138). Ferrar was probably born at Ewood, Yorkshire (*DNB*, Art. "Robert Ferrar"). Moreover, Wordsworth, *Ecclesiastical Biography*, V, p. 75, says on the authority of Dr. P. Peckard's *Memoirs of the Life of Nicholas Ferrar*, Cambridge, 1790, that "Nicholas was very nearly related to that pious and resolute martyr Robert Ferrar, Bishop of St. David's." Nicholas Ferrar himself was descended from a Yorkshire branch of the de Ferrariis family who theoretically could trace their genealogy back to the days of William the Conqueror. In fact, all the known records of Bishop Robert Ferrar's background lead to Yorkshire and there certainly were Ferrars or Farrars living at Ewood in the sixteenth century. The Bishop was, in all probability, related to William Farrar of Ewood who married Margaret dr. of John Lacy of Brearley (cf. his coat of arms with those of the Bishop—*Visitations of Hertford-shire*, H.S., XXII, p. 53, and Bedford, *Blazon of Episcopacy*, p. 40).

SECTION C

Considerably less is known about the final seven bishops. Anthony Kitchen, alias Dunston, is said by the *DNB*, and by J. C. Whitebrook, *The Consecration of Matthe Parker*, p. 19, to have been born in 1477. However, he did not receive his B.D. till 1525 and his D.D. till 1538. Though he might have received these degrees at the ages of 48 and 61, it seems improbable. Again, it is possible, but unlikely, that he should have died at the age of 86 or 87. Whitebrook states that he received a bachelor's degree in canon law in 1493 from Cambridge and was "probably" born at Dunstan, near Bolsover, of "a fairly well-to-do family." Also the Bishop may have been related to Robert Kitchen of Leeds, Yorkshire, whose arms are very similar to those of Anthony (cf. *Visitation of Hertfordshire*, H.S., XXII, p. 70, and Bedford, *Blazon of Episcopacy*, p. 79). Paul Bush, Bishop of Bristol, is said by A. Wood and the *DNB* to have been born in Somerset "of honest and sufficient parents"—a statement which seems to be confirmed in part at least by the fact that he was a friend of Walter, Lord Hungerford and is referred to in a letter from Lord Hungerford to Cromwell as "Sir Paul Bushe" (*L.P.*, XIII, pt. i [1538], No. 1064). The genealogy of Robert Aldridge, though better documented than Bishop Bush's, is even more obscure. A. Wood, *Athenae Oxonienses*, I, p. 232, states that he was born at Burnham in Buckinghamshire. There was certainly a William Aldrich living in Burnham whose will is dated October 1511, and who left his cousin Robert, "a scholar," a bequest of 40 pounds (see his will, Somerset House, Fetiplace—3). However, J. C. Smith in *N. and Q.*, Ser. 13, I (1923) p. 369, says that a John Aldryge, of London, grocer, died and his will was proved in the Prerogative Court of Canterbury, on 11 Feb., 1517-18 by his brother, Master Robert Aldryge, clerk. This Robert, Mr. Smith says, "was doubtless the headmaster of Eton, afterwards prominent as the Bishop of Carlisle. By giving a bequest to his father, Richard Aldryge, the testator incidentally supplies the hitherto unrecorded Christian name of the Bishop's father." Finally, there seems to be no evidence that Robert Aldridge was in any way related to the influential and wealthy Aldridges of Yarmouth and Norwhich (see their pedigree in the *Visitations of Norfolk*, H.S., XXXII, pp. 2-3). John Bird, Bishop of Chester, is connected by A. Wood (I, p. 238) to the Birds of Broxton (see their pedigree in Ormerod, *History of the County Palatine and City of Chester*, II, pt. ii, p. 675). Bishop

Godwin, *Catalogue of Bishops*, B.M., Harl. 2039, f. 163, says that he was born in Coventry in Warwickshire. If he was connected with the Broxton Birds, he came from a distinguished and powerful county family. The history of John Chambers, alias Borowe, is equally difficult. Gunton, *History of the Church of Peterburgh*, p. 57, merely says that the Bishop was born at Peterburgh. C. H. Garrett, *Marian Exiles*, p. 111, suggests that Richard Chambers, the important Marian exile, was the natural son of the Bishop who was in turn the base offspring of Laurence Chamber (or Chambers), "fourth son of Thomas Chamber of Wolsted Castill, Cumberland, in the reign of Henry VII, and himself Lord Abbot of Peterborough." However, if John Chambers' real name was Borowe as Bishop Kennett says (B.M., Add. 5828, p. 150), this would invalidate Miss Garrett's suggestions. As for John Salcot, alias Capon, and Robert Warton, alias Parfew, Purefoy, and Parfey, I can find nothing concerning their pasts.

APPENDIX IV

CLASSIFICATION OF BISHOPS

NAMES	RELIGIOUS STATUS	DEGREES	PREVIOUS STATUS
Conservatives			
Dead by 1548			
Bell, J.	Secular	B.C.L.	Lawyer & Councilor.
Clerk, J.	Secular	LL.D.	Lawyer, Councilor, Diplomat.
Fox, Edw.	Secular	D.D.	Councilor & Diplomat.
Kite, J.	Secular	?	Diplomat.
Knight, W.	Secular	D.C.L.	Lawyer, Councilor, Diplomat.
Lee, Edw.	Secular	D.D.	Councilor & Diplomat.
Lee, R.	Secular	B.C.L.& D.Can.L.	Lawyer & Councilor.
Longland, J.	Secular	D.D.	Confessor to H. VIII, and Councilor.
Sherborn, R.	Secular	M.A.	Diplomat.
Stokesley, J.	Secular	D.D.	Vice-Pres. Magdalen Col., Almoner, Councilor, Diplomat.

NAMES	RELIGIOUS STATUS	DEGREES	PREVIOUS STATUS
Living in 1548			
Aldridge, R.	Secular	D.D.	Univ. Preacher, Provost of Eton, Registrar of the Order of the Garter, Diplomat.
Bonner, E.	Secular	D.C.L.& B.Can.L.	Lawyer, Councilor, Diplomat.
Bulkeley, A.	Secular	D.C.L.& B.Can.L.	Lawyer & Councilor.
Day, G.	Secular	D.D.	Vice-Chancellor, & Provost of King's College.
Gardiner, S.	Secular	D.C.& Can.L.	Lawyer, Councilor, Diplomat.
Heath, N.	Secular	D.D.	Almoner, Councilor, Diplomat.
Rugge, W.	Regular	D.D.	Abbot, St. Bennet's, Hulme.
Skip, J.	Secular	D.D.	Master of Gonville Hall, Almoner and Councilor.
Thirlby, T.	Secular	D.C.& Can.L.	Lawyer, Councilor, Diplomat.
Tunstal, C.	Secular	LL.D.	Lawyer, Councilor, Diplomat.
Voysey, J.	Secular	D.C.L.	Lawyer and Councilor.

Total: 22	Total:	Total:	
	Regular:1	D. or B. of L.	11
	Secular: 21	D. of Div.	9
		M.A.	1
		Unknown	1

Reformers			
Martyrs			
Cranmer, T.	Secular	D.D.	Fellow of Jesus Col., Univ. Preacher, Diplomat (?).
Ferrar, R.	Regular	B.D.	Can. Regular, St. Austin Order.
Hooper, J.	Regular	B.A.	Cistercian Monk.
Latimer, H.	Secular	B.D.	Fellow of Clare Col., Univ. Preacher.
Ridley, N.	Secular	D.D.	Master of Pembroke College.

Appointed After 1547			
Coverdale, M.	Regular	D.D.	Augustinian Friar.

NAMES	RELIGIOUS STATUS	DEGREES	PREVIOUS STATUS
Harley, J.	Secular	B.D.	Master of Magdalen School, Chaplain to John Dudley.
Poynet, J.	Secular	B.D.	Dean of Queen's Col., & Chaplain to Archbp. Cranmer.
Scory, J.	Regular	B.D.	Dominican Friar.
Taylor, J.	Secular	D.D.	Master of St. John's Col.

Other Reformers

Barlow, W.	Regular	?	Can. Regular, St. Austin Order, Prior of Bromehill, Diplomat (?).
Bird, J.	Regular	D.D.	Provincial of the Carmelite Friars, Suffragan to Bp. Holgate.
Bush, P.	Regular	B.D. (D.D.?)	Bonhomme of the Reformed Order of the St. Austin Monks.
Goodrich, T.	Secular	D.D.	Fellow of Jesus Col., Univ. Proctor.
Hilsey, J.	Regular	B.D. (D.D.?)	Black Friar, Dom. Order.
Holbeach, H.	Regular	D.D.	Benedictine Monk.
Holgate, R.	Regular	D.D.	Gilbertine Canon, Univ. Preacher.
Shaxton, N.	Secular	D.D.	Fellow of Gonville Col., Univ. Preacher.

Doubtful

Chambers, J.	Regular	B.D.	Abbot of Peterborough.
King, R.	Regular	D.D.	Abbot of Oseney and Thame.
Kitchen, A.	Regular	B.D.	Abbot of Eynsham.
Salcot, J.	Regular	D.D.	Abbot of Hyde.
Wakeman, J.	Regular	B.D.	Abbot of Tewkesbury.
Warton, R.	Regular	B.D.	Abbot of Bermondsey.

Total: 24	Total:	Total:
	Regular:16	D. or B. of Law 0
	Secular: 8	D. or B. of Div. 22
		B.A. 1
		Unknown 1

APPENDIX V

THE MARIAN APPOINTMENTS

NAME	RELIGIOUS STATUS	DEGREES	PREVIOUS STATUS
Bayne, R.	Secular	D.D.	Professor of Hebrew, Paris (?).
Bourne, G.	Secular	B.D.	Chaplain to Bp. Bonner; Rector of High Ongar, Essex.
Brooks, J.	Secular	D.D.	Master of Balliol Col.; Chaplain & Almoner to Bp. Gardiner.
Christpherson, J.	Secular	B.D.	Exile in Louvain (1547-53); Master of Trinity Col.
Coates, G.	Secular	D.D.	Master of Balliol Col.
Glynn, W.	Secular	B.D.	Lady Margaret prof. of theology; Dean of Queen's Col.
Goldwell, T.	Regular	B.D.	Exile in Italy; Theatine monk.
Griffin, M.	Regular	B.Can.L.	Archdeacon of Rochester; Chancellor of St. Asaph.
Holyman, J.	Regular	D.D.	Monk of St. Mary's Abbey, Reading; Vicar of Winge, Bucks.
Hopton, J.	Regular	D.D.	Dominican monk; Chaplain & confessor to Princess Mary.
Morgan, H.	Secular	D.C.L. B.Can.L.	Principal of St. Edward's Hall.
Oglethorpe, O.	Secular	D.D.	President of Magdalen Col.
Pate, R.	Secular	B.D.	Archdeacon of Lincoln; diplomat; exile; made Bp. of Worcester by Paul III in July of 1541.
Pole, D.	Secular	D.C.L.& B.Can.L.	Dean of the Arches; Chancellor of Coventry & Lichfield.
Pole, R.	Secular	B.A.	Dean of Exeter; Scholar; exile; made a Cardinal in October of 1536.
Scott, C.	Secular	D.D.	Master of Christ's Col.; Vice Chancellor of Cambridge.
Turberville, J.	Secular	D.D.	Rector of Hartfield, Sussex; Canon of Winchester.
Watson, T.	Secular	D.D.	Master of St. John's Col.
White, J.	Secular	D.D.	Warden of Wykeham's School.

| Total: 19 | Total: Regular: 4 Secular: 15 | Total: D. or B. of L. 3 D. or B. of Div. 15 B.A. 1 | |

[308]

BIBLIOGRAPHY

OF PRINTED BOOKS

Alane, A. *Of the Auctorite of the Word of God against the Bishop of London.* Printed in H. Ellis, *Original Letters.* 3rd Ser., Vol. III, p. 196.

Allen, P. S. and H. M. *Opus Epistolarum Des. Erasmi Roterodami.* 11 vols. Oxford, 1906-1947.

Archaeologia: or, Miscellaneous Tracts relating to Antiquity. Vol. XXIII. London, 1831.

Archaeologia Cantiana; being Transactions of the Kent Archaeological Society. Vol. I. London, 1858.

Atterbury, F. *Rights, Powers, and Privileges of an English Convocation Stated and Vindicated.* London, 1700.

Bailey, A. "A Legal View of Cranmer's Execution," *English Historical Review,* Vol. VII, pp. 466-470. London, 1892.

Bailey, T. *The Life and Death of the Renowned John Fisher.* London, 1739.

Barnes, R. *Supplication.* Printed in *The Whole Works of W. Tyndall, John Frith, and Doctor Barnes.* London, 1573.

Baskerville, G. *English Monks and the Suppression of the Monasteries.* Bedford Historical Series, Vol. VII. London, 1940.

Beckett, W. A. *The English Reformation.* Church History Series, Vol. VII. London, 1890.

Bedford, W. K. R. *The Blazon of Episcopacy.* Oxford, 1897.

Birt, H. N. *The Elizabethan Religious Settlement.* London, 1907.

Bonner, Edmund. *Homelies sette forth by the Right Reverende Father in God, Edmund, Byshop of London.* London, 1555.

Bretschneider, C. G. *Corpus Reformatorum.* 3 vols. Halle (Saxony), 1836.

Brewer, J. S. *The Reign of Henry VIII.* 2 vols. London, 1884.

Brinklow, H. *The Lamentacyon of a Christen agaynst the Cytye of London.* Printed in Early English Text Society, Vol. XXII. London, 1874.

Burke, S. H. *Historical Portraits of the Tudor Dynasty and the Reformation Period.* 4 vols. London, 1879-1883.

Burnet, G. *The History of the Reformation.* Ed. E. Nares. 4 vols. London, 1839; Ed. N. Pocock. 7 vols. Oxford, 1865.

Bush, D. *The Renaissance and English Humanism.* Toronto, 1939.

Calendar of Letters, Dispatches, and State Papers Relating to the Negotiations between England and Spain. Ed. G. A. Bergenroth, *et al.* 11 vols. London, 1862-1896. (Cited as *Cal. St. P. Span.*)

Calendar of State Papers and Manuscripts Relating to English Affairs, Preserved in the Archives of Venice. Ed. R. Brown, *et al.* 9 vols. London, 1864-1898. (Cited as *Cal. St. P. Ven.*)

Calendar of State Papers, Domestic Series, of the Reigns of Edward VI, Mary, Elizabeth, 1547-1580. Ed. R. Lemon. London, 1856.

Calendar of State Papers, Foreign Series, of the Reign of Elizabeth, 1561-2. Edw. J. Stevenson. London, 1866. (Cited as *Cal. St. P. Foreign.*)

Cardwell, E. *Documentary Annals of the Reformed Church of England.* 2 vols. New Edition. Oxford, 1844.

Carthew, G. A. *History of the Hundred of Launditch, Norfolk.* Norwich, 1878.

Cavendish, G. *The Life of Cardinal Wolsey.* Ed. H. Morley. 3rd Edition. London, 1890.

Chambers, R. W. *Thomas More.* Bedford Historical Series, Vol. II. London, 1938.

Clark, W. K. L. and Harris, C. *Liturgy and Worship.* London, 1932.

Clerk, John. "Oration." Printed as a preface to *Assertio Septem Sacramentorum: or an Assertion of the Seven Sacraments Against Martin Luther by Henry VIII.* Tr. T. W. Gent. London, 1687. •

Colliers, J. *An Ecclesiastical History of Great Britain.* Ed. T. Lathbury. 9 vols. London, 1852.

Constant, G. "Politique et dogme dans les confessions de foi de Henri VIII, roi d'Angleterre." *Revue Historique,* Vol. CLV, pp. 1-38. Paris, 1927.

The Reformation in England. Vol. I, *The English Schism: Henry VIII.* Tr. R. E. Scantlebury. New York, 1934.

The Reformation in England. Vol. II, *Introduction of the Reformation into England: Edward VI.* Tr. E. I. Watkin. New York, 1942.

Cooper, C. H. and T. *Athenae Cantabrigienses.* 2 vols. Cambridge, 1858-1861.

Cootes, C. *Sketches of the Lives and Characters of Eminent English Civilians.* London, 1804.

Corpus Reformatorum. See Bretschneider, C. G.

Cranmer, T. *Miscellaneous Writings and Letters.* Ed. J. E. Cox.
Parker Soc. Cambridge, 1846.
Works. See above.
Writings and Disputations. Ed. J. E. Cox. Parker Soc. Cam-
bridge, 1844.

Dasent, J. R. Acts of the Privy Council of England. Vols. II, III,
& VII. New Series. London, 1891. (Cited as Dasent, *A.P.C.*)

Davis, J. "Doctors' Commons, its Title and Topography." *London Topographical Record.* Vol. XV, pp. 36-50. London,
1931.

Dickens, A. G. "The Marriage and Character of Archbishop Holgate." *English Historical Review.* Vol. LII, pp. 428-442. London, 1937.

Dictionary of National Biography. Ed. L. Stephen and S. Lee. 63
vols. London, 1885-1900. (Cited as *DNB*)

Dixon, R. W. *History of the Church of England.* 6 vols. London,
1878-1902.

Dodds, M. H. and R. *The Pilgrimage of Grace, 1536-37, and*
the Exeter Conspiracy, 1538. 2 vols. Cambridge, 1915.

Ducarel, A. C. *A Summary Account of the Society of Doctors'*
Commons. London, 1753. (Lambeth Lib. Ms. 958)

Earwaker, J. P. *East Cheshire.* 2 vols. London, 1877.

Einstein, L. *Tudor Ideals.* New York, 1921.

Elliot-Binns, L. F. *England and the New Learning.* London,
1937.

Ellis, H. *Original Letters Illustrative of English History.* 11 vols.
London, 1824; 1827; 1846.

Encyclopaedia Britannica. Eleventh Edition. Vols. XVII, XXV. New
York, 1910-1911.

Erasmus, D. *Epistolae.* See Allen, P. S. and H. M.
Epistles. See Nichols, F. M.
Praise of Folly. Tr. H. H. Hudson. Princeton, 1945.
The Whole Familiar Colloquies. Tr. N. Bailey. Glasgow,
1877.

Fiddes, R. *The Life of Cardinal Wolsey.* London, 1724.

First and Second Prayer Books of Edward VI. Everyman Edition.
London, 1910.

Foster, J. *Alumni Oxonienses: the Members of the University of*
Oxford, 1500-1714. Part I. 4 vols. Oxford, 1891-1892.
*Pedigrees Recorded at Heralds' Visitations of Northumber-
land, 1615 and 1665.* Newcastle, 1891.

[311]

Foxe, J. *Acts and Monuments.* Ed. G. Townsend. 8 vols. London, 1843-1849.

Friedmann, P. *Anne Boleyn.* 2 vols. London, 1884.

Fuller, T. *Church History of Britain.* London, 1655.
 History of the University of Cambridge. London, 1655.
 The Worthies of England in Church and State. London, 1684.

Gairdner, J. *Lollardy and the Reformation.* 4 vols. London, 1908-1913.
 The English Church in the Sixteenth Century. London, 1902.

Gardiner, S. *A Declaration of suche true articles as George Joye hath gone about to confute as false.* London, 1546.
 A Detection of the Devils Sophistrie, wherewith he robbeth the unlearned people, of the true byleef, in the most blessed Sacrament of the aulter. London, 1546.
 A Discussion of Mr. Hopers oversight where he entreateth amonge his other Sermons the matter of the Sacrament of the Bodye and Bloode of Christe, 1550. P.R.O., S.P. 10, Vol. XII.
 De Vera Obedientia. "Roane" Edition, 26 October, 1553. Tr. John Bale (?).
 Letters. See Muller, J. A.

Garrett, C. H. *The Marian Exiles.* London, 1938.

Gasquet, F. A. *Cardinal Pole and his Early Friends.* London, 1917.
 Henry VIII and the English Monasteries. 2 vols. London, 1895.
 The Eve of the Reformation. New Edition. London, 1900.

Gasquet, F. A. and Bishop, E. *Edward VI and the Book of Common Prayer.* London, 1890.

Gee, H. and Hardy, W. J. *Documents Illustrative of English Church History.* London, 1896.

Gentleman's Magazine and Historical Review. Vol. xv, pt. ii. London, 1863.

Gillow, J. *A Literary and Biographical History, or Bibliographical Dictionary, of the English Catholics from the Breach with Rome to the Present Time.* 5 vols. London, 1885-1903.

Grace Book B. Part I (1488-1511), Part II (1511-1544). Ed. M. Bateson. Cambridge, 1903; 1905.

Greenslade, S. L. *The Works of William Tindale.* London, 1938.

Gunton, S. *History of the Church of Peterburgh.* London, 1686.

Haile, M. *Life of Reginald Pole.* London, 1910.

Hall, E. *Henry VIII.* Ed. C. Whibley. 2 vols. London, 1904.

Harbison, E. H. *Rival Ambassadors at the Court of Queen Mary.* Princeton, 1940.

Harpsfield, N. *A Treatise on the Pretended Divorce between Henry VIII and Catharine of Aragon.* Ed. N. Pocock. Cam. Soc. 2nd Ser., Vol. XXI. London, 1878.

The Life and Death of Sir Thomas More. Ed. E. V. Hitchcock and R. W. Chambers. Early English Text Society. London, 1932.

Hayward, J. *Annals of the First Four Years of the Reign of Elizabeth.* Cam. Soc. Vol. VII. London, 1840.

Henry VIII. *Assertio Septem Sacramentorum: or an Assertion of the Seven Sacraments Against Martin Luther.* Tr. T. W. Gent. London, 1687.

Herbert, Lord Edward (of Cherbury). *The Life and Raigne of King Henry the Eighth.* London, 1649.

Holinshed, R. *Chronicles of England, Scotland, and Ireland.* 6 vols. London, 1807-1808.

Hooper, J. *Early Writings.* Ed. S. Carr. Parker Soc. Cambridge, 1843.

Later Writings. Ed. C. Nevinson. Parker Soc. Cambridge, 1852.

Hunter, J. *Familae Minorum Gentium.* Ed. J. W. Clay. 4 Parts. Harl. Soc. Vols. XXXVII-XL. London, 1894-1896.

Janelle, P. *L'Angleterre Catholique à la Veille du Schisme.* Paris, 1935.

Obedience in Church and State: Three Political Tracts by Stephen Gardiner. Cambridge, 1930.

Jessopp, A. *One Generation of a Norfolk House.* London, 1879.

Johnson, J. N. *Linacre.* London, 1835.

Journals of the House of Lords. Vols. I & IV. London, n.d. (Cited as *Lords' Journal*).

Joye, G. *The refutation of the Byshop of Winchesters derke declaratiõ of his false articles, once before confuted by George Ioye.* London, 1546.

Kaulek, J., et al. *Correspondance politique de MM. de Castillon et de Marillac.* Paris, 1885.

Kautsky, K. *Thomas More and his Utopia.* Tr. H. J. Stenning. London, 1927.

[313]

Latimer, H. *Sermons*. Everyman Edition. London, 1926.
  Sermons and Remains. Ed. G. E. Corrie. Parker Soc. Cambridge, 1845.
Leland, J. *Antiquarii de Rebus Britannicis Collectanea*. Ed. T. Hearn. 6 vols. London, 1770. (Cited as Leland, *Collectanea*)
Le Neve, J. *Fasti Ecclesiae Anglicanae*. Ed. T. D. Hardy. 3 vols. Oxford, 1854.
Letters and Papers, Foreign and Domestic of the Reign of Henry VIII. Ed. J. Gairdner and R. H. Brodie. 21 vols. London, 1862-1910. (Cited as *L.P.*)
Lever, T. *Sermons*. London, 1550. Printed in *Arber Reprints*. London, 1871.
Lincolnshire Pedigrees. Ed. A. R. Maddison. 4 Parts. Harl. Soc. Vols. L-LII, LV. London, 1902-1904, 1906.
Lloyd, C. *Formularies of the Faith put Forth by Authority During the Reign of Henry VIII*. Oxford, 1825.
Longlond (Longland), J. *A Sermon Spoken before the Kinge, his Maiestie at Grenwiche, Upon Good Fryday*. London, 1536.
Machyn, H. *The Diary of*. Ed. J. G. Nichols. Cam. Soc. Vol. XLII. London, 1848.
Maitland, F. W. *English Law and the Renaissance*. Cambridge, 1901.
  Roman Canon Law in the Church of England. London, 1898.
Maitland, S. R. *Essays on Subjects Connected with the Reformation in England*. London, 1849.
Makower, F. *The Constitutional History and Constitution of the Church of England*. New York, 1895.
Merriman, R. B. *Life and Letters of Thomas Cromwell*. 2 vols. Oxford, 1902.
Messenger, E. C. *The Reformation, the Mass and the Priesthood*. 2 vols. London, 1936-1937.
Meyrick, S. R. *Visitations of Wales*. 2 vols. Llandovery, 1846.
More, T. *Correspondence*. See Rogers, E. F.
  English Works. Published by W. Rastell. London, 1557.
Muller, J. A. *Stephen Gardiner and the Tudor Reaction*. London, 1926.
  The Letters of Stephen Gardiner. Cambridge, 1933.
Mullinger, J. B. *The University of Cambridge from the Earliest Times to the Accession of Charles the First*. 2 vols. Cambridge, 1875-1884.

Nichols, F. M. *The Epistles of Erasmus*. 3 vols. London, 1918.

Nichols, J. G. *Literary Remains of King Edward VI*. 2 vols. Roxburghe Club. London, 1857.

Notes and Queries: a Medium of Intercommunication for Literary Men, General Readers, etc. London.

Ogle, A. *The Tragedy of Lollards' Tower*, Oxford, 1949.

Oliver, G. *Lives of the Bishops of Exeter*. Exeter, 1861.

Original Letters Relative to the English Reformation. Ed. H. Robinson. Parker Soc. 2 vols., continuously paged. Cambridge, 1846-1847.

Ormerod, G. *History of the County Palatine and City of Chester*. 3 vols. London, 1819.

Parker, M. *Correspondence*. Ed. J. Bruce and T. T. Perowne. Parker Soc. Cambridge, 1853.

Phillips, G. E. *The Extinction of the Ancient Hierarchy*. London, 1905.

The Truth about Bishop Bonner. Catholic Truth Society. London, 1903.

Pickthorn, K. *Early Tudor Government, Henry VIII*. Cambridge, 1934.

Pocock, N. *Records of the Reformation*. 2 vols. Oxford, 1870.

"The Conditions of Morals and Religious Beliefs in the Reign of Edward VI." *English Historical Review*, Vol. x, pp. 417-444. London, 1895.

Troubles Connected with the Prayer Book of 1549. Cam. Soc. New Series, Vol. xxxvii. London, 1884.

Pollard, A. F. *England under Protector Somerset*. London, 1900.

Henry VIII. London, 1934.

The Political History of England. Vol. vi, *The History of England from the Accession of Edward VI to the Death of Elizabeth, 1547-1603*. London, 1919.

Thomas Cranmer and the English Reformation. New York, 1904.

Tudor Tracts. London, 1903.

Wolsey. London, 1929.

Powicke, F. M. *et al. Handbook of British Chronology*. London, 1939.

The Reformation in England. London, 1941.

Prescott, H. F. M. *A Spanish Tudor, the Life of "Bloody Mary."* New York, 1940.

Reid, R. R. *The King's Council in the North*. London, 1921.

[315]

Ridley, N. *Works.* Ed. H. Christmas. Parker Soc. Cambridge, 1841.

Robinson, C. J. *A History of the Mansions and Manors of Herefordshire.* London, 1873.

Rogers, E. F. *The Correspondence of Sir Thomas More.* Princeton, 1947.

Rose-Troup, F. *The Western Rebellion of 1549.* London, 1913.

Rupp, E. G. *Studies in the Making of the English Protestant Tradition.* Cambridge, 1947.

Sanders, N. "Report to Cardinal Moroni on the change of religion in 1558-59." Ed. F. A. Gasquet. *Catholic Record Society.* I (1904-1905), pp. 1-46.
Rise and Growth of the Anglican Schism. Tr. D. Lewis. London, 1877.

Schenk, W. *Reginald Pole, Cardinal of England.* London, 1950.

Seebohm, F. *The Oxford Reformers, John Colet, Erasmus, and Thomas More.* 3rd Edition. London, 1887.

Smith, H. M. *Henry VIII and the Reformation.* London, 1948.
Pre-Reformation England. London, 1938.

Smith, P. *The Life and Letters of Martin Luther.* Boston and New York, 1911.

Smith, Sir Thomas. *De Republica Anglorum.* Ed. L. Alston. Cambridge, 1906.

Smyth, G. H. *Cranmer and the Reformation under Edward VI.* Cambridge, 1926.

Spelman, Sir Henry. *The History and Fate of Sacrilege.* Ed. C. F. S. Warren. London, 1895.

Stapleton, T. *The Life and Illustrious Martyrdom of Sir Thomas More.* Tr. P. E. Hallett. London, 1928.

Starkey, T. *England in the Reign of King Henry the Eighth.* Ed. S. J. Herrtage. Early English Text Society. London, 1878.

State Papers during the Reign of Henry VIII. 11 vols. London, 1830-1852. (Cited as *St. P.*)

Statutes of the Realm. Vol. III. Ed. T. E. Tomlins and W. E. Taunton. London, 1817.

Stowe, J. *Survey of London.* Everyman Edition. London, n.d.

Strype, J. *Annals of the Reformation and Establishment of Religion in the Church of England.* 4 vols. in 7. Oxford, 1824.
Ecclesiastical Memorials. 3 vols. in 6. Oxford, 1822. (Cited as Strype, *Ecc. Mem.*)

Memorials of the Most Reverend Father in God, Thomas Cranmer. 2 vols. Oxford, 1812.

Sturge, C. *Cuthbert Tunstal.* London, 1938.

Tawney, R. H. *Religion and the Rise of Capitalism.* Pelican Edition. New York, 1947.

The Agrarian Problem in the Sixteenth Century. London, 1912.

Tierney, M. A. *Dodd's Church History of England.* 5 vols. London, 1839-1843.

Tunstal, C. *Contra impios Blasphematores Dei Praedestinationis.* Antwerp, 1555.

Turner, W. *The huntyng and fyndyng out of the Romyshe foxe, which more then seuen yeares hath bene hyd among the bisshoppes of Englonde.* Basle, 1543.

The Rescuynge of the romishe fox otherwise called the examination of the hunter deuised by Steuen gardiner. Zurich (?), 1545.

Tytler, P. F. *England under the Reigns of Edward VI and Mary.* 2 vols. London, 1839.

Venn, J. *Biographical History of Gonville and Caius College.* 2 vols. Cambridge, 1897.

Venn, J. and J. A. *Alumni Cantabrigienses.* Part I, vols. I-IV. Cambridge, 1922.

Visitation of Cheshire, 1580. Ed. J. P. Rylands. Harl. Soc. Vol. XVIII. London, 1882.

Visitations of Berkshire, 1532, 1563, 1623, and 1664-66. Ed. W. H. Rylands. 2 Parts. Harl. Soc. Vols. LVI-LVII. London, 1907-1908.

Visitations of Essex, 1552, 1558, 1612, and 1634. Ed. W. C. Metcalfe. 2 Parts. Harl. Soc. Vols. XIII-XIV. London, 1878-1879.

Visitations of Hampshire and the Isle of Wright, 1530, 1575, and 1622-1634. Ed. W. H. Rylands. Harl. Soc. Vol. LXIV. London, 1913.

Visitations of Hertfordshire, 1572 and 1634. Ed. W. C. Metcalfe. Harl. Soc. Vol. XXII. London, 1886.

Visitation of London, 1568. Ed. J. J. Howard and C. J. Armytage. Harl. Soc. Vol. I. London, 1869.

Visitation of London, 1633-34. Ed. J. J. Howard. 2 Parts. Harl. Soc. Vols. XV and XVII. London, 1880 and 1883.

Visitations of Norfolk, 1563, 1589, and 1613. Ed. W. Rye. Harl. Soc. Vol. XXXII. London, 1891.

Visitations of Nottinghamshire, 1569 and 1614. Ed. G. W. Marshall. Harl. Soc. Vol. IV. London, 1871.

Visitation of Shropshire, 1623. Ed. G. Grazebrook and J. P. Rylands. 2 Parts. Harl. Soc. Vols. XXVIII-XXIX. London, 1889.

Visitation of Staffordshire. Staffordshire Historical Collections. Vol. V. London, 1884.

Visitation of Warwickshire, 1619. Ed. J. Fetherston. Harl. Soc. Vol. XII. London, 1877.

Visitation of Worcestershire, 1569. Ed. W. P. W. Phillimore. Harl. Soc. Vol. XXVII. London, 1888.

Visitation of Yorkshire, 1564. Ed. C. B. Norcliffe. Harl. Soc. Vol. XVI. London, 1881.

Wegg, J. *Richard Pace, a Tudor Diplomatist.* London, 1932.

White, H. C. *Social Criticism in Popular Religious Literature of the Sixteenth Century.* New York, 1944.

Whitebrook, J. C. *The Consecration of Matthew Parker.* London, 1945.

Wilkins, D. *Concilia Magnae Britanniae.* 4 vols. London, 1737.

Willis, B. *History of the Cathedral Church of Chester.* London, 1793.

— *Survey of the Cathedral Church of Bangor.* London, 1721.

Wood, A. *Athenae Oxonienses.* Ed. P. Bliss. 6 vols. London, 1813.

Wordsworth, C. *Ecclesiastical Biography.* 6 vols. London, 1818.

Wraghton, W. See Turner, W.

Wright, T. *Letters Relating to the Suppression of Monasteries.* Cam. Soc. Vol. XXVI. London, 1843.

Wriothesley, C. A. *A Chronicle of England.* Ed. W. D. Hamilton. 2 vols. Cam. Soc. Vols. XI and XX. London, 1875, 1877.

Zeeveld, W. G. *Foundations of Tudor Policy.* Cambridge (Mass.), 1948.

Zurich Letters, or the Correspondence of several English Bishops and others with some of the Helvetian Reformers during the Reign of Queen Elizabeth. Ed. H. Robinson. Parker Soc. 2nd Edition, 2 vols. in one and arranged chronologically. Cambridge, 1846.

117-8, 124-5; belief in the Mass till 1540, 132, 140; death, 139; promotes conservatives, 28, 142-5; conservativism, 157 and note; associates Catholicism with the Papacy, 164; states aim of the re-formers, 171-2; attitude toward images, 176; account of the plague, 196-7; argument with Henry VIII, 200; contempt for law, 225-6, 228; grief at Henry VIII's death, 251; *Book of Hom-ilies*, 254, 262; attitude toward the Mass, 270; pedigree, 301; mentioned, 44, 46, 51, 64, 106, 110, 112, 123, 149, 155, 181, 184, 186, 194, 195, 205-6, 210, 213, 242, 256, 278, 280, 282, 291

Crome, Dr. Edward, 162-3, 170

Cromwell, Gregory, 153, 240

Cromwell, Thomas, Vicar-general, Earl of Essex: patron of the con-servatives, 10, 74, 141-5; em-ployed by Wolsey, 41, 72; his fall from power, 88, 98, 209, 213-9; his fall the signal for re-action, 145, 182, 222; troubles with Barlow, 114; troubles with Shaxton, 115; friendship with Roland Lee, 153-4; role in the suppression of the monasteries, 167-8; role in the Pilgrimage of Grace, 192; created Earl of Es-sex, 218; mentioned, 58, 60, 76-7, 85, 174, 186, 188, 194, 195, 196, 210, 259, 264

Crowley, Robert, 130

Day, George, Bishop of Chichester (1543-1551, 1553-1556): social status, 12; at Cambridge, 28; on communion in both kinds, 135; attitude toward transubstantia-tion, 137; promoted by Cromwell, 143, 145; one of the authors of *The King's Book*, 244, 247; at-titude toward altars, 268-9; ef-forts to reconcile faith and obedi-ence, 266, 268-70; supports the papal supremacy, 288; defies the

Edwardian government, 268-9, 272; deprivation, 256n, 268, 272; imprisonment, 268; pedi-gree, 301; mentioned, 12, 56, 57, 64, 66, 67, 91, 93, 97, 139, 148, 149, 201, 218, 258, 279, 284, 294

Day, William, Bishop of Winchester (1596), 12

diplomacy: training for, 13; dan-gers of, 80-1, 85-91; influence on the conservatives, 94-105, 226-32; monopolized by laymen under Mary, 282-3. *See also* ambassa-dors; bishops; conservatives

divorce of Catherine of Aragon, 18, 71, 77-8, 90, 181; effect on bishops, 19, 40; effect on mar-riage, 202

Doctors' Commons: meeting place for lawyers, 42-3; center of hu-manistic interests, 49-50

Dorset, Thomas, 188

Dowes, Henry, 240-1

Dudley, John, Earl of Warwick, Duke of Northumberland, 139, 253, 263, 282

Duns Scotus, 135

Dunston, Anthony, *see* Kitchen

Durham, Bishop of, *see* Tunstal

Edward VI: Reformation under, 168-9, 172, 249-50, 252-6; con-servatives omitted from his gov-ernment, 249; nature of his gov-ernment, 252-3; efforts to enforce religious conformity, 255-6; ap-peal of his government to national unity, 263-4; tables replace altars under, 268-70; economic condi-tions under, 276; death, 282; mentioned, 147, 159, 251, 262

Elizabeth I, 172, 273, 286, 287, 293, 294

Ely, bishops of, *see* Goodrich, Thirl-by, West

enclosures, 126, 127, 166; a cause of rebellion, 193, 276; a cause of vagabondage, 247

Episcopal Bench: middle class origin of, 14-5; social and economic